New Approaches to Evaluating Community Initiatives

Volume 2
Theory, Measurement, and Analysis

Roundtable on Comprehensive Community Initiatives for Children and Families

Edited by
Karen Fulbright-Anderson,
Anne C. Kubisch, and
James P. Connell

The Aspen Institute

The Aspen Institute
Suite 1070
1333 New Hampshire Avenue, N.W.
Washington, D.C. 20036
Published in the United States of America
in 1998 by The Aspen Institute

ISBN 0-89843-249-9

**Publications of the Aspen Institute Roundtable on
Comprehensive Community Initiatives for Children and Families**

*Voices from the Field: Learning from the
Early Work of Comprehensive Community Initiatives* $10.00

*New Approaches to Evaluating Community
Initiatives, Vol. 1: Concepts, Methods, and Contexts* $12.00

*New Approaches to Evaluating Community
Initiatives, Vol. 2: Theory, Measurement, and Analysis* $12.00

To preview our publications, visit our web site at www.aspenroundtable.org

To order, send check payable to the Aspen Institute or credit card information
(including type of card, account number and expiration date) to:

> The Aspen Institute
> Publications Office
> P.O. Box 222
> 109 Houghton Lab Lane
> Queenstown, MD 21658
> Fax: (410) 827-9174

Shipping costs are included in the price.

Contents

Evaluating Community Initiatives: A Progress Report

Anne C. Kubisch, Karen Fulbright-Anderson, and James P. Connell

The Roundtable on Comprehensive Community Initiatives for Children and Families is a forum where representatives of many groups engaged in comprehensive community initiatives (CCIs) can meet to discuss lessons emerging from this relatively new approach to community revitalization. Established in 1992, the Roundtable moved to the Aspen Institute in 1994 and now includes approximately 30 foundation sponsors, program directors, technical assistance providers, evaluators, and public sector officials. Also in 1994, the Roundtable formed the Steering Committee on Evaluation, which attempts to address problems encountered by stakeholders in their efforts to learn from and judge the effectiveness of CCIs. (Members of the Roundtable and the Steering Committee on Evaluation are listed on pages 253-56 of this volume.)

Soon after its formation, the Steering Committee on Evaluation commissioned several papers on some of the more pressing issues in CCI evaluation. The papers were published in 1995 in *New Approaches to Evaluating Community Initiatives: Concepts, Methods, and Contexts,* edited by James Connell, Anne Kubisch, Lisbeth Schorr, and Carol Weiss. The current volume follows up on concerns raised in that first collection, hereinafter referred to as Volume 1.

The Emergence of Comprehensive Community Initiatives

In the United States, the history of locally based initiatives to improve poor urban neighborhoods and the lives of their residents dates back to the late nineteenth century. Comprehensive community initiatives (CCIs) represent the most recent generation in a line of neighborhood-level efforts that includes settlement houses, Grey Areas, Model Cities, Community Action

Programs, and community development corporations.[1] CCIs build on and incorporate lessons from each of these models.

Individual CCIs take different forms and structures, yet all are guided by principles of comprehensiveness and community building. As comprehensive initiatives, CCIs seek to strengthen all sectors of neighborhood well-being, including social, educational, economic, physical, and cultural aspects, and in so doing seek to achieve a level of synergy among them. Although CCIs may not implement programmatic strategies for all sectors at the outset, they pay attention to the interrelationships among sectors while pursuing opportunities to improve community conditions. By claiming comprehensiveness, CCIs also indicate a commitment to change at many levels, including individual, family, institutional, and community-wide, through processes that involve collaboration and coordination within the community and between the community and the broader society.

The community-building dimension of CCIs emphasizes *how* this change should come about. It places priority on a resident-driven approach that values local knowledge and participation in all stages of the revitalization effort, from initial goal setting through evaluation and policy change. It aims to build capacity at the neighborhood level for a continuous process of local improvement. It also aims to build or rebuild "social capital"—that is, the social fabric among residents—in the community. Finally, community building operates according to values of racial equity, social and economic justice, and respect for community assets, including local culture and history.

Most CCIs have been created by, and receive support from, private foundations, although there is a growing number of federal, state, and locally sponsored initiatives. In addition, many institutions have undertaken activities designed to provide technical assistance to CCIs, to evaluate and carry out research in order to increase understanding of their work, and to share knowledge among CCIs and disseminate information about them to a broader audience. Perhaps more important, however, is the way in which the principles that underlie CCIs are increasingly guiding a wide range of publicly and privately sponsored social welfare and economic development efforts. A growing number of sector-specific or outcome-specific initiatives in education, health, youth development, crime prevention, substance abuse, child development, child welfare, and other areas are being guided by principles of comprehensiveness and community building. Thus, while CCIs may represent the "purest" application of comprehensiveness and community building, they are by no means the exclusive expressions of those principles.

Why is Good Evaluation of CCIs So Important?

CCIs bear an enormous responsibility to ensure that we learn as much as possible from their collective experience for three sets of reasons, one political, one practical, and one more technical.

Politically, CCIs are public efforts that seek to be both democratic in process while also committed to results. As such, they benefit from the support of a wide range of constituents, all of whom need to be kept informed of progress and outcomes. Funders look for evidence that their investments are "paying off," quite often within the time frame of their funding cycles. But in CCIs, neighborhood residents and "influentials" outside the community are equally important audiences for information about the initiative. They too need evidence that their investments—whether in time, energy, or social or political capital—are having an effect. Other partners in the public, nonprofit, and corporate sectors also need to be kept informed of progress.

The second press for good evaluation is the need to generate useful feedback to guide implementation. Surely any good program or agency manager wants formative feedback to inform planning, management and administration, and mid-course correction. In CCIs, this need is intensified by the defining mandate to create new and different ways of doing business at the neighborhood level. No stock blueprint shows how this should happen: structures and activities must be tailored to individual neighborhood circumstances. Thus, contemporaneous learning from each CCI's unique, progressive experimentation is necessary to guide practitioners' decisions and actions and to help ensure that CCIs have the best chance of success.

The third reason for good evaluation has to do with what Alice O'Connor (1995) calls the need for "social learning" over the longer run. Essentially laboratories for applying the best lessons from previous inner city revitalization efforts, CCIs offer opportunities for practitioners and researchers to test their knowledge and experience and to examine some of the most fundamental and cutting-edge questions in the antipoverty field today—questions concerning the configuration of model programs, for example, or the role that "social capital" and "neighborhood capacity" play in promoting healthy communities. This information, ultimately, cycles back to inform and shape both the policy and research agendas.

The Challenge of Evaluating CCIs

Broad interest in CCIs means that CCI evaluations are being asked to serve multiple purposes for a host of audiences. Fortunately, many CCI funders have recognized the value of investing in learning as much as possible from the current cohort of interventions, and a number of evaluations are underway.[2]

At the same time, the very characteristics of CCIs that give hope to both stakeholders and observers are also the ones that challenge our ability to evaluate and learn from them. In their introduction to the first Aspen Roundtable volume on evaluation, Kubisch and colleagues (1995) describe these CCI features and why they raise evaluation-related difficulties:

- **Horizontal complexity.** They work across multiple sectors (social, economic, physical, political, and others) simultaneously and aim for synergy among them.

- **Vertical complexity.** They aim for change at the individual, family, community, organizational, and systems levels.

- **Community building.** They aim for strengthened community capacity, enhanced social capital, an empowered neighborhood, and similar outcomes.

- **Contextual issues.** They aim to incorporate external political, economic and other conditions into their framework, even though they may have little power to affect them.

- **Community responsiveness and flexibility over time.** They are designed to be community-specific and to evolve in response to the dynamics of the neighborhood and the lessons being learned by the initiative.

- **Community saturation.** They aim to reach all members of a community, and therefore individual residents cannot be randomly assigned to treatment and control groups for the purposes of assessing the CCI's impact; finding equivalent comparison communities is also not feasible.[3]

This enumeration of evaluation-related difficulties helped identify the scope of the problem facing the field, yet a different framework was required for structuring work to address those difficulties. One of the first priorities of the Roundtable's Steering Committee on Evaluation was to reshape this list of complex and inter-related challenges into a more manageable and accessible framework within which to organize new thinking and new work. That process led to the identification of three fundamental questions that have guided the committee's work over the last three years; those questions, in turn, form the structure of this volume.

- Given the breadth, complexity, and evolving nature of CCIs, what can be done to clarify the short, interim, and long-term outcomes of an initiative, as well as the projected pathways for achieving them, in a way that guides initiative evaluation?

- Given the value that CCIs place on community building, on the process of change, and on community-level change, what are compelling indicators of all CCI outcomes—early, interim and long-term—and how should they be measured?

- Given the community-specific and community-wide goals of CCIs, how should data be collected and analyzed to ensure that the causal links between initiative activities and outcomes—and the role of contextual variables in those links—are as fully understood as possible?

Volume 1: Concepts, Methods, and Contexts

Perhaps the most important contribution of Volume 1 was to introduce the potential applicability of theory-based evaluation to the CCI field. In "Nothing as Practical as Good Theory: Exploring Theory-Based Evaluation for Comprehensive Community Initiatives," Carol Weiss hypothesized that a key reason that CCIs and other complex programs are so difficult to evaluate is that the "theories of change" that underlie the structures, strategies, and goals of CCIs are poorly articulated. Weiss challenged CCI designers to be specific about theories of change and suggested that doing so would improve their overall evaluation plans while also providing guidelines for data collection and analysis.[4]

In the three years since the publication of Weiss's paper, the importance of achieving clarity about the theory of change underlying a CCI has gained considerable popularity among CCI funders, evaluators, and practitioners. This turn of events was perhaps predictable, given that many CCIs did indeed begin with only very general theories of change: as funders and communities entered into agreements to work together toward neighborhood transformation, they deliberately left aspects of their initiatives open so that collaborative processes of planning and implementation could unfold. But why were concerns about the clarity of the theory of change triggered by questions regarding CCI *evaluation*, as opposed to, say, planning or technical assistance? There are two answers to that question.

One answer, offered in this volume by James Connell and Anne Kubisch, is that the process of designing an evaluation requires participants to be explicit about aspects of an initiative that might otherwise be left vague for technical, political, administrative, or conceptual reasons. The authors state that "it is in the process of designing an evaluation that specific decisions must be taken regarding what is meant by key terms (such as 'collaboration'), the type and degree of change being sought, and the measures that would indicate whether change is occurring."

The second answer is that many CCI funders decided early in the process that good evaluation should accompany these new and high-risk efforts, not only as a means for tracking their considerable investments closely and gathering formative feedback but also to ensure that these important social experiments would generate useful knowledge along the way. As a result, evaluation became an important locus for creative thinking about the range of planning, implementation, and research challenges facing CCIs.

These circumstances meant that, at each stage, CCI evaluators have been confronted with challenges for which traditional evaluation tools have seemed inadequate. Problems at the outset included vaguely defined interventions; at the measurement stage, the absence of indicators for many of the community-building concepts; and at the analysis stage, the difficulty of causal attribution. For CCI evaluators, the "theory of change" notion offers a framework for breaking down this complex set of problems into discrete and more manageable questions.

Volume 2: Theory, Measurement, and Analysis

This second volume offers a progress report on work accomplished over the last few years. The first paper, by Connell and Kubisch, attempts to take Carol Weiss's formulation of a theory of change evaluation to the next level: that is, to apply it specifically to the circumstances of a CCI. They define a theory of change approach to CCI evaluation and describe steps stakeholders can follow to carry one out.

In the five contributions that follow, several practitioners share their experiences with the theory of change approach to evaluation, together providing an up-to-date portrait of the field. As a group, the papers provide an overview for understanding how to apply the approach and examples of its benefits and challenges when used in different settings and at different stages of an initiative.

The paper by Sharon Milligan, Claudia Coulton, Peter York, and Ronald Register was written as part of an effort by the Aspen Roundtable's Steering Committee on Evaluation to "field test" the concept on the ground, in the context of a comprehensive community initiative. A fortunate convergence of interests and timing enabled the Roundtable to form a partnership with the Cleveland Community-Building Initiative in the early phases of its evaluation design process. The Cleveland site benefited from technical and financial resources provided by the Roundtable, while the Roundtable gained from the opportunity to test the approach. In addition, evaluators whose recent work incorporates a theory of change approach were invited to write short, analytical papers describing the strengths and weaknesses of the approach. The contributions by Prudence Brown, Lynn Kagan, Susan Philliber, and Scott Hebert and Andrea Anderson are intended to give readers a broad set of perspectives on how the approach actually works, in practice, for evaluators.

The volume then turns to issues regarding measurement of change and the availability of data. The problem of measuring the range of types and levels of change that CCIs expect to influence has been at the forefront of the agenda of the Steering Committee on Evaluation since its inception. Because CCIs aim for change at many levels (individual, family, personal network, institutional, and community), across many domains (economic, social, physical, and community building), and over different time periods (near-term, interim, and long-term or ultimate), the measurement task is substantial. Surveying even well-understood measures in so many areas would be a daunting process for any evaluator—but for CCI evaluators, good measures simply do not exist for many of the most important desired outcomes, such as community building.

Since the publication of Volume 1, the Roundtable has embarked on several activities to identify measurement issues and organize measures of community-level change. One step was to convene a meeting of researchers and evaluators in December 1996. Michelle Gambone took that wide-ranging discussion and distilled from it a framework, presented in this volume, for thinking through the various CCI dimensions that need measuring, covering context, progress, and early, interim, and long-term outcomes. The Steering Committee on Evaluation also prevailed upon two of its members, Claudia Coulton and Robinson Hollister, to share their extensive knowledge of administrative, census, and survey data in a paper that reviews the use of existing data to measure change at the neighborhood level.

Turning to the thorny issue of attributing causality—the problem that dominates evaluators' discussions about CCIs—Robert Granger takes up a challenge issued by Hollister and Hill in Volume 1 and suggests several strategies evaluators can use to strengthen the case that neighborhood outcomes can be attributed convincingly to a CCI.

A final theme woven throughout the discussion is the changing role of the evaluator in the context of CCIs and other complex community-based initiatives. In Volume 1, Prudence Brown argued for a more engaged role than the evaluator has traditionally adopted, and the authors in this volume for the most part concur. The five "practitioner reflections" presented here all describe significant participation in the theory articulation process, the research design, collection of data, and other steps. The papers are rich in their discussion of the advantages of this approach, but they are also honest about the difficulties that arise.

This, in turn, raises the question of who should be responsible for the theory articulation process. A theory of change that is accepted by all stakeholders is a product of a CCI's work.[5] It comes out of an in-depth planning process, but as Connell and Klem (1996) and Schorr (1997) suggest, theories can be informed by knowledge and experience from outside the community, implying a different, and perhaps less intensive, process of producing a theory of change that is nonetheless community owned. Experts in fields relevant to community revitalization, therefore, may be more appropriate facilitators of the process of creating the theory of change than are evaluators.

How do we define a CCI's theory of change? How should we measure the change? How can we be sure that the CCI caused the change? What is the role of the evaluator in this new approach? This volume describes the progress that has been made in the field as a whole on each of those questions over the last three years. Greater advances have been made in some areas than in others, and in some cases the progress has been more conceptual than applied. Nonetheless, the members of the Roundtable's evaluation committee believe that the papers included here offer new ways of thinking, new insights, and new information, which together can help CCI stakeholders approach the evaluation enterprise with greater confidence that the result will meet their various needs.

Notes

1   For further discussion of the evolution CCIs and the state of the field today, see Kubisch et al., 1995; Kingsley et al., 1997; Stone, 1996; Walsh, 1996; Lieterman and Stillman, 1993; Kubisch et al., 1997; Pitcoff, 1997, 1998; Jackson and Marris, 1996; Halpern, 1994; O'Connor, 1995; O'Connor, forthcoming; Ferguson and Dickens, forthcoming; and Wright, 1998.

2   See, for example, Chapin Hall Center for Children, 1997; Chaskin, 1992; Chaskin and Joseph, 1995; Chaskin, Dansokho, and Joseph, 1997; Hirota, Brown, and Butler, 1998; Sviridoff and Ryan, 1996; Nathan, 1997; OMG, Inc., 1995, 1998; Hebert and Anderson, this volume; Milligan et al., this volume; and Stillman et al., 1996.

3   The lack of suitable comparison groups in CCI evaluations is discussed at greater length in Hollister and Hill, 1995.

4   Chen (1990) and Weiss (1995, 1997) offer further thoughts on the challenges of theory-based evaluation.

5   For more on the role of the evaluator, see Connell, 1997.

References

Chapin Hall Center for Children. 1997. *The Partnership for Neighborhood Initiatives: Report of the Chapin Hall Center for Children at the University of Chicago.* Chicago: Chapin Hall Center for Children.

Chaskin, Robert. 1992. *The Ford Foundation's Neighborhood and Family Initiative: Toward a Model of Comprehensive Neighborhood-Based Development.* Chicago: Chapin Hall Center for Children.

Chaskin, Robert, Selma Chipenda Dansokho, and Mark Joseph. 1997. *The Ford Foundation's Neighborhood and Family Initiative: The Challenge of Sustainability.* Chicago: Chapin Hall Center for Children.

Chaskin, Robert, and Mark Joseph. 1995. *The Neighborhood and Family Initiative: Moving toward Implementation.* Chicago: Chapin Hall Center for Children.

Connell, James P. 1997. "Render unto Evaluators...: Some Cautions from Early Experience with a Theory of Change Approach." Paper presented at the Annie E. Casey Foundation Evaluation Conference, Baltimore.

Connell, James P., and Adina Klem. 1996. "Using a Theory of Change Approach to Evaluate Investments in Public Education." Paper presented at a meeting convened by Independent Sector, Washington, DC.

Chen, Huey-tsyh. 1990. *Theory Driven Evaluations.* Thousand Oaks, CA: Sage Publications.

Ferguson, Ronald, and William T. Dickens, eds. Forthcoming. *Urban Problems and Community Development.* Washington, DC: Brookings Institution.

Halpern, Robert. 1994. *Rebuilding the Inner City: A History of Neighborhood Initiatives to Address Poverty in the United States.* New York: Columbia University Press.

Hirota, Janice M., Prudence Brown, and Benjamin Butler. 1998. *Neighborhood Strategies Project: Report on Initial Implementation, July 1996-March 1998.* Chicago: Chapin Hall Center for Children.

Hollister, Robinson G., and Jennifer Hill. 1995. "Problems in the Evaluation of Community-Wide Initiatives." In *New Approaches to Evaluating Community Initiatives: Concepts, Methods, and Contexts,* ed. James Connell et al. Washington, DC: Aspen Institute.

Jackson, Maria-Rosario, and Peter Marris. 1996. *Collaborative Comprehensive Community Initiatives: Overview of an Emerging Community Improvement Orientation.* Washington, DC: Urban Institute.

Kingsley, Thomas G., Joseph McNeely, and James O. Gibson. 1997. *Community Building: Coming of Age.* Washington, DC: Urban Institute.

Kubisch, Anne C., Prudence Brown, Robert Chaskin, Janice Hirota, Mark Joseph, Harold Richman, and Michelle Roberts. 1997. *Voices from the Field: Learning from Comprehensive Community Initiatives.* New York: Roundtable on Comprehensive Community Initiatives for Children and Families, Aspen Institute.

Kubisch, Anne, Carol H. Weiss, Lisbeth B. Schorr, and James P. Connell. 1995. *New Approaches to Evaluating Community Initiatives: Concepts, Methods, and Contexts,* ed. James Connell et al. Washington, DC: Aspen Institute.

Leiterman, M., and J. Stillman. 1993. *Building Community.* New York: Local Initiatives Support Corporation.

Nathan, Richard, P. 1997. *Empowerment Zone Initiative: Building a Community Plan for Strategic Change: Findings from the First Round of Assessment.* Albany: Nelson A. Rockefeller Institute of Government, State University of New York.

O'Connor, Alice. Forthcoming. "Swimming Against the Tide: A Brief History of Federal Policy in Poor Communities." In *Urban Problems and Community Development.* Washington, DC: Brookings Institution.

O'Connor, Alice. 1995. "Evaluating Comprehensive Community Initiatives: A View from History." In *New Approaches to Evaluating Community Initiatives: Concepts, Methods, and Contexts,* ed. James Connell et al. Washington, DC: Aspen Institute.

OMG, Inc. 1998. *Final Assessment Report: Comprehensive Community Revitalization Program in the South Bronx.* New York: Comprehensive Community Revitalization Program.

OMG, Inc. 1995. *Final Assessment Report: The Planning Phase of the Rebuilding Communities Initiative.* Baltimore: Annie E. Casey Foundation.

Pitcoff, Winton. 1998. "Redefining Community Development, Part II: Collaborating for Change." *Shelterforce* 20 (1):2-17.

Pitcoff, Winton. 1997. "Redefining Community Development." *Shelterforce* 19 (6):2-14.

Schorr, Lisbeth. 1997. *Common Purpose.* New York: Doubleday.

Stillman, Joseph, Benjamin Butler, Prudence Brown, and Lenneal J. Henderson. 1996. *Sandtown-Winchester Community Building in Partnership: 1990-1994: Interim Evaluation Report.* New York: Conservation Company.

Stone, Rebecca. 1996. *Core Issues in Comprehensive Community-Building Initiatives.* Chicago: Chapin Hall Center for Children.

Sviridoff, Mitchell, and Willam Ryan. 1996. *Investing in Community: Lessons and Implications of the Comprehensive Community Revitalization Program.* New York: Comprehensive Community Revitalization Program.

Walsh, Joan. 1996. *Stories of Renewal: Community Building and the Future of Urban America.* New York: Rockefeller Foundation.

Weiss, Carol Hirschon. 1997. "How Can Theory-Based Evaluation Make Greater Headway?" *Evaluation Review* 21, no. 4.

Weiss, Carol Hirschon. 1995. "Nothing as Practical as Good Theory: Exploring Theory-based Evaluation for Comprehensive Community Initiatives for Children and Families." In *New Approaches to Evaluating Community Initiatives: Concepts, Methods, and Contexts,* ed. James Connell et al. Washington, DC: Aspen Institute.

Wright, David J. 1998. "Comprehensive Strategies for Community Renewal." *Rockefeller Institute Bulletin,* pp. 48-66.

Applying a Theory of Change Approach to the Evaluation of Comprehensive Community Initiatives: Progress, Prospects, and Problems

James P. Connell and Anne C. Kubisch

Since its birth in the late 1980s and early 1990s, the field of comprehensive community initiatives (CCIs) has been struggling to find evaluation strategies and methodologies that correspond well to the goals and designs of the initiatives themselves. Up to this point, CCIs have had three general options to follow: (1) retreat to process documentation of the initiatives and greatly reduce expectations about obtaining credible evidence of their impacts; (2) try to "force fit" the initiatives themselves into the procrustean bed of existing and accepted evaluation methods in order to estimate their impacts; and (3) put off evaluating CCIs until the initiatives are more "mature" and "ready" to be evaluated using existing strategies.

The field needs better options than these. Specifically, the field is seeking alternative approaches to evaluating CCIs that will meet both the need to estimate these initiatives' effects on interim and longer-term outcomes and the need for information on how the interventions produce those outcomes. This paper is a progress report on one such approach.

In this paper, we present what we are calling a "theory of change approach" to evaluating CCIs. We describe three stages in carrying out this approach:

- surfacing and articulating a theory of change

- measuring a CCI's activities and intended outcomes

- analyzing and interpreting the results of an evaluation, including their implications for adjusting the initiative's theory of change and its allocation of resources

In many ways, these stages—and the questions they raise—are similar to those of any evaluation process: What is the treatment or intervention? What are its intended and measurable outcomes? And, how are the data to be collected and analyzed such that the causal links between treatments and outcomes are described in the most compelling way? What is different about evaluating CCIs is that the answers to these three questions are often much more elusive.

For example, as we describe the steps that are necessary to surface and articulate a theory of change, the reader will see that, at their most general level, CCI theories are quite similar to many program theories: the initiative plans to do X in order to accomplish Y and Z. But, this similarity—and its implications for evaluating CCIs—vanishes quickly when one realizes that, unlike most programs, CCI theories have multiple strands (economic, political, and social), which operate at many levels (community, institutional, personal network, family, and individual), are co-constructed in a collaborative process by diverse stakeholders, and evolve over the course of the initiative. Each of these complicating factors can plague evaluation of more circumscribed programs, to be sure, but in CCIs these factors are defining traits. They are the rule, not the exception. Moreover, these complicating factors spill over into the other stages of evaluation; in later sections of the paper, we explore their implications for measurement, analysis, and interpretation.

We conclude the paper with reflections on the constraints and promise of the approach, including its capacity to reinforce the basic principles of a CCI and contribute to a knowledge base that can inform future neighborhood-based interventions.

Defining a Theory of Change Approach to Evaluation

What Is a Theory of Change Approach to Evaluation?

Weiss (1995) defines a theory of change quite simply and elegantly as a theory of how and why an initiative works.[1] Building on her work, we have defined a theory of change approach to CCI evaluation as *a systematic and cumulative study of the links between activities, outcomes, and contexts of the initiative.*

This definition suggests that the first step toward evaluating a CCI is to determine its intended outcomes, the activities it expects to implement to achieve those outcomes, and the contextual factors that may have an effect on implementation of activities and their potential to bring about desired outcomes. For example, the goal of many CCIs is to improve the well-being of children and families in the neighborhood. In this case, one of an initiative's primary activities might be to replace categorical and centralized services with integrated neighborhood-based family resource centers. An important contextual factor might be the policy environment, including the presence or absence of legislation allowing for pooled funding of state resources for innovative community-based initiatives. Another central activity might be to build social networks among families with young children, which in turn could be affected by local contextual factors such as the racial make-up of the neighborhood and its history of intergroup relations.

How do such theories of change assist CCI stakeholders? In 1972, Carol Weiss described the value of having any program evaluation rooted in good theory (1972). In a 1995 paper, Weiss described the potential contribution of this approach to the evaluation of CCIs. We now identify at least three reasons to begin the design and evaluation of a CCI with a good theory of change.

A theory of change approach can sharpen the planning and implementation of an initiative. Used during the design phase, it increases the likelihood that stakeholders will have clearly specified the initiative's intended outcomes, the activities that need to be implemented in order to achieve those outcomes, and the contextual factors that are likely to influence them. These are the building blocks of any good evaluation, but they are especially useful for mid-course feedback to managers and for developing a knowledge base about how and why CCIs work.[2]

With a theory of change in hand, the measurement and data collection elements of the evaluation process will be facilitated. For example, a theory of change asks that participants be as clear as possible about not only the ultimate outcomes and impacts they hope to achieve but also the avenues through which they expect to achieve them (Weiss, 1995). An evaluation based on a theory of change, therefore, identifies what to measure—ultimate and interim outcomes, and the implementation of activities intended to achieve these outcomes—and helps to guide choices about when and how to measure those elements. By providing guidelines for deciding among the various tools in the evaluation toolbox, the approach helps avoid the risk that evaluations will be driven by the tools themselves.

Articulating a theory of change at the outset and gaining agreement on it by all stakeholders reduces, but does not eliminate, problems associated with causal attribution of impact. A theory of change specifies, up front, how activities will lead to interim and longer-term outcomes and identifies the contextual conditions that may affect them. This helps strengthen the scientific case for attributing subsequent change in these outcomes (from initial levels) to the activities included in the initiative. A theory of change approach would seek agreement from all stakeholders that, for example, activities A1, A2, and A3, if properly implemented (and with the ongoing presence of contextual factors X1, X2, and X3), should lead to outcomes O1, O2 and O3; and, if these activities, contextual supports, and outcomes all occur more or less as expected, the outcomes will be attributable to the intervention. Although this strategy cannot eliminate all alternative explanations for a particular outcome, it aligns the major actors in the initiative with a standard of evidence that will be convincing to *them*. Clearly, this will not be as powerful as evidence resulting from randomly assigned control and treatment groups, but, as has been noted elsewhere, random assignment of communities is not a feasible avenue of evaluation for CCIs (Hollister and Hill, 1995).

It should be noted at this point that we are advocating a theory of change *approach* to evaluation; it is not an evaluation *method* that stands on its own. Indeed, the approach relies upon and uses many methodologies that have been developed and refined over the years—quantitative and qualitative, impact and process oriented, traditional and non-traditional, and so on—for information collection, measurement, and analysis. But, if we are right about its promise to generate credible evidence of CCI impact, along with insight into the reasons for that impact, results from evaluations using a theory of change approach should respond to current needs in the field for information about whether CCIs are "working" and generate useful new scientific knowledge to enrich the design of future CCIs.

What Is a *Good* Theory of Change?

For the approach to achieve its potential, the theory of change guiding the CCI and its evaluation needs to be a good one. We have identified three attributes of a good theory of change that stakeholders should confirm are present before committing to an evaluation and, indeed, should revisit throughout the implementation and evaluation of the initiative:[3]

- **It should be *plausible*.** Do evidence and common sense suggest that the activities, if implemented, will lead to desired outcomes?

- **It should be *doable*.** Will the economic, technical, political, institutional, and human resources be available to carry out the initiative?

- **It should be *testable*.** Is the theory of change specific and complete enough for an evaluator to track its progress in credible and useful ways?

To develop plausible, doable, and testable theories of change, CCIs need to draw upon various sources of information—program experience, scientifically generated knowledge, and community residents' insights, to name some of the most important.[4] This is, in part, because neither social science nor experience-to-date nor participants' insights alone yet offers a complete picture of the processes of change that CCIs are seeking. Social science research and evaluation research, for example, are just beginning to investigate unplanned and planned community change (Sullivan, 1996) and how community change impinges on the lives of residents (Connell, Aber, and Walker, 1995; Aber, Berlin, Brooks-Gunn, and Love, 1997). This emerging research base must be combined with the insights and experience of past CCIs (for example, O'Connor, 1995; Halpern, 1995) and the new insights and experience of contemporary CCIs (for example, Kubisch et al., 1997; Stone, 1996) in the development of theories of change.

For example, suppose a CCI sets crime reduction in the target neighborhood as one of its longer-term desired outcomes. If the information guiding the selection of interim and early outcomes and initial activities for the CCI were drawn primarily from the field of law enforcement, the CCI designers might develop a theory of change that highlights increased police presence in the neighborhood. If the information were drawn from urban planning, the theory might focus on improving the condition of open spaces in the neighborhood or tearing down abandoned housing. If the information were drawn from the field of family therapy, the theory might include activities designed to provide developmental supports for adolescents in households with track records of child or spousal abuse. Or, if the information were drawn from community residents' knowledge, well-known drug dealers might be identified for sting operations. By enriching the construction with information from all these sources, the planning process should yield a more plausible theory of change with respect to the longer-term outcome of crime reduction.

O'Connor (1995) has emphasized that one element that must also be incorporated into the theory of change is the external environment. Careful consideration of context helps the designer and evaluator gain clarity about factors that may have a significant bearing on a CCI's chances for achieving its intended outcomes but that the initiative itself is not initially able to influence. This should help ensure that activities are strategically implemented and that the evaluation yields sharp and compelling tests of its hypotheses. In the hypothetical theory of change for education reform presented later in this paper (grid 2), for example, the local school task forces need to be aware of upcoming board elections at the local level, regulations for allocation of state education funds, and federal timelines for phasing out court-ordered bussing.

Carrying Out a Theory of Change Evaluation

Having attempted to describe a theory of change, we now turn to the task of describing how an evaluation based on a theory of change might proceed. On this front, we have made some progress and met some difficult challenges, and, in the next three sections, we share both. The first step is to map out a process that should produce a plausible, doable, and testable theory of change. This is where we have the most experience, and we discuss how to go about getting the theories surfaced, articulated, and aligned. We then turn to the questions of how and when to measure activities and outcomes included in the theories. And finally, we examine whether the information being generated is credible enough to make judgments about how well the initiative is working.

Surfacing and Articulating a Theory of Change

In the introduction to *New Approaches to Evaluating Community Initiatives* (1995), Kubisch, Weiss, Schorr, and Connell conclude that CCIs are difficult to evaluate in part because their designs are underspecified at the outset of an initiative. As a consequence, one of the first things evaluators are commonly asked to do is help specify the theory underlying the intervention and thereby "unpack" the intervention itself.

Chen (1990) and Patton (1986) describe a process in which stakeholders and evaluators "co-construct" the initiative's theory so as to maximize its utility for all, as a planning and management tool, as a vehicle for participant empowerment, as a guide to resource allocation, and as a way of communicating with the field as a whole. This approach resonates with the CCI field's limited experience in this area (see, for example, the practitioners' reflections in this volume).

In our experience, surfacing and articulating a theory of change through a collective and collaborative process is as fraught with difficulties as it is full of promise. The case study by Milligan, Coulton, York, and Register in this volume confirms this and provides more detail about the nature of the real-life discussions that occur on the ground in order to produce such theories of change. Although we are still in the early stages of learning about how to carry out a theory of change evaluation, some lessons and challenges that appear to be particular to the theory articulation process are beginning to emerge. They fall into two broad categories: generating a theory of change and reconciling multiple theories of change.

GENERATING A THEORY OF CHANGE

From our perspective, the goal of the participatory planning process is to generate a theory of change that is viewed by its stakeholders as plausible, doable, and testable. With these three criteria in mind, we recommend that the following questions be considered as part of the planning process:

• What longer-term outcomes does the CCI seek to accomplish?

• What interim outcomes and contextual conditions are necessary and sufficient to produce those longer-term outcomes, beginning with penultimate outcomes and moving through intermediate to early outcomes?

• What activities should be initiated and what contextual supports are necessary to achieve the early and intermediate outcomes?

• What resources are required to implement the activities and maintain the contextual supports necessary for the activities to be effective, and how does the initiative gain the commitment of those resources?

If there is a gap between existing or projected resources available to the initiative and those deemed necessary to implement activities that will produce outcomes, the initiative will have to raise the resources necessary to close the gap. If the gap cannot be closed, first outcomes and then activities will have to be adjusted in order for the theory of change to remain "doable."

We believe that the sequence of steps shown in the diagram below is important to maintain: start with long-term outcomes, work backward toward initial activities, and then map required resources against existing resources. Beyond the general frame, however, much has to be determined locally. Who participates in the conversations? How, when, and where should these conversations take place? These questions must be resolved within the community setting.

STEP 6 — Resource Mapping → STEP 5 — Initial Activities → STEP 4 — Early Outcomes → STEP 3 — Intermediate Outcomes → STEP 2 — Penultimate Outcomes → STEP 1 — Long-term Outcomes

Experience from a wide range of programs and CCIs shows that identifying and agreeing upon long-term outcomes is relatively easy, in part because long-term outcomes are generally so broad as to be uncontroversial: for example, improved high school graduation rates, greater "sense of community," or increased income levels. Likewise, identifying early activities is relatively straightforward. Intermediate and early outcomes are more difficult to specify because scientific and experiential knowledge about links between early, interim, and long-term outcomes is not well developed in many of the key areas in which CCIs operate. Defining interim activities and interim outcomes, and then linking those to longer-term outcomes, appears to be the hardest part of the theory articulation process.

For the purposes of this paper, we have generated two theories of change that could have resulted from this process. Each illustrates, at an admittedly general level, what an early version of a theory of change might look like for a CCI that is focusing on community building (grid 1) or education reform (grid 2).[5] Each grid includes longer-term outcomes, a set of interim outcomes that should lead to these longer-term outcomes, some early outcomes that logically precede the intermediate ones, and the initial activities that are meant to lead to the early outcomes. Each grid is also divided into four levels of outcomes that appear to be most relevant for current CCIs: community, organizational/institutional, family/personal network, and individual.

The process of constructing these theories of change highlights the tenuous nature of the causal linkages guiding many CCIs. In the education reform theory of change (grid 2), evidence from school-reform research tells us that the long-term, individual outcome of improved student performance will probably occur when the specified changes at the school, or institutional, level are put in place. There is much weaker support, however, for the part of the theory that identifies the formation and activation of an education task force within the CCI as a critical step toward producing institutional change in the schools. In the case of the community building theory of change (grid 1), we have even weaker scientific and practical knowledge about how to produce some of the longer-term outcomes

Grid 1: Hypothetical Theory of Change for Community Building

	Early Activities	Early Outcomes
Community	• Publicity about initiative • Neighborhood celebration • Neighborhood clean-up • Mapping of neighborhood resources and needs assessment • Neighborhood newsletter	• Large numbers of residents come to initiative meetings • Neighborhood assets are mapped and priority problems identified • New "vision" of neighborhood developed, articulated, and agreed upon

Organizational/ Institutional	• Formation of multi-institutional, multi-purpose governing entity for initiative
	• Funding solicited/received
		• Governing entity well functioning with:
		  • good representation, good leadership, trained board
		  • management and staffing structure in place
		  • accountability clear
		  • shared vision, long-term goals, and action plan developed

Personal Network/ Family	• Mutual support groups formed (e.g., teen parents, grandparents, alcohol abuse) • "Sub-neighborhood" social and civic activities (e.g., block or building associations)	• Residents know more neighbors' names and faces • Increased resident participation in voluntary associations • Residents know of safe places to go in case of problems
Individual	• Leadership development programs launched	• Residents trained in conflict resolution, community organizing, and leadership skills

Intermediate Outcomes	Long-Term Outcomes
• Residents' attitudes shifting to view that "neighborhood is getting better" • Increase in percentage of residents who voted at last election • Fewer negative events/behaviors such as graffiti, public substance abuse, littering	• Residents believe theirs is a good neighborhood to raise children • Inter-group relations harmonious • Improved neighborhood-level outcomes on income, education, crime, physical infrastructure, health, and well-being • Residents believe that neighborhood has capacity to achieve goals • Residents not moving out even when their income increases
• "Visible" projects successfully implemented • Resources (financial, political, or technical) leveraged from outside neighborhood • Research and evaluation information used as management tool, community organizing tool • Service institutions more flexible, family- and community-oriented • Increase in activities of cultural, recreational, religious, social, and civic institutions • Resident-driven economic and physical revitalization	• Neighborhood projects have provided systematic reform in public and private institutions outside of neighborhood • Neighborhood institutions (service, economic, civic, etc.) have strong resource base
• Increases in number of informal associations (bowling leagues, holiday events, cooking clubs, savings clubs) • Neighbors more willing to ask one another for help (borrowing tools, watching kids) • Vulnerable populations (aged, disabled) well cared for	• Residents feel comfortable about taking action when neighbor does something wrong (using drugs publicly, kids misbehaving) • Residents help one another get jobs, get access to political leadership • Volunteerism is strong neighborhood practice
• New nontraditional leadership emerging in neighborhood activities	• Residents running most of the significant civic, cultural, economic, social and political institutions in the community

Grid 2: Hypothetical Theory of Change for Educational Reform

	Early Activities	Early Outcomes
Community	• Overall CCI collaborative formed • Collaborative identifies meaningful improvement of educational outcomes as part of mission	• Residents meet to discuss strategic plan as it pertains to their local schools

Organizational/ Institutional	• Collaborative forms education task force to:
	  • study school outcomes and practices
	  • review best practices (local and national)
	  • discuss promising change models for getting best practices implemented
	• Education task force creates plan for instigating and supporting local school reform that includes:
	  • critical features for schools to be successful with all students in community
	  • changes in roles and responsibilities
	  • school and community resources (human and financial) required for change
		• Education task force and CCI leadership and supporters obtain written commitment from key stakeholders at all levels to see critical features of plan for schools and school system implemented
		• Education staff on task force convenes colleagues at local schools to discuss strategic plan
		• School planning teams develop local implementation plans for putting critical features in place along with resource maps
		• School-site planning teams coordinate with district support team to assure systemic change in support of school-site change

Personal Network/ Family	• School sends home regular newsletters about plans and activities
	• New afterschool social and cultural activities initiated
		• Caregivers initiate and have regular contact with school personnel
		• Families participate in school-sponsored activities:
		  • at the school, such as governance opportunities, celebrations, fundraising
		  • in the community, such as learning fairs, board elections, and meetings
		• Peer networks form around positive school-related activities, such as afterschool clubs

Individual		• Individual students report higher levels of interpersonal and instructional supports from their teachers

Intermediate Outcomes	Long-Term Outcomes
• Members of CCI educational task force and local school task forces meet with community residents regularly to discuss progress on ways to support implementation of critical features of educational reform plan • Local school task forces coordinate to help develop platforms and campaign for school board	• Families move less often in order to keep children in same schools and do not choose private or religious schools • The prevalence of idle school-age adolescents decreases during school hours • School staff viewed as engaged in community efforts • Youth viewed as contributing to the community, respectful and employable

• Initial implementation of "critical features" of successful schools:
  • <15:1 student/adult ratios during core instructional periods
  • teachers staying with students for multiple years
  • high, clear, and fair standards for academic performance and conduct
  • enriched opportunities for learning
  • collective responsibility for student performance
  • instructional autonomy and support
  • flexible allocation of resources
	• Full implementation of "critical features" of successful schools in all schools serving community's children and youth

• Families know each other through school initiated activities and provide mutual support for student learning • Families can state examples of school personnel being available, accessible, responsive, and/or proactive • Peer networks engage more frequently in school- and career-related discourse • Youth gangs are less prevalent	• Caregivers are assisting with homework and monitoring progress and dedicating discretionary resources—time, effort, and money—to educational materials and activities • Peer networks are engaging less frequently in anti-social activities

• Individual students show improvement in attendance and disciplinary referrals
• Individual students report greater:
  • sense of support from peers for academic achievement
  • involvement by caregivers and teachers
  • interest in and effort toward school work
  • personal connections with teachers
  • responsibility for own education and belief in own competence
	• Individual students show meaningful improvement in their knowledge and performance:
	  • within the academic disciplines (mathematics, history, science, languages)
	  • in cross-cutting competencies (communications, reasoning, problem solving, workplace and higher education readiness, citizenship, functioning in multicultural contexts)

specified in the theory. Consider, for example, the outcome of residents feel-
ing comfortable about taking action when a neighbor "does something
wrong," such as using drugs publicly. Given that we have little evidence
about how to produce that outcome, how can we have confidence that its
hypothesized precursors—say, creating new block-level civic and social
activities so that more residents know their neighbors—even if implemented, will take us down the right path?

In addition, specifying intermediate outcomes and how they may lead
to long-term change can be a politically charged process, especially if those
outcomes might imply major resource reallocation or power shifts. For
example, in the educational reform theory of change (grid 2), we hypothe-
size that the strategic plan of the CCI education task force has the goal of
making significant changes in school operations. These changes may
require different uses of funds, new job descriptions, and perhaps even laying people off. Gaining consensus among all stakeholders, especially the
education professionals, on those changes and how they will be made is
more difficult than simply pronouncing that all children will show meaningful improvement in their educational performance.

With regard to a CCI's activities, early activities proposed by the CCI are
often fairly well specified, while later activities and their links to later outcomes
tend to remain underspecified. This lack of detail reflects the fact that few CCIs
have gotten much beyond early outcomes in any of their operational areas.
Moreover, CCIs are meant to be dynamic enterprises, and the initial theory of
change serves as a map of mostly uncharted territory, a map that the CCI itself
will have to revise as it makes its voyage. Thus, our experience suggests that a
common answer to the question, "What do you expect to be doing in the fifth
year of the initiative?" is "Ask us in the fourth year, and we'll tell you."

The inability of many stakeholders to make linkages between early
activities and longer-term outcomes raises significant problems for evaluation design. Perhaps the greatest factor in determining the feasibility of the
theory of change approach is the capacity of a CCI's stakeholders and
evaluators to identify, prioritize, and then measure the key activities and
contextual factors, *not in retrospect but in advance*. Evaluators and stake-

holders alike are quite good at looking back on interventions and constructing compelling tales of why a particular result did or did not occur.
The challenge posed by the theory of change approach is to theorize
prospectively about these issues. This requires balancing the need for the
theory of change to remain responsive to emerging opportunities and
challenges with the need for investors in CCIs (including funders,
implementers, and participants) to have some basis upon which to judge
the likelihood of reaching the intended long-term outcomes.

RECONCILING MULTIPLE THEORIES OF CHANGE

Once the theory specification process begins, it quickly becomes apparent
that various stakeholders in the initiative can, and often do, hold different
views about what it will take to produce the long-term outcomes of the initiative. Indeed, one of the important contributions of this approach is that
it points out that multiple theories of change may be operating simultaneously within a single CCI and that various CCI stakeholders may be working under different, and possibly even competing, theories of change.

For example, Weiss (1995) pointed out several assumptions CCI archi-
tects and funders are including in their theories of change: that $250,000-
$500,000 per year is a significant enough amount of money to cause change
at the neighborhood level; that a neighborhood is an appropriate unit on
which to target an initiative's efforts; and that agency collaboration is required
at the neighborhood level. One can imagine the director of a lead agency chosen to implement a new foundation-funded CCI operating under quite different assumptions. She might believe that $250,000-$500,000 is not nearly
enough to implement the activities required to achieve the CCI's stated outcomes. She might think, therefore, that the initial grant should be seen as a
vehicle to leverage additional funds. She might also believe that the neighborhood is not capable of achieving the change on its own and that significant
efforts must be made to involve the neighborhood in citywide efforts. Finally,
she might think that agency collaboration is nice but takes a lot of time and
preempts the agencies' time to deliver specialized services that are badly needed in the neighborhood. In what ways are these different hypotheses in har-
mony, and possibly reinforcing, and in what ways do they imply different

activities, timelines, and even outcomes? These views should be uncovered as stakeholders move through the steps presented earlier of surfacing and articulating the theories of change guiding the CCI.

It is not uncommon for CCIs to be launched without the various theories of change being articulated, much less reconciled. Some experts have noted that one of the great strengths of the CCI phenomenon might well be that it can accommodate multiple theories of change and move forward without their reconciliation. But CCIs that remain inclusive enough to accommodate these multiple theories cannot avoid integrating the theories at two points: the allocation of resources and the evaluation. It is, after all, in the decisions about which activities to invest in that priorities must be developed about which of the various hypotheses that link activities to outcomes are most promising. And it is in the process of designing an evaluation that specific decisions must be taken regarding what is meant by key terms (such as "collaboration"), the type and degree of change being sought, and the measures that would indicate whether change is occurring.[6]

In the example above, the difference between the funder's and director's views of the importance of agency collaboration would emerge as they decide upon early and interim outcomes that each believes will lead to long-term change. In the funder's eyes, credible evidence of collaboration might involve building structural institutional links, such as joint staffing of a new family service program and pooled resources. The lead agency director, on the other hand, might view collaboration so differently that her marker of progress might simply be increased evidence of referrals among agencies.

Resolving the challenges that these multiple theories pose is a political as well as scientific process. Patton (1996) and Usher (1996) warn that imposing strict standards of theory articulation too early in the process can undermine participation and stifle the dynamic nature of the CCI enterprise. At the same time, as suggested above, leaving the CCI's theory of change ambiguous permits, and indeed encourages, various stakeholders to project their own preferences about activities and outcomes onto the initiative. This Rorschach-test model for CCI theories of change can set up false and unrealizable expectations among stakeholders that could become problematic during resource allocation and evaluation planning. The political question that confronts the

CCI manager becomes: When is the CCI robust enough to have the true diversity of its stakeholders' theories surfaced and integrated into its overall theory? Or, when can it no longer operate without doing so? Will these different theories of change be included as parallel, integrated, or competing strands in the overall theory, or will some be selected for inclusion in the implementation and evaluation of the initiative and others not? The task of addressing these issues should not fall solely, or even primarily, to the evaluator, but the evaluation discussion may serve as the context within which they are played out.

The requirements that theories be articulated and that they be specific enough for stakeholders to make judgments about whether or not they are plausible, doable, and testable do not preclude those theories from incorporating multiple perspectives on what long-term outcomes are important, what the interim steps are to getting to those long-term outcomes, and what activities should be implemented. Our two hypothetical theories of change are complex and include multiple strategies for achieving long-term outcomes.[7] Plausible theories of change will no doubt be complex and pluralistic, but if they are to be implemented (doable) they cannot be contradictory and if they are to be evaluated (testable) they cannot be unarticulated.

Measuring Activities and Outcomes

In any evaluation, outcomes and activities must be translated into observable measures: How do we know that the treatment or program occurred, and how do we measure its results? That measurement process in CCIs is likely to be more complex and demanding than in typical program evaluations.

Even in evaluations of multifaceted programs—having different combinations of elements, multiple mediators and moderators of treatment effects, and multiple desired outcomes—the measurement process tends to reside at one unit of observation, typically the individual, and to occur in a fixed order, with treatment assessed first, mediators next, and outcomes last. Moreover, measurement in more circumscribed program evaluations tends to draw primarily on quantitative techniques, such as enumerating participation through administrative records, surveying clients to gauge exposure and experience, and actuarial activities to measure discrete client outcomes.

The measurement demands placed on evaluators of CCIs by a theory of change approach are quite different. Measures of outcomes and activities must be developed at multiple levels. In the case of outcomes, as in any other evaluation, some are more difficult to measure than others. CCI outcomes such as improvements in infant mortality, high school graduation, and employment rates are relatively easy to measure.[8] Measures of community attributes such as social capital, shared values, and strong networks are more elusive, as are institutional change indicators of service integration, responsiveness to community needs, and systems reform. CCI "treatments" are sets of activities that occur over time in inter-related clusters at different levels of observation, with later activities being shaped by the outcomes of earlier activities. Therefore, traditional single-point or fixed-interval longitudinal assessments of outcomes will not effectively capture the change process in CCIs, and staggered baselines may even be necessary. Clearly, the measurement burden in a theory of change evaluation is likely to be heavy.[9]

Although most CCIs are still in the early stages of measuring activities and outcomes, three measurement issues are emerging that are specific to a theory of change evaluation.[10]

Measurement of a CCI's activities is as important as measurement of its outcomes. To make a case for impact, the theory of change approach seeks to accumulate rigorous tests of links between an initiative's activities and their expected outcomes. Therefore, it must have compelling measures of both activities and outcomes and then link, through causal inference, change in one to change in the other, repeatedly and cumulatively over the early, intermediate, and later stages of the initiative. Thus, in this approach, process is recast into activities, and outcomes are expanded to include results occurring over the entire course of the initiative, not just the long term, and at multiple levels, not just the individual level. Some of those activities might relate more to the creation of the conditions or capacities for achieving outcomes, and their outcomes might be indicators of readiness to continue with the next set of activities.

The measurement discussion must resolve the issue, "How good is good enough?" For a theory of change to guide an initiative and its evaluation, performance standards must be set for the outcomes included in the theory as well as for the implementation of activities. In our education reform example, many of the critical features of school site reform included in the theory of change have specific targets in the intermediate and long terms: for example, reducing student/adult ratios to less than 15/1 during core instructional periods. For the evaluation to be useful during early stages, stakeholders will have to be precise about what the initial activities should look like and what early outcomes will be required to produce desired thresholds on intermediate outcomes. For example, what form of commitment from school officials to the reform plan will be sufficient to proceed to the first implementation step? Or, in our community building example, how will we know whether the CCI governing entity has good representation, good leadership, an adequate management structure, and appropriate staffing?

Certainly any evaluation would be well served by establishing expected threshold levels of change, but this issue is crucial in a CCI theory of change evaluation. Stakeholders must have a clear idea of how much change is "good enough" for them because there may not be an *ex post* analysis of whether CCI-induced change, particularly on early and intermediate outcomes, was "statistically" significant.

The process of surfacing and articulating the theory of change will provide important information about measuring activities and outcomes. For example, a good theory of change provides some rational structure for determining measurement points. Instead of setting arbitrary and perhaps inappropriate data-collection points (or expecting "constant" data gathering from the evaluator), the approach suggests that measurement points be based on when activities specified in the theory of change should occur and when their intended outcomes should occur. If a strong collaborative process is established in the early stages of a theory of change evaluation, it can help assure that stakeholders will work with the evaluator to explore creative measurement strategies.

Making the Case for Impact

The question of how to make a convincing case that a CCI has or has not worked remains problematic. The paper by Robert Granger in this volume takes up this topic in much greater detail, so we will raise only a few points at this time.

At the most general level, the theory of change approach contends that the more the events predicted by theory actually occur over the course of the CCI, the more confidence evaluators and others should have that the initiative's theory is right. We suggest, then, that the major audiences for an evaluation of a CCI—including community residents, initiative managers and funders, and policy makers—should be convinced that the initiative "worked" if four points can be demonstrated:

• up front and along the way, a well-specified and plausible theory of change described steps toward an anticipated change (from historical baselines) in important outcomes for the community, its institutions, and its residents

• the activities of the CCI that were part of these steps were implemented at expected thresholds

• the magnitude of changes in the early, intermediate, and long-term outcomes that followed these activities met predicted thresholds

• no obvious and pervasive contextual shift occurred that could otherwise account for all these predicted sequences of activities and outcomes

Would these criteria be sufficient for the most skeptical researchers to agree that the CCI worked, that it had impact? Probably not. But ruling out all alternative explanations through randomized experimental methods is not feasible as the *primary* inferential tool for attributing impact to a CCI. The theory of change approach for establishing impact draws on tried and true scientific traditions of testing hypotheses about cause and effect relationships, including methods used in physical, biological, and other social sciences.

What sets the social policy evaluation field apart from most of the rest of the scientific world has been its conclusion that all forms of hypothesis-testing are inadequate relative to experimental approaches that include random assignment of units of observation (individuals, institutions, communities) to treatment and control conditions (Hollister and Hill, 1995). The argument made by those who seek to retain this single standard of evidence for impact is that it is the *only* way to establish a convincing counterfactual. But, part of the reason for the dominance of the experimentalists is that the magnitude of the change expected to occur as a function of many social interventions has been very small. The smaller the change expected, the more solid the counterfactual must be in order to attribute cause. However, in most current CCIs, the magnitude of change expected in the long-term outcomes is *not* small. They seek neighborhood transformation and meaningful improvements in individual and family well-being. Whether or not stakeholders agree that these expectations are realistic— that is, whether the theory of change is plausible and doable—should be determined before they are tested in an evaluation. The more significant the change that occurs, we and others (such as Gueron, 1996) would argue, the less the need for airtight counterfactuals to attribute impact to CCIs.

Theory of Change Evaluation Reports

The theory of change approach recasts traditional distinctions made in the program evaluation literature. For example, *a systematic and cumulative study of links between activities and outcomes* replaces process documentation, implementation, and outcome studies. This recasting has implications for what the products of such an evaluation might look like.

Most evaluations of complex initiatives focus their measurement activities on long-term outcomes. As a secondary component, "process" or "documentation" studies collect descriptive data (usually qualitative) on planning and implementation activities. Implementation studies discuss whether or not and how completely the program or initiative was implemented. These studies are then written up separately from the outcomes studies or loosely coupled in a summary report. The message delivered by this form of reporting is clear: what is really important is whether the long-term outcomes changed; how the change occurred and why the intervention did or didn't work are secondary.

Alternatively, and more frequently in evaluation reports on CCIs, process documentation and implementation studies are *all* that is presented because long-term outcomes are not expected to have shown any change until years after the initial activities are implemented and because there is no strong, *a priori* theory of change linking early activities to early outcomes. Process documentation has not been unwelcome, since it often provides both funders and directors of initiatives with formative feedback on operational issues useful for mid-course corrections. Even so, those who have been involved with CCIs for some time are well aware that it is important for evaluators to avoid becoming so enmeshed in information about process that they lose sight of the importance of whether and how activities are leading to desired outcomes. Assessing quality of implementation is a necessary but not a sufficient condition for good evaluation, even in the short term. What early outcomes are these activities supposed to affect? How are these outcomes being measured? How are the links between initial activities and early outcomes established? How is the movement toward intermediate and longer-term outcomes being tracked?

Thus, the theory of change approach replaces the two principal, and often independent, types of evaluation reports with one that explicitly and deliberately covers both activities (formerly process and implementation) and outcomes (formerly long-term outcomes only). As in most approaches to evaluation, the very first reports are likely to provide baseline readings on desired early, intermediate, and long-term effects. But soon thereafter, we should expect evaluation reports to focus on links between initial activities and early outcomes. We believe that this form of reporting helps the theory of change approach supply all stakeholders with timely, useful, and rigorous information about the progress of their initiative and can provide early guidance if the theory of change needs to be revised.

Strengths and Challenges of the Theory of Change Approach

The major strength of the theory of change approach is its inherent common sense. Its major *competitive* advantage is the inability of other currently available approaches to do the job.

We have described the potential benefits of the theory of change approach from the initial planning of a CCI, through the measurement of its outcomes and activities, to the analysis and interpretation of the data. It should generate useful learning over the life span of the initiative and could spawn cross-initiative learning as well. But perhaps its most powerful contribution to the evaluation endeavor is its emphasis on understanding not only *whether* activities produce effects but *how* and *why,* throughout the course of the initiative. This is useful at the level of the CCI itself, where feedback from the evaluation can help stakeholders make informed decisions about whether to stay the course or modify goals and strategies. But the audience for information about the "how" and "why" is also much wider. It includes other program directors, designers, or funders who need guidance as they develop new efforts or attempt to learn from successful initiatives. They need specific information about actual mechanisms that are related to good outcomes, and an evaluation guided by a theory of change can provide that level of detail (Weiss, 1997). And, given that CCIs are explicitly designed as experiments in how to transform distressed communities, a theory of change evaluation contributes to the "social learning" objectives of evaluations and gives them a national and perhaps even international audience in policy and research. For example, the approach exposes gaps in existing knowledge and helps lay out a research agenda in many fields of inquiry.

The theory of change planning and evaluation process can also reinforce the broader goals of the initiative. In particular, the process can be a powerful tool for promoting collaboration and engagement at the community level focused on products and outcomes. For example, building capacity for ongoing problem solving at the community level is a goal of virtually all CCIs, and, because a theory of change evaluation explicitly values community knowledge, vehicles for resident involvement are easily built into its structure. Brown (1995) suggests that an evaluation, if so designed, can contribute to that goal by ensuring that data about the community are collected, analyzed, and then fed back in a way that can educate and mobilize residents to participate in an ongoing community planning process. Also, although all participants may agree that evaluation is important, it can be difficult to get agency staff or residents to invest the requisite time and energy in the evaluation enterprise, which often seems secondary to activities that lead more directly to improved outcomes. We suggest that a theory of change approach to evaluation, when developed with or shared with staff and residents, can help to overcome that reluctance. It helps to make explicit the capacity-building agenda of the initiative and the role evaluation can play in that agenda.

At the same time, creating new partnerships, fostering collaboration, and developing community capacity can lead to a diffusion of responsibility that is detrimental to the impact and sustainability of an initiative. Again, a theory of change is helpful, in this case to clarify accountability pathways in the initiative. The more explicit the theory of change, the more explicit and consensually validated the accountability structure can be.

Thus, the approach breaks down the line between formative and summative evaluation. It diminishes the perceived trade-off between rigor and programmatic utility of information being collected. It aspires to both simultaneously, while adding the goals of social learning and capacity building. The approach, as we see it, recognizes that there is neither the need nor the time to collect separate kinds or different qualities of information in order to serve all of these important goals.

Before closing, however, we feel obligated to be clear about what we foresee as some of the burdens of a theory of change approach to evaluation. In order for it to be most useful, all stakeholders will need to invest time and political capital in developing plausible, doable, and testable theories of change. This is true for all participants but especially for evaluators, who will need to broaden their view of their role to include eliciting complex theories of change and translating them into evaluation designs; using or developing multiple, and often sophisticated, measures of activities and outcomes; ascertaining linkages between activities and outcomes on a continuous basis; detecting differences between espoused theories and program implementation; and supporting strategic efforts to convince skeptics that evaluation results are compelling.

Of course, many of these investments would be required for any good evaluation. What is not yet known is whether a theory of change approach suggests still greater investments on these fronts or whether a well-articulated theory of change will create offsetting efficiencies as well. In all likelihood, the answer will vary greatly by initiative, by evaluator, and by the availability of funding.

Finally, it is important to reiterate that the theory of change approach to CCI evaluation is *only an approach.* It provides a framework for embarking on the evaluation of a complex initiative that promises to be useful to the evaluator and other stakeholders. It helps to identify what should be evaluated and clarifies the research questions. But it will employ familiar methodological tools to measure outcomes and activities and to strengthen the credibility of its conclusions. It does not solve all the evaluator's challenges in working with these complex initiatives, but it might make the job more tractable, useful, and rewarding.

The next and most important question is how this approach holds up in the crucible of practice. Fortunately, versions of the approach are already being tested in a number of initiatives, some of which are described elsewhere in this volume. Some insights on the utility of the approach should be forthcoming from these initiatives and others in the near future. The true test of the approach will come as stakeholders in these and other CCIs take stock and decide whether the evaluation results are clear, compelling, and useful for their purposes.

Notes

Many people shared their time and wisdom with us in order to make this paper possible. Janice Hirota, a consultant to the Roundtable, took the first step in testing out the concepts of a "theory of change" approach to CCI evaluations on the ground. The following people endured long interviews and were very generous with their time: Otis Johnson, Don Mendoza, and Mary Willoughby at the Chatham-Savannah Youth Futures Authority; Eric Brettschneider and his colleagues at Agenda for Children Tomorrow in New York City; Marvin Cohen and his colleagues at the Chicago Community Trust's Children, Youth and Families Initiative; Arthur Bolton, Rosalind Garner, James Johnson, Jan Reeves, and their colleagues in Sacramento; and Ronald Register, Sharon Milligan, Claudia

Coulton, and their colleagues in Cleveland. Throughout the paper, we weave in information about current and planned CCIs in order to ground the points we are making. The examples are synthetic ones, drawn from and combined across these and other CCIs. We mean to implicate none of the above-mentioned initiatives in the paper. In addition, Margery Turner, Lisbeth Schorr, Langley Keyes, Sheila Smith, Peter Rossi, Michael Patton, Lynn Usher, Lynn Kagan, John Gaventa, and many other colleagues in the field have shared their views on the issues presented herein and have provided invaluable feedback on earlier drafts. We are grateful to them all.

1   Carol Weiss introduced the notion of theory-guided program evaluation in 1972 (Weiss, 1972). Huey-tsyh Chen has been working on theory-driven evaluation approaches since 1981, particularly as applied to program evaluation, and many others have contributed to its elaboration and evolution along the way. See, for example, Bickman, 1987; Chen, 1990; Chen and Rossi, 1992; Fetterman et al., 1996; Gaventa, 1995; Patton, 1986; Yin, 1989.

2   See Connell (1996) for a fuller elaboration of these arguments.

3   Recent field-based work by Connell suggests that a fourth criterion be added: that outcomes included in the theory of change be *meaningful* to all stakeholders. One can imagine a theory of change that meets the first three criteria but is focused on goals and outcomes that are considered unimportant or even trivial by one or more stakeholder groups.

4   Existing literature on program evaluation suggests that there are different types of theories and that, for both design and evaluation purposes, there are tradeoffs among them. For example, Chen (1990) makes the distinction between normative (experience based) and causative (scientifically based) program theories, and Rossi (1996) argues that scientifically based theories are more useful for program evaluation. Our view is that CCIs are such new and complex phenomena that we must mine multiple sources of information in order to try to develop the strongest possible theories of change.

5   See Connell (1996) for a fuller examination of an education reform theory of change.

6   If, on the other hand, the initiative and the evaluation are extremely well funded, multiple theories of change might be implemented and tested.

7   We have encountered other cases where multiple strategies are being pursued in the service of a common goal: for example, building developmental supports for youth by establishing service-based referrals to church youth groups, community service programs for youth, and support networks for their grandparents. In

other cases, multiple goals are served by a single set of activities: for example, putting resources into an existing "community kitchen" to improve physical health by providing nutritious meals, to offer jobs to otherwise unemployed residents, and to build "individual responsibility" by insisting that those who receive free meals contribute time to the kitchen or other neighborhood service activity.

8 The "face validity" of any measure could be questioned by some stakeholders in CCIs. For example, change in the proportion of students completing high school is relatively easy to measure, but some stakeholders may challenge this as an indicator of "progress" if they perceive standards being lowered to increase proportions of students achieving this outcome.

9 These challenges of measurement and others—when and how often to collect measures of these activities and outcomes, or who or what should be measured to capture neighborhood, institutional, family and individual change—are discussed in more detail in the chapter by Michelle Gambone in this volume. The Roundtable's steering committee on evaluation is also developing an annotated catalogue of measures that will give potential users important information about available instruments and strategies.

10 These issues are addressed in greater depth by Michelle Gambone, in this volume.

References

Aber, J. Lawrence, Lisa Berlin, Jeanne Brooks-Gunn, and John Love. 1997. "Comprehensive Community Initiatives: Their Role in Promoting the Development of Young Children and Their Families." Draft report. Washington, DC: Aspen Institute.

Argyis, Chris, and Donald Schon. 1992. *Theory in Practice: Increasing Professional Effectiveness.* San Francisco: Jossey-Bass.

Brown, Prudence. 1995. "The Role of the Evaluator in Comprehensive Community Initiatives." In *New Approaches to Evaluating Community Initiatives: Concepts, Methods, and Contexts,* ed. James Connell et al. Washington, DC: Aspen Institute.

Chen, Huey-tsyh. 1990. *Theory Driven Evaluations.* Thousand Oaks, CA: Sage Publications.

Chen, Huey-tsyh, and Peter H. Rossi., eds. 1992. *Using Theory to Improve Program and Policy Evaluations.* New York: Greenwood Press.

Connell, James P. 1996. *First Things First: A Framework for Successful School-site Reform.* White paper prepared for the E. M. Kauffman Foundation. Kansas City: E. M. Kauffman Foundation.

Connell, James P., Anne C. Kubisch, Lisbeth B. Schorr, and Carol H. Weiss, eds. 1995. *New Approaches to Evaluating Community Initiatives: Concepts, Methods, and Contexts.* Washington, DC: Aspen Institute.

Connell, James P., J. Lawrence Aber, and Gary Walker. 1995. "How Do Urban Communities Affect Youth? Using Social Science Research to Inform the Design and Evaluation of Comprehensive Community Initiatives." In *New Approaches to Evaluating Community Initiatives: Concepts, Methods, and Contexts,* ed. James Connell et al. Washington, DC: Aspen Institute.

Fetterman, David M., Shakeh J. Kaftarian, and Abraham Wandersman, eds. 1996. *Empowerment Evaluation: Knowledge and Tools for Self-Assessment and Accountability.* Thousand Oaks, CA: Sage Publications.

Gaventa, John, Janice Morrissey, and Wanda Edwards. 1995. *The Evaluation and Learning Initiative of the National Empowerment Zone and Enterprise Community Program: Review and Recommendations for Phase II Support.* Volumes I and II. Knoxville: University of Tennessee.

Granger, Robert. 1995. Personal communication.

Gueron, Judith. 1996. Personal communication.

Halpern, Robert. 1995. *Rebuilding the Inner City: A History of Neighborhood Initiatives to Address Poverty in the United States.* New York: Columbia University Press.

Hirota, Janice. 1995. *Interim Report: Fieldwork and a Theory-based Approach to Evaluation.* Draft report to the evaluation steering committee of the Roundtable on Comprehensive Community Initiatives for Children and Families. Washington, DC:Aspen Institute.

Hollister, Robinson G., and Jennifer Hill. 1995. "Problems in the Evaluation of Community-Wide Initiatives." In *New Approaches to Evaluating Community Initiatives: Concepts, Methods, and Contexts,* ed. James Connell et al. Washington, DC: Aspen Institute.

Kubisch, Anne C., Carol H. Weiss, Lisbeth B. Schorr, and James P. Connell. 1995. "Introduction." In *New Approaches to Evaluating Community Initiatives: Concepts, Methods, and Contexts,* ed. James Connell et al. Washington, DC: Aspen Institute.

Kubisch, Anne C., Prudence Brown, Robert Chaskin, Janice Hirota, Mark Joseph, Harold Richman, and Michelle Roberts. 1997. *Voices from the Field: Learning from Comprehensive Community Initiatives.* Washington, DC: Aspen Institute.

Milligan, Sharon, Claudia Coulton, Peter York, and Ronald Register. 1996. *Implementing a Theories of Change Evaluation in the Cleveland Community Building*

Initiative. Cleveland: Center on Urban Poverty and Social Change, Case Western Reserve University.

Mueller, Elizabeth, Xavier de Souza Briggs, and Mercer Sullivan. 1996. *From Neighborhood to Community: Evidence on the Social Effects of Community Development.* New York: Community Development Research Center, New School for Social Research.

O'Connor, Alice. 1995. "Evaluating Comprehensive Community Initiatives: A View from History." In *New Approaches to Evaluating Community Initiatives: Concepts, Methods, and Contexts,* ed. James Connell et al. Washington, DC: Aspen Institute.

Patton, Michael. 1986. *Utilization-Focused Evaluation.* Newbury Park, CA: Sage Publications.

Patton, Michael. 1996. Personal communication.

Rossi, Peter. Forthcoming. "Evaluating Community Development Programs: Problems and Prospects." In *Urban Problems and Community Development,* ed. Ron Ferguson and William Dickens. Washington, DC: Brookings Institute.

Stone, Rebecca, ed. 1996. *Core Issues in Comprehensive Community-Building Initiatives.* Chicago: Chapin Hall Center for Children.

Sullivan, Mercer. 1996. "Where Is the Community in Comprehensive Community Initiatives? Lessons from Community Studies for Design and Evaluation." Draft Report. Washington, DC: Aspen Institute.

Trochim, William M. K., and Judith Cook. 1992. "Pattern Matching in Theory-Driven Evaluation: A Field Example from Psychiatric Rehabilitation." In *Using Theory to Improve Program and Policy Evaluations,* ed. Huey-tsyh Chen and Peter H. Rossi. New York: Greenwood Press.

Usher, C. Lynn. 1996. Personal communication.

Weiss, Carol Hirschon. 1997. "How Can Theory-Based Evaluation Make Greater Headway?" *Evaluation Review* 21, No. 4.

Weiss, Carol Hirschon. 1995. "Nothing as Practical as Good Theory: Exploring Theory-based Evaluation for Comprehensive Community Initiatives for Children and Families." In *New Approaches to Evaluating Community Initiatives: Concepts, Methods, and Contexts,* ed. James Connell et al. Washington, DC: Aspen Institute.

Weiss, Carol Hirschon. 1972. *Evaluation Research: Methods of Assessing Program Effectiveness.* Englewood Cliffs, NJ: Prentice-Hall.

Yin, Robert K. 1992. "The Role of Theory in Doing Case Study Research and Evaluations." In *Using Theory to Improve Program and Policy Evaluations,* ed. Hueytsyh Chen and Peter H. Rossi. New York: Greenwood Press.

Implementing a Theory of Change Evaluation in the Cleveland Community-Building Initiative: A Case Study

Sharon Milligan, Claudia Coulton,
Peter York, and Ronald Register

Introduction

Comprehensive community initiatives have proven difficult to evaluate because they do not lend themselves to traditional experimental methods. Nevertheless, many audiences are interested in the effectiveness of these efforts in actually creating change and improving the lives of residents. The theory of change approach to evaluation is intended to respond to these challenges.

In a theory of change approach, evaluators, program designers and staff, and other stakeholders work together to make explicit the important pathways of change they expect to follow. Further, they specify key steps along those pathways so those steps can be measured. The steps include both initiative strategies and the anticipated short- and long-term outcomes of the initiative. The evaluation determines the degree to which the change process is unfolding as expected and links strategies to outcomes.

Although this approach does not yield the type of impact estimate that can come from an experimental design, it does have several advantages. First, it can be applied to whole community interventions, within which untreated control groups are not possible. Second, it makes explicit many assumptions about the ingredients of community and system change and how those are expected to improve conditions for residents and their local institutions. Third, by tracking progress along the steps of the change process, it can provide corrective feedback that distinguishes failures of theory from failures in implementation. If the initiative's programs and activities are shown to lead to expected outcomes over time, the evaluation begins to build a case for the effectiveness of the initiative. Even without a control group to provide a counter-factual, the order of occurrence of the outcomes and the resemblance of those outcomes to those predicted can support inferences about effectiveness.

The Cleveland Community-Building Initiative (CCBI), in collaboration with the Center on Urban Poverty and Social Change, has begun the process of implementing a theory of change approach to evaluation. CCBI and the evaluators have participated in the work of the evaluation committee of the Aspen Institute's Roundtable on Comprehensive Community Initiatives for Children and Families and are one of the first teams to operationalize concepts from the theory of change approach.

Because there is little extant experience with the theory of change approach, this paper describes how the evaluators, staff, board, and community stakeholders launched the evaluation and what they learned from the experience. Specifically, the processes of involving stakeholders in the evaluation, delineating the elements of the theory, and choosing and defining the concepts to be studied are explicated. Before depicting these experiences, however, we present background on CCBI and the evaluation.

The Cleveland Community-Building Initiative

The Cleveland Community-Building Initiative (CCBI) builds on the work of the Cleveland and Rockefeller foundations to reverse growing and persistent poverty and related deteriorating conditions in urban neighborhoods. Through its six-city Community Planning and Action Project, the Rockefeller Foundation sought to analyze local data on these conditions and to find the appropriate local partners to galvanize communities to address poverty. In 1987, the two foundations provided support to Case Western Reserve University's Mandel School of Applied Social Sciences (MSASS), which in turn created the Center on Urban Poverty and Social Change. After a detailed study, the center produced the 1990 report "An Analysis of Poverty and Related Conditions in Cleveland Area Neighborhoods."

The report articulated a growing consensus that it was time to take bold action. As a result, the Cleveland Foundation formed the Commission on Poverty, a 30-member group charged with developing a long-term strategy to address Cleveland's persistent poverty. The commission's work was guided by five principles:

• Cleveland's plan must be comprehensive and integrated.

• Strategies should be tailored to individual neighborhoods.

• An individual community strategy should begin with an inventory of the community's assets, not its deficits.

• Local communities themselves must be actively involved in shaping strategies and choices.

• The approach should be tested in pilot areas and carefully evaluated before being replicated in other Cleveland neighborhoods.

In support of its first principle, the commission identified five program frameworks: health, investment, education, family development, and human resource development. Realizing that implementing these program frameworks consistent with the guiding principles required considerable community-wide commitment and effort, the commission issued recommendations on how best to implement this community-building approach in its 1992 final report.

After the Commission on Poverty concluded its work, a group of six commission members and six other public and private sector leaders continued to work on ways to implement the principles through a long-term strategy to address persistent poverty in the city of Cleveland. This group, called the Cleveland Community-Building Initiative Council (CCBIC), worked in collaboration with MSASS's Center for Community Development to prepare an implementation plan. CCBIC selected four geographic areas for testing the new approach. Referred to as "villages," the areas selected were East (Fairfax), Central (King Kennedy Estates), West (Ohio City and a portion of Detroit Shoreway), and Mount Pleasant. CCBIC, with continuing support from the Cleveland Foundation, determined that the most viable mechanism for implementing the recommendations of the commission report was a new, independent organization. As implementing organization, CCBI received its nonprofit charter from the State of Ohio in September 1993 and its 501(c)(3) designation letter from the IRS in August 1994.

CCBI was incorporated by the original twelve CCBIC members and is presently governed by a board of trustees composed of eleven of those original members and seven others, including a representative from each of the four village councils. Each board member also participates on one of the village councils. The village councils, which seek to be inclusive and representative of various stakeholders, are charged with developing action plans to address poverty in the local neighborhood. Board members provide links to financial, intellectual, and technical expertise to implement the village-based agendas.

CCBI is staffed by a three-member administrative team and a coordinator for each village. Once organized, village councils participate in the selection of the village coordinators. Each coordinator is responsible for working with the executive director and the council to develop and maintain the functioning of the council and to provide technical assistance in support of village-based change strategies. To support the village-level work, a capacity-building component focuses on developing a core training curriculum based on recommendations from the councils.

Each village is a distinct geographic area whose residents are linked by a cluster of local institutions or a commercial center. By definition, the village concept suggests the interdependence of people who live in or do business within a geographic area; the village council is the mechanism to bring groups of stakeholders together. The village councils were organized over a two-year period. Start-up activities included establishing the geographic boundaries of the village, strategic planning, expanding membership to be more inclusive and diverse, conducting an asset inventory, establishing operating procedures and by-laws, and launching pilot projects.

Each village council deliberated about whether to maintain or revise the geographical boundaries identified by the Commission on Poverty in

1992. Thus far, three villages have redefined their geographical boundaries to include a larger population in the intervention area. All have developed operating procedures and by-laws. The councils vary in size, ranging from 13 members in East village to 27 members in West village. The composition of the membership also varies, with residents, social service providers, businesspeople, educators, and clergy represented on most councils. The councils have given considerable attention to composition, with at least one village developing very specific membership guidelines.

Although the method of work differs among the villages, each council has embarked on a process to develop collective vision, strategies, and activities for social change. Two councils—East and Mount Pleasant—called this a community strategic planning process, which included sessions to develop the local mission, strategies, activities, and goals, and produced a document charting a plan of activities to reach their goals. In contrast, the West village council opted not to conduct an extensive planning process, choosing instead to develop a mission statement, council composition guidelines, common themes for change, an operations statement for community outreach and communication, and a committee structure to address priority issues. West village has also developed a workplan identifying potential partners located in the village and the larger Cleveland community.

Village Characteristics and Assets

The West Village focus area is located on the west side of the city of Cleveland, Mount Pleasant is situated at the eastern border, and Central and Fairfax are centrally located, contiguous to one another. The villages vary in population size, ranging from slightly under 1,900 people in Central village to more than 31,000 in Mount Pleasant (table 1). The population is predominantly African American in Central, East, and Mount Pleasant, while West village is racially and ethnically diverse.

All four villages have poverty rates above city averages. Poverty is extremely high in Central village, especially among children. Mount Pleasant is the most affluent of the villages. All villages have unemployment rates that exceed city and county averages, ranging from a high in Central

Table 1. Cleveland Community-Building Initiative Village Areas
Selected Demographic and Housing Characteristics

Categories	Central Village	East Village
Vital Statistics		
Total Population	1,899	10,454
By Race		
White	39 (2%)	218 (2%)
African American	1,855 (98%)	10,201 (97%)
Asian	4 (0%)	8 (<1%)
Native American	1 (<1%)	12 (<1%)
Other	0 (0%)	15 (<1%)
By Age		
0 to 17 years	789 (42%)	2,887 (28%)
18 to 64 years	779 (41%)	5,075 (48%)
65 years and over	331 (17%)	2,492 (24%)
Poverty		
Total Persons below Poverty Line (% base)	1,597 (84%)	5,365 (51%)
Percentage within Age Group Poor		
0 to 17 years	91%	69%
18 to 64 years	94%	56%
65 years and over	46%	46%
Education Attainment		
Persons 25+ Years	960	6,660
Non high school graduate	707 (74%)	3,544 (53%)
High school graduate	187 (19%)	1,702 (26%)
Some college, no degree	47 (5%)	887 (13%)
College degree	19 (2%)	527 (8%)
Family		
Total Family Households with Children	207	1,128
Female headed households with children <18 (% total)	185 (89%)	806 (71%)
Housing		
Total Housing Units	1,317	4,886
Occupied (% total)	681 (52%)	4,130 (85%)
Owner Occupied (% occupied)	26 (4%)	1,183 (29%)
Employment*		
Persons 16+ Years	1,184	7,944
Employed (% total)	92 (8%)	2,180 (27%)
Unemployed (rate**)	130 (58.5%)	798 (26.8%)
Not in labor force (% total)	962 (81%)	4,966 (63%)

*Note: Universe is all civilians 16 years old and over. Not in labor force includes all persons not classified as members of the labor force. This category consists mainly of students, housewives, retired persons and institutionalized persons.

**Note: Unemployment Rate = Unemployed/Employed+Unemployed.

Analysis by Center on Urban Poverty and Social Change, Mandel School of Applied Social Sciences, Case Western Reserve University.

Mt. Pleasant Village	West Village	Cleveland	Cuyahoga
31,512	19,897	505,616	1,412,140
790 (3%)	13,037 (66%)	250,234 (49%)	1,025,756 (73%)
30,556 (97%)	3,224 (16%)	235,405 (47%)	350185 (25%)
33 (<1%)	293 (1%)	5115 (1%)	18085 (1%)
77 (<1%)	62 (<1%)	1562 (<1%)	2533 (<1%)
56 (<1%)	3281 (16%)	13,300 (3%)	15581 (1%)
8,939 (28%)	6,214 (32%)	136,117 (27%)	339,199 (24%)
18227 (58%)	11,805 (59%)	298,746 (59%)	714,248 (51%)
4346 (14%)	1,878 (9%)	70,753 (14%)	358,693 (25%)
9,368 (30%)	8,952 (45%)	142,217 (28%)	191,149 (14%)
43%	63%	42%	21%
26%	39%	24%	14%
19%	24%	18%	6%
19,432	10,797	316,673	943,924
7,811 (40%)	5,726 (53%)	130,584 (41%)	245,297 (26%)
5,770 (30%)	2,658 (25%)	99,449 (32%)	291,883 (31%)
3,412 (18%)	1,462 (13%)	48,507 (15%)	169,957 (18%)
2,439 (12%)	951 (9%)	381,33 (12%)	236,787 (25%)
3,726	2,763	60,875	165,364
2,216 (59%)	1,460 (53%)	27,098 (45%)	44,465 (27%)
13,155	9,391	224,311	604,538
11,822 (90%)	7,451 (79%)	199,787 (89%)	563,243 (93%)
5,804 (49%)	2,300 (31%)	95,765 (47%)	348,985 (62%)
23,451	11,136	381,896	1,107,886
10,623 (45%)	7,106 (64%)	182,225 (48%)	629,512 (57%)
2,195 (17.1%)	1,748 (19.7%)	29,749 (14.0%)	51,371 (7.5%)
10,633 (45%)	2,282 (20%)	169,922 (44%)	427,003 (39%)

Sources: Cleveland and Cuyahoga County, U.S. Bureau of the Census 1990 stf1 and stf3; Can Do Data Base.
Central Village: Census Tracts 1138, 1139; East Village: Census Tracts 1131, 1132, 1134, 1135, 1136, 1141, 1189;
Mt. Pleasant: Census Tracts 1196, 1198, 1199,1205,1206,1207.01,1208.02,1208.01,1834.02; West Village: Census
Tracts 1026, 1031, 1032, 1033, Block Group 2 only, 1034, 1035, 1036, 1037, Block Group 1 only,1038, 1039.

village of 59 percent to a low in Mount Pleasant of 17 percent. Central also has the highest rate of adults over age 25 without a high school diploma and the highest proportion of female-headed households.

The villages are also quite diverse in terms of housing. Central and West villages encompass two public housing estates each, which typically have high vacancy rates. Nearly all Central village residents live in public housing, where many units are being internally demolished and renovated through a major modernization effort called Central Vision/Hope VI. Hope VI is a national initiative to renovate and create defensible space in public housing estates. West village, however, has more private market housing and a substantially lower vacancy rate. In Mount Pleasant, the rate of owner occupied housing units (49 percent) is similar to the citywide rate (43 percent) but lower than the county rate (62 percent).

Despite poverty and other less desirable indicators, the villages have several assets located in or nearby their geographic boundaries. East village, for instance, has a number of large institutions in the neighborhood, which could provide a range of resources, from job training and employment to health care services, housing, and community and business development. Additionally, East village is within the Cleveland Empowerment Zone, a designation that has the potential to bring additional job training programs and employment, business development, and housing resources to the village. Each village has numerous places of worship, representing a range of denominations, many of which provide social and other services to village residents. Community development corporations and other institutions are working within each village to improve the supply and quality of housing units. Other common assets include public and independent educational institutions from early childhood education through high school. Located near the East and Central villages are a community college, a public university, and an independent university.

The CCBI Evaluation

When the Cleveland Commission on Poverty proposed a set of principles, guidelines, and actions to reverse persistent poverty in 1992, it was agreed that the initiative would have to undertake a program of cross-sector, cross-system reform (Cleveland Commission on Poverty, 1992; Connell et al., 1995). These actions were to be implemented and tested in a few areas, with the clear expectation that they would be transferable to other locations.

Evaluation was embedded in the commission's report. The report identified the Center on Urban Poverty and Social Change as the entity to develop a full assessment strategy, based on an initial evaluation plan constructed by the center and included in the report. After further work with the Aspen Institute Roundtable and in collaboration with CCBI, the center proposed a theory of change approach for evaluating the initiative. Baseline data collection was conducted in 1995-96.

An important aspect of the change process in Cleveland has been the notion that all stakeholders should be involved in designing and using the evaluation. Neighborhood residents and public and private sector leaders are all key stakeholders, including those who are involved in the initiative, potential users, and those affected indirectly by the strategies designed. Agency staff and volunteer leaders are also important stakeholders and need to be closely involved in the evaluation process. Area institutions, agencies, and organizations also have a stake in the direction and effectiveness of the initiative. Finally, those outside the target area, such as city and county government officials whose operations may be affected by the initiative or who may have a role in transferring successful programs and strategies to other areas, have a stake in the evaluation process.

The theory of change approach to evaluation is compatible with the way Cleveland stakeholders have conceived their role in the change process. Stakeholders view this approach to evaluation as a natural extension of the collaborative process of the Commission on Poverty and CCBI. Stakeholders have welcomed the opportunity to work with the evaluation team to specify the assumptions and hypotheses that guide decisions about the structure and components of the initiative. Early involvement in the evaluation process seems to have built trust among the stakeholders.

A theory of change approach is complex, intermingling the initiative's strategies and its anticipated outcomes. It is explicit about the short-term and interim outcomes that will lead to the long-term goals desired. Similarly, evaluating an initiative like CCBI is a complex undertaking, requiring an explicit plan for the collaborative and analytic activities that make up the evaluation design.

Terms and Definitions

To reduce the confusion that can arise from the complexity of a theory of change approach, evaluators and stakeholders may want to adopt common language for referring to elements within the initiative and its guiding theory. CCBI uses the following definitions:

• **Strategy.** Set of actions to achieve a purpose

• **Activities.** Actions that make up the strategy

• **Outcomes.** Early, interim, and long-term results of the chosen strategies

• **Benchmark.** Specified point in an activity or strategy that is agreed to be a sign of accomplishment

• **Indicator.** Defined manifestation of an outcome

Initiating the CCBI Evaluation

In designing a theory of change evaluation for the Cleveland Community-Building Initiative and laying out a plan of action, the evaluators envisioned a series of specific but related steps:

• articulate theories of change as viewed by multiple stakeholders

• identify important concepts and key benchmarks along the change pathway

• design methods to measure important outcomes and the related strategies

• collect data to measure the outcomes and benchmarks at specified points in time

- conduct analyses to determine whether outcomes and strategies are related to one another as specified by the theory of change

- modify theories as needed, based on experience

- provide regular feedback to stakeholders on progress and results

Although the steps themselves are well articulated, little is currently known about the procedures evaluators should follow in carrying them out. The CCBI evaluation therefore presents an important opportunity to consider the practical aspects of such crucial early activities as eliciting theories of change from key groups, defining and reconciling theories to track, operationalizing key concepts of those theories, and establishing measures and data sources. Our recent experience in implementing these start-up activities in Cleveland may prove helpful to other initiatives and evaluators.

Eliciting Theories of Change from Stakeholder Groups

To define CCBI's overall theory of change, the evaluation team and CCBI staff jointly identified three groups of key stakeholders who would be asked to describe their theories of community change under the initiative: CCBI staff, CCBI board members, and members of the four village councils. Each group plays a relevant and distinct role in defining CCBI's theory of change.

The CCBI executive director manages overall operations and monitors programs and activities according to CCBI's mission, goals, and objectives. The four village coordinators aid their respective village councils by providing technical assistance and advocacy and by helping to link village stakeholders with assets located inside and outside the community. The CCBI board—consisting of Cleveland-area business, church, educational, legal, medical, and social service leaders—provides direct guidance and assistance for CCBI program planning and development and oversees the financial administration of CCBI activities. The four village councils are made up of local residents and leaders. The councils play a critical role in developing and implementing programs, projects, and activities, as well representing the recipients of the services.

ELICITING THEORIES FROM CCBI STAFF

The evaluators and the executive director of CCBI began the process of eliciting theories of change from CCBI staff by conducting a small group interview with the village coordinators. Prior to the session, the evaluation team reviewed CCBI written materials and circulated a paper on the theory of change approach to evaluation to the coordinators. The executive director was interviewed separately to avoid undue influence on the views of staff members.

The initial meeting with village coordinators included the evaluation team leaders and consultants from the Aspen Institute. The evaluators oriented the group to the task by explaining the theory of change approach and indicating that the meeting's goal was to form a beginning sense of how each coordinator expected the change process to unfold. The following questions were used by the evaluators to guide the group interview:

• What kinds of activities are you doing or planning to do in your role in the Cleveland Community-Building Initiative?

• What are you trying to accomplish with the neighborhood, families, or individuals in the villages?

• What initial results do you expect from your involvement in the project?

• What short-term results do you expect in the next year for the neighborhoods, families, and individuals in the villages?

• What results do you expect in the next five years for the neighborhoods, families, and individuals in the villages?

• How will the actions or activities lead to the short-term results?

• What long-term outcomes do you expect from your involvement in the initiative?

• How will the actions or activities lead to the long-term results?

• What barriers do you foresee in implementing the actions or activities?

The evaluators guided the initial conversation toward short-term strategies and outcomes, recognizing that some of the steps leading to initial outcomes had already been put into motion. The intention of beginning with short-term strategies and outcomes was to provide participants with a foundation upon which intermediate and long-term strategies and outcomes could be developed. After eliciting immediate strategies and outcomes, ensuing strategies and outcomes were gleaned until long-term goals were finally identified. Questions like "What would you do next?" and "What would happen next?" served this process. The separate interview with CCBI's executive director was conducted in a similar fashion.

During the small group interview, evaluators diagrammed the evolving theory on large sheets of white paper taped to the walls of the room. The evaluators also took written notes, documenting the details of what participants said regarding strategies and short-term, intermediate, and long-term outcomes. Theory-eliciting questions were asked by the evaluators, as well as the evaluation consultants from the Aspen Institute. The evaluators conducting the group interview ensured that every participant contributed to the discussion equally and that personal experiences with community-building initiatives were brought to the fore.

The evaluators observed that the village coordinators were specific when discussing the short-term strategies and outcomes they sought but became more abstract as the discussion moved toward long-term strategies and outcomes. The long-term strategies and outcomes tended to be more universal, often reflecting commonly held values. Overall, the evaluators present at the group interview noted that, when long-term strategies and outcomes were being proffered, values played a strong role in the development of the staff's theory of change.

Group members appeared to be enthusiastic, engaged, and excited about the theory-eliciting process, and all four village coordinators said they had enjoyed the discussion. Further, the village coordinators found that the process of eliciting theories was not unlike the organizational planning process they had been through with CCBI. They stated that previous

CCBI planning meetings had fostered a high level of involvement and participation in the group interview by increasing their capacity for thinking about and discussing ways to achieve organizational goals.

The evaluators took the information gleaned from the group interview and the interview with the executive director and developed a diagrammatic representation of the staff's theoretical model for change. The first draft was disseminated to all relevant staff members in preparation for a second meeting, at which modifications and further elaboration of the theories were solicited. The recommended changes were made by the evaluation team and sent back to the staff members for further input. No more changes were suggested. Figure 1 represents the staff's theory of change.

ELICITING THEORIES FROM THE BOARD OF TRUSTEES

To ease scheduling burdens and assure the full participation of highly vocal and more reticent members, the evaluation team and the CCBI executive director decided to elicit board members' theories of change through individual interviews. The chairman of the board sent letters to all members in advance, informing them that evaluators would be scheduling interviews to seek information about activities CCBI was seeking to initiate, benchmarks indicating accomplishments, and the role of the board in the CCBI initiative. The letter also explained that the interview would take approximately 1.5 hours, that it would be conducted in-person, and that all comments would be confidential.

Each interview was tape recorded and documented through written notes. As a theory developed for each individual, the interviewer constructed a conceptual diagram of what was being stated. A draft of the board's theory of change, in flow chart form, was later developed and sent to all board members.

An evaluation team leader presented the draft at a meeting of the board to confirm the accuracy of the evaluators' interpretation. Although discussion was brief because of time constraints, the evaluators described a strand of the theory to explain the flow of the model and clarified relationships between activities and outcomes. Board members pointed out that two important concepts—training and entrepreneurial activity—were missing from the model.

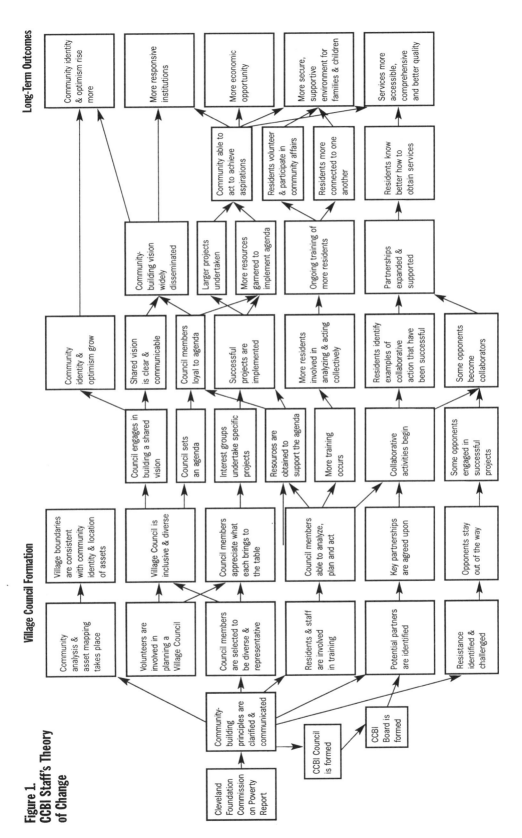

Figure 1.
CCBI Staff's Theory of Change

Village Council Formation

Long-Term Outcomes

The board delegated further refinement of the theory of change to its program and planning board subcommittee. The evaluators are working with the subcommittee to prepare a final draft of the board's theory of change, for submission to the entire board for approval. Figure 2 represents the board's current theory of change.

ELICITING THEORIES FROM THE VILLAGE COUNCILS

When the evaluation began, each of the four villages councils was at a different stage of development. One council was newly formed, while another had completed a strategic planning process. The remaining two were engaged in project activities, having gone through their initial planning processes. The evaluators and village coordinators decided that eliciting theories of change should be coordinated with these developmental activities and should not be introduced too soon to a newly formed council.

Evaluators and village coordinators deliberated about methods of eliciting theories of change from the relatively large and diverse village councils before deciding to use focus groups led by a professional facilitator. Although interviewing a smaller group of village council representatives was discussed, it was determined that convening the entire council would serve the process best. Several village coordinators also raised concerns about ideological differences within the councils and their possible effect on the theory-eliciting process. Last, village coordinators agreed their own presence might inhibit village council members' input.

An additional concern discussed by the evaluation team and village coordinators was that, as research, the evaluation would need to comply with Case Western Reserve University regulations for the protection of human subjects. The university's internal review board required that village council members be informed of the purposes of the evaluation and their rights as participants. An information sheet was prepared using straightforward, non-technical language for use in obtaining informed consent from village council members prior to the focus group meeting.

Although the focus groups were expected to provide important information for theory development, the evaluators subsequently realized that

**Figure 2.
CCBI Board's
Theory of Change**

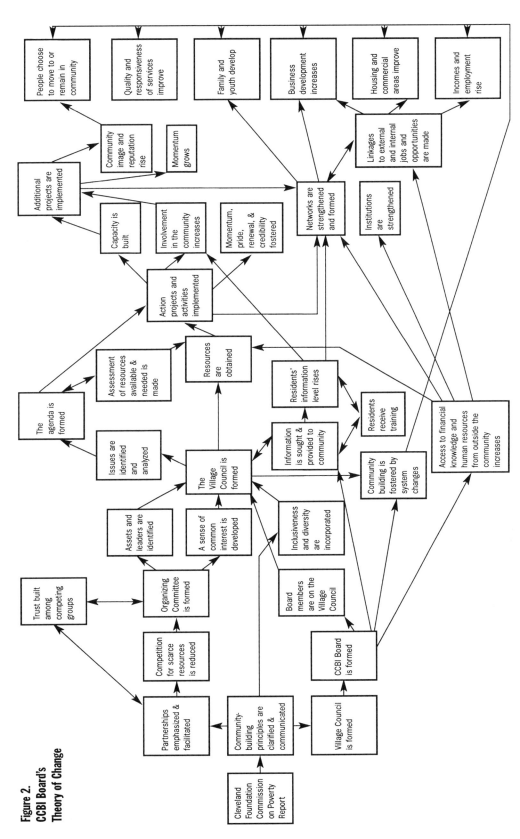

the village councils' strategic planning work was also pertinent. The evaluation team believed that each village's strategic planning process should be linked to the theory-eliciting process, and vice versa, if the theory guiding the evaluation was to incorporate activities being implemented within each village. The evaluation team therefore decided to observe strategic planning meetings and review planning documents, as well.

Mount Pleasant, the village farthest along in articulating a theory of change, had completed its strategic planning process prior to the decision to use a theory of change approach to evaluation. The evaluators and village council members therefore had strategic planning documents in hand during the first theory-eliciting focus group. The focus group began with an explanation by the evaluators of the theory of change approach and an orientation to the kind of discussion anticipated. Each member had a chance to ask questions and was asked to give informed consent. The council members then engaged in a facilitated discussion of their expectations and thinking about changing the Mount Pleasant community. Because the strategic planning document had already been ratified, they were asked to build upon it, adding additional thoughts about their vision and relationships between activities and outcomes.

Overall, the council members participated actively, elaborating upon most of the ideas represented in the planning document and contributing some new activities and outcomes. The responses of the council members were recorded in written form throughout the process. The theory elicited from this focus group was diagrammed by the evaluators and presented to a feedback focus group, which suggested some modifications. The current version appears in figure 3.

Defining and Reconciling Stakeholders' Theories

Having begun to elicit theories of change from the staff, board, and village councils, the evaluators' next steps were to define the overall theory for each stakeholder group and find common and unique elements within and among the theories. These elements were identified by reconciling and combining individual differences within each group, comparing theories

Figure 3. Mount Pleasant Village Council's Theory of Change

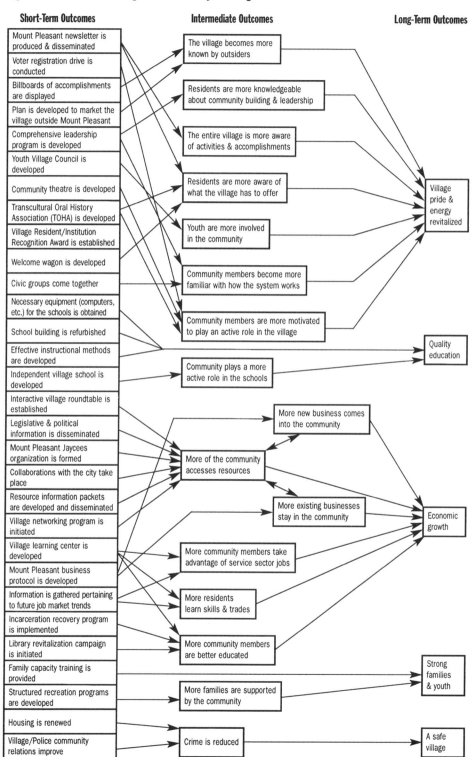

within and between groups, and determining whether there were one or several theories or theories within theories.

DEFINING THE STAFF'S THEORY OF CHANGE

The staff's theory of change was developed primarily during the theory-eliciting group process. More specifically, the small group interview was structured so that questions pertained directly to strategies and outcomes for CCBI as the organization moved from the present to the future. This structure provided evaluators the opportunity to construct and diagram the first draft of the theory as the meeting unfolded. During the interview, each village coordinator was given an opportunity to propose strategies and outcomes relevant to particular points in the initiative's time frame. If coordinators disagreed with each other about the strategy that best served a specific outcome and a compromise was not reached through discussion, then all the strategies were placed in the theory. For example, to reach the intermediate outcome of "successful projects are implemented," two strategies were suggested: "interest groups undertake specific projects" and "resources are obtained to support the agenda." Since the village coordinators believed these strategies to be important for the implementation of successful projects, they were both included in the theory. Similarly, if a strategy was proposed and agreed upon, but more than one outcome was proffered, then all outcomes were placed in the theory.

To complete the theory, the evaluators examined the executive director's theory of change and integrated it with the staff's theory. When aspects of the two theories were in agreement, no changes were made; but when the executive director suggested novel strategies and outcomes, these were added to the staff's overall theory. After evaluators refined the staff's first theory of change, it was presented to the staff for further modification. Then, the theory was finalized.

DEFINING THE BOARD'S THEORY OF CHANGE

The board's theory of change was developed and diagrammed during an evaluation team meeting that followed individual interviews with ten of the sixteen board members. The evaluation team first examined all ten theories of change for common or similar strategies and short-term, intermediate, and long-term outcomes. In general, these were noted when more than one board member expressed a similar idea. An example of a common strategy was "to identify community leaders, assets, and resources," and the common outcome associated with this strategy was "the formation of a strong village council."

The evaluation team then examined each board member's theories for unique elements. When a strategy or outcome was proposed by only one board member, the evaluation team discussed whether or not to incorporate it into the theory. Although most of these unique elements were included in the board's theory, some were left out for further clarification during the feedback process. The first draft of the board's theory, represented during the evaluators' meeting on a poster-sized flow chart, was generated by computer and sent to board members for review and discussion at the next board meeting.

Defining Theories of Change of the Village Councils

Although the evaluators drew mainly on strategies and outcomes which an entire village council had agreed upon, the first draft also included elements that had been proposed vigorously by particular participants. For example, one council member felt strongly that more community residents should take advantage of service sector jobs. Others disagreed, stating that service sector job opportunities offer limited income potential and leadership opportunities. Evaluators incorporated service sector job opportunities into the theory with the assumption that the feedback process would ultimately determine whether or not it was included in the final theory.

In Mount Pleasant, planning documents and focus group notes were used to diagram the village council's theory of change. The evaluators first listed all outcomes and strategies. Each strategy and outcome was then placed within the initiative's time frame according to the village council's specification, and links between strategies and outcomes were established. Last, Mount Pleasant's theory of change was diagrammed using a computer presentation program and presented to the village council for feedback during a monthly meeting.

RECONCILING THE STAKEHOLDERS' THEORIES OF CHANGE

As figures 1, 2, and 3 show, the theories of the CCBI staff, the CCBI board, and the Mount Pleasant village council are similar with respect to long-term outcomes. More specifically, the staff's ultimate outcome, "community identity and optimism rise more," is similar to the board's "people choose to move to or remain in the community" and the village council's "village pride and energy revitalized." Each theory also contains ultimate outcomes pertaining to the development of strong families and youth and a more robust business and economic environment. Both the staff and board theories include long-term outcomes related to improving the quality and responsiveness of neighborhood institutions and services. The staff and village council theories include long-term outcomes pertaining to safety. The only unique ultimate outcomes are quality education, part of the village council theory, and improved housing and commercial areas, included by the board.

In general, the staff and board theories contain more similarities than differences. Many of the steps leading to village council formation are similar: both theories stress identifying community assets and leaders, developing a sense of common interest, training resident leaders, and recruiting a diverse group of volunteer council members. Also, after the village council is formed, the steps toward realizing ultimate outcomes are similar in the staff and board theories, including agenda development, capacity building or resident training, networking and collaboration, acquiring resources, and activity or project development. The staff and board theories are also similar in their lack of specificity regarding methods for conducting each step. For example, the "agenda is formed" step in the board's theory and the "council sets an agenda" step in the staff's theory do not explicate the "micro-steps," or activities needed to form an agenda. The evaluators did not see this as problematic because village council theories would likely specify those activities.

The Mount Pleasant village council's theory of change does not differ from the staff and board theories as much as it elucidates steps that focus on capacity building, resident training, networking and collaboration, acquiring resources, and activity or project development. For example, both the staff and board theories mention the need to get access to resources. The village council theory elaborates the activities that Mount Pleasant intends to implement, including developing an interactive village roundtable, disseminating legislative and political information, forming a Jaycees organization, collaborating with the city, developing and disseminating resource information packets, and initiating a village networking program. Some of the council's intermediate outcomes closely resemble staff and board general steps as they move toward ultimate outcomes.

Using the Theories of Change to Design the Evaluation

Although the theories of change are incomplete, they have been useful in guiding the early stages of the evaluation. Data collection and measurement strategies have been planned to establish baselines and cover the initiative's initial stages, since the three sets of theories show considerable agreement and clarity about how early activities will lead to short-run changes or accomplishments. The evaluators believe that stakeholders cannot yet be explicit about steps in the intermediate and long term, but the theories will be revisited periodically to see when and if further elaboration becomes possible.

It is important that the evaluation move forward, since stakeholders are eager to know how they are progressing. Thus, the evaluators have produced an early, streamlined version of the theory of change, defined key concepts and definitions, developed preliminary benchmarks, and begun to gather baseline information about longer-term outcomes for which there is considerable support.

Streamlining the Early Theory

Some stakeholders expressed the view that the complexity of the theories made it difficult to see how those theories would lead to meaningful evaluation findings. When the evaluators confronted the task of operationalizing and measuring the elements of the theory, they too acknowledged the need to simplify. After examining the board, staff, and village council theories of change, the evaluators concluded that the elements could be grouped tentatively into sets of major strategies and outcomes, each of which could then be further specified for evaluation.

The general theory of change that seems to fit CCBI early in its development is shown in figure 4. The formation and operation of village councils is the first outcome. Each village is to establish an inclusive, representative, and collaborative structure that can effectively move the village toward its goals using the community-building principles established by CCBI. The process of establishing the village council and its work in identifying community assets begins to unleash greater participation of residents in community affairs, while also serving as a forum for collaboration as groups and institutions are brought into the planning activities. The work of the village council builds upon, celebrates, and enhances the assets of its community.

A focused agenda—established by the council—garners resources and directs the community's energy toward comprehensive change consistent with its long-term objectives. For example, well-defined projects move the community toward its goals while building capacity and increasing involvement within the community. Growing civic involvement and the action projects themselves build social capital by creating new social connections and forms of organization. Communication channels become more effective as a result of rising participation and action projects such as newsletters and bulletin boards.

The growing implementation capacity serves as a magnet for additional internal and external resources. Some projects are deliberately structured to involve actors and systems outside the village, thus beginning to strengthen external relations. The agenda may also include expanding and improving services, which requires specific community actions directed toward systems and agencies.

The community's growing capacity to achieve its goals allows advancement in areas it considers important, while stronger social structures sustain this movement. Thus, neighborhood identity, security, service quality, economic opportunity, and family development are all promoted by the strengthened social organization within the community and the improved connections to the larger society.

Figure 4. CCBI Generalized Theory of Change

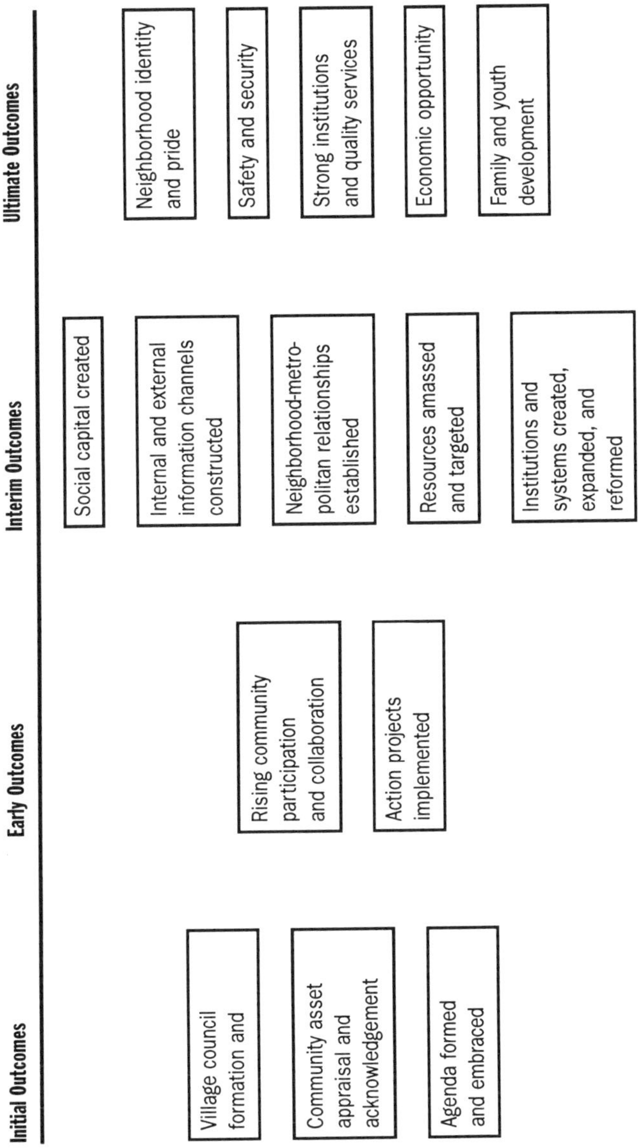

Initial Outcomes	Early Outcomes	Interim Outcomes	Ultimate Outcomes
Village council formation and		Social capital created	Neighborhood identity and pride
Community asset appraisal and acknowledgement	Rising community participation and collaboration	Internal and external information channels constructed	Safety and security
Agenda formed and embraced	Action projects implemented	Neighborhood-metro-politan relationships established	Strong institutions and quality services
		Resources amassed and targeted	Economic opportunity
		Institutions and systems created, expanded, and reformed	Family and youth development

This general theory will change as several of the villages begin to put forward details of their strategies. Specific steps linking interim to long-term outcomes will be added as the initiative unfolds.

DEVELOPING BENCHMARKS

Before these strategies can be evaluated, they needed to be broken down into elements about which judgments can be made. In explaining this to stakeholders, the CCBI evaluators found the term *benchmark* to be useful. Achieving a benchmark is a sign that a strategy is progressing in a desirable and effective manner.

Benchmarks suggest implicitly that performance can compared against some standard of achievement or definition of what is acceptable or desirable. The establishment of benchmarks can draw on the experience of the stakeholders, expert opinion, literature on best practices, or scientific research. CCBI plans to use all these sources, but at present the process is incomplete. Even so, the evaluators have developed a beginning set of benchmarks, some of them drawn from what was learned in the theory-eliciting process and others based on literature and the advice of experts.

A list of benchmarks for the initial CCBI outcomes is presented in table 2. Each benchmark is related to an important aspect of the success of the strategy, and, where possible, a threshold for accomplishment is specified. For example, while stakeholders assume that councils must be inclusive in their membership, the benchmarks specify categories of individuals to be included and reference points for determining adequacy. At selected points in time, the evaluation can compare actual performance with these benchmarks. For each strategy, numerous benchmarks have been proposed, each of which requires consideration of the evidence—and the measurement procedure—that will be required to know its status. Where possible, established measurement methods will be used.

To ensure that stakeholders are aware of and agree upon these benchmarks as visible signs of progress, the evaluation team conducted meetings with all stakeholder groups. For example, the evaluation team met with the Mount Pleasant village council to verify their agreement with the benchmarks, establish priorities, and review the criteria for measurement. The council agreed with the concepts but had concerns about timing. Also, the council was dissatisfied with the dichotomous nature of the operational definitions, which measured only presence or absence of a phenomenon. The evaluation staff agreed that most of the benchmarks did not adequately specify an established standard and that a continuum should be used, rather than a dichotomy. It was also agreed that, for some villages, the current measurement would constitute a baseline.

The evaluators also met with the CCBI staff to discuss priorities regarding the benchmarks and criteria for measurement. The staff thought the benchmarks were helpful but suggested a few changes in wording.

Collecting Baselines for Long-Term Outcomes

CCBI has also begun to track long-term outcomes. Although the theories are not fully developed and the path to long-term results remains unclear, it is important to begin defining these ultimate outcomes so that a baseline can be obtained. Further, tracking these outcomes as part of the evaluation process should help keep the initiative's long-term aims visible and aid in sustaining its focus.

The theories of change from all three stakeholder groups have specified long-term outcomes. An examination of these suggests that there is considerable agreement among the stakeholders on the following general outcome categories:

- **Economic opportunity.** The economic potential and well being of residents and the economic vitality of the neighborhood is improved.

- **Neighborhood identity and pride.** The neighborhood is viewed positively and valued by residents and outsiders.

- **Safety and security.** Community residents and visitors are not threatened or harmed and their property is secure.

- **Strong institutions and services.** Educational, cultural, religious, service, and civic organizations are effective and serve and involve residents.

- **Family, child, and youth development.** Families are stable and supported, and children and youth are healthy and developing.

Table 2. Benchmarks for Initial Outcomes

Outcome	Definition
1. Village Council Formation and Operation	
1a. Inclusiveness	• Is there an even representation of age categories among the village council members?
	• Are the racial proportions about the same as in the community's population?
	• Are all sectors of the community (business, residents, government, church, etc.) represented on the village council?
	• Are social class proportions about the same as in the general population?
	• Are all geographic sections within the village represented?
	• Are many types of skills represented?
1b. Practices	• Has a decision-making process been formalized?
	• Is there an accountability mechanism?
	• Do conflict of interest policies exist?
	• Does a committee structure exist?
	• Is there a method for assuring input/participation?
	• Is there a council member training/orientation process?
	• Is there a method of membership maintenance?
	• Is there an established method of conflict resolution?
	• Are there established dissemination practices?
	• Are community input mechanisms in place?
	• Is evaluation feedback utilized on an ongoing basis?
1c. Participation	• Do members regularly attend council meetings?
	• Do all the village council members speak during meeting?
	• Is the workload evenly distributed?
	• Do members feel engaged in council activities?
	• Do members perceive a high level of collective engagement and equity in workload distribution?
1d. Perceived adequacy of resources	• Are the following resources adequate: staff, technical assistance, evaluation, information sources, space/accessibility, equipment, communication capacity, training to use resources?
	• Are long-term goals well specified?
	• Are long-term goals comprehensive?
2. Community Asset Appraisal, Analysis, and Acknowledgment	
2a. Community asset appraisal	• Have assets been identified in each of the following categories?
	• Institutions/Organizations: service, cultural, recreational, educational, spiritual, civic, financial, business
	• Physical: land, buildings, transportation, utilities

Outcome	Definition
2a. Community asset appraisal *(continued)*	• Technological • Financial: contributors, lending • Human Resources • Political • Have the locations of these assets been identified?
2b. Community asset analysis	• Has there been an examination of the current status of long-term outcomes? • Have existing assets been examined in relation to what is needed to achieve long-term outcomes? • Are the methods for closing the gap between idealized and actual assets specified?
2c. Community asset acknowledgment	• Are assets communicated through informal (word-of-mouth) means? • Are the assets of the community communicated through formal means, such as publications, briefings, or media presentations? • Has training occurred regarding how to acknowledge community assets?
3. Agenda Formation	• Has information been gleaned regarding available resources for the agenda? • Are near-term outcomes specified and prioritized? • Are activities targeting near-term outcomes specified? • Are links between near- and long-term outcomes specified? • Have the responsibilities for carrying out the activities been designated? • Have resources been allocated for the activities? • Have practices developed for conducting activities (see 1b) been applied to the agenda formation process?
4. Action Projects	• Are there action projects in the village council? • Are the action projects sustainable? • Are diverse constituencies working on the projects? • Is there a perceived urgent need for the action projects being implemented? • Are the action projects highly visible? • Are the action projects linked to near-term outcomes? • Do the action projects contribute to relationships and networks external to the village? • Do the action projects succeed in achieving stated outcomes? • Do the action projects benefit residents? • Is training and technical assistance sought in relation to the development and implementation of action projects?

CCBI staff and evaluators have just begun to consider the possible indicators that could be used to define each of the categories. Initially, we expect to choose indicators that can be drawn from available data in order to create a retrospective baseline. This will help establish reasonable expectations for the rate and amount of change that can be expected as a result of CCBI's work. Further, it is important that stakeholders be prepared to review the indicators and interpret the measurements realistically, so that the data are not perceived as discouraging or excessively negative. Both evaluators and stakeholders need assurances that the information will be interpreted in the proper context and used to promote positive planning and action.

ESTABLISHING MEASURES AND DATA SOURCES

Although some important CCBI elements are only in their beginning stages, it has become apparent that certain basic data collection mechanisms must be implemented immediately. Otherwise, important information may be lost or forgotten. These mechanisms include:

• **Documentation of activities.** Specific activities carried out by staff, village councils, residents, and others will be documented in a data base by CCBI staff. Documents such as minutes, reports, and memos will also be collected. Special data collection instruments may be developed but will be kept to a minimum.

• **Key informant interviews.** Measurement of early benchmarks will probably rely on questions posed to staff, board members, village councils, and residents. Questionnaire items will be developed and tested for validity and reliability. Interviewers will be trained to administer these questions and record and code the answers.

• **Social and economic indicators.** The Center on Urban Poverty and Social Change maintains a detailed longitudinal data base of social and economic indicators for all Cleveland neighborhoods. Drawn from administrative agencies and the census, these data will be valuable in calculating baseline and ongoing measures for many of the long-term outcomes. For some outcomes, the center will add new data sources, especially in the areas of educational and developmental outcomes for children and youth and service and institutional effectiveness.

• **Oral history/archiving.** Working with a historian, an oral history group of selected residents will record the process of community building within their villages. The transcribed oral records will be used by the evaluators and will also serve to communicate the principles and promise of community building within the village and externally.

• **Resident surveys.** A survey of neighborhood residents will probably be necessary to obtain measures of some outcomes. In particular, a survey could focus on residents' perceptions of their neighborhood's identity, cohesiveness, and effectiveness and on changes in individuals and families.

• **Surveys of institutions and organizations.** The theories as they now stand are not explicit about how institutions and organizations in the community will need to change in order to produce the desired long-term changes. Surveys of institutions and organizations may be needed to measure those concepts as they are specified.

Issues in the Theory of Change Approach

Traditional evaluation designs can rely on well-established protocols and standards, but these are not yet available to evaluators using a theory of change approach. From our initial steps toward evaluating CCBI, we offer several reflections upon the method and some recommendations to the field.

Considering the Role of the Evaluator

The role of the evaluator—a key issue in the application of the theory of change approach to evaluating CCIs (Brown, 1995; 1996)—has also been an important issue in the early steps of the CCBI evaluation. The very nature of eliciting theories of change from stakeholders placed the evaluators into new and less traditional roles, as stakeholders and evaluators interacted mutually as teachers and learners through an iterative and ongoing process. Early experiences in evaluating CCBI raised several issues regarding relationships between the evaluator and stakeholder groups and the evaluator's effectiveness as a trainer.

Relationships with the Board, Staff, and Village Councils

The CCBI evaluators had previous experience with the initiative and its stakeholders, having earlier provided information and data analysis to community stakeholders to increase their understanding of the nature of poverty and its consequences in Cleveland neighborhoods. Thus, the capacity of the evaluators to provide a detailed longitudinal data base on social and economic indicators from administrative agencies and census information was widely known and utilized by CCBI. This capacity to gather, manage, and analyze geographic-specific data continues to meet the needs of the board and staff in the planning and implementation process. Together, CCBI and the evaluators have examined trends that provide a better understanding of the villages.

All stakeholders were eager to participate in defining the CCBI theory of change. The evaluators, staff, board, and village councils worked together as collaborators and inquirers to elicit theories of change, and the meetings where theories were elicited functioned as open exchanges with opportunities for all present to participate in the discussion. Work to date has promoted stakeholder participation in the theory development process and clarified the roles and responsibilities of stakeholders.

In many ways the collaborative process has created demands for the evaluation work by stakeholders. The goal for the evaluation is not only to contribute to an understanding of the effects of the initiative, but also to use information for community and organizational decision making. Stakeholders have asked, "How are we doing on accomplishing our goals?"

Collaborative decision making has been central to theory development and measurement. Early on, village coordinators convinced evaluators to delay theory development work in two of the four villages where the respective councils were organizing their strategic planning process. The evaluators agreed, in order to be supportive of the growth of the organizations and to fit into a naturalistic process.

THE EVALUATOR AS TRAINER AND CONSULTANT

Training is an important part of the evaluators' role in the CCBI experience, especially in surfacing theories of change. Formal and informal training can help participants understand the theory of change approach while also demystifying the evaluation process, clarifying roles and expectations, building trust, and helping evaluators and stakeholders get to know one another and understand and acknowledge fears (Sonnischsen, 1994).

The evaluators had several opportunities to train and consult with stakeholders on understanding the theory of change approach. Each stakeholder group was given the opportunity to grapple with the concept in initial and feedback sessions, and board members and staff were given access to selected literature on evaluating CCIs. Moreover, in the iterative process of specifying the theories of change, evaluators have helped stakeholders reflect upon the plausibility of the strategies planned or being implemented and the outcomes stated. This process has put the evaluators in the role of consulting with stakeholders on the development of program strategies and outcomes and of articulating underlying assumptions. In one feedback session, for example, the evaluation team challenged the notion put forward by the village council that involving young people in physical cleanup of the neighborhood would build youth leadership. This challenge led to a discussion of other youth development strategies that the literature has identified as promising contributors to youth leadership.

The use of verbal and written progress reports is also part of the training process. The evaluators have met regularly with staff and board members to discuss progress and have provided quarterly written progress reports to the CCBI board and staff, thus encouraging multiple stakeholders to explore strategies and benchmarks. If the process of clarifying the theory of change serves as a model for subsequent processes, stakeholders can be expected to be closely involved in developing the evaluation design and in the final selection of measures.

Ultimately, the evaluator may also be instrumental in uncovering biases inherent in the various roles of stakeholders regarding the initiative. Such biases inform the perspectives of each stakeholder group, which in turn can yield significant information about how the initiative is working. The evaluator could also facilitate interactions among the groups and help them attain a unified view of the initiative.

Working with Funders

The evaluators, CCBI staff, board members, and village councils have been involved in eliciting the theories of change and the iterative process of defining the assumptions that underlie the initiative. Yet funders—another stakeholder group—have not yet participated directly in the CCBI theory of change process.

CCBI has worked with two funders, a foundation and a government agency. For the foundation, a program officer has been involved with CCBI since its origins through the Cleveland Foundation Commission on Poverty, and the chief executive officer has been aware of the development of the initiative. Recently, the foundation conducted an unprecedented all-staff site visit to provide program officers in different funding areas with first hand knowledge of the initiative. During the site visit, the evaluators had an opportunity to present the theory of change approach and to provide each program officer with literature about the approach.

Both funders have expressed an interest in the evaluation and see it as integral to the initiative's implementation. Even so, the processes of eliciting theories and defining measurements have so far focused on institutional and programmatic assumptions rather than funder expectations. The CCBI evaluation may be somewhat unique in this regard, since many previous and current evaluations have had considerable funder involvement in their design.

Eliciting and Defining Theories of Change

FACILITATING EFFECTIVE GROUPS

In this first phase of evaluating CCBI, both individual and group approaches to eliciting theories were tried. We conclude that the group process added value: not only does it serve to build consensus and yield a common theory, but it also seems to allow group members to see one other's perspectives more clearly.

Even so, there are limits on the ideal size of the group. We have found that, to allow participants adequate time to relate their theories and be pressed for clarification, groups should be no larger than eight. For larger groups, the task of working directly with the evaluators has been delegated to a subcommittee, which routinely reports issues to the larger group for discussion. This strategy can be supplemented with individual interviews.

MAPPING THEORIES OF CHANGE

Communicating the developing theories of change to the groups at each stage has proven somewhat unwieldy. Detailed theories are very difficult to display on paper, especially at early stages when there is uncertainty about concepts and language. For example, it is difficult to tell at the outset whether people have truly different concepts or are using different words to describe the same idea. The temptation to simplify prematurely, just to fit the theory on paper, can be very strong.

To maintain underlying complexity without confusing the audience, we have experimented with layering levels of detail on computer screens that can be tied to more comprehensive concepts on a screen with a simpler diagram. Microsoft PowerPoint has proved to be a useful piece of software for this purpose. However, displaying these diagrams to a large group requires projection equipment that is not readily available to many neighborhood organizations.

The fact that many strategies and outcomes occur repeatedly and over time presents an additional difficulty in diagramming theories of change. In the CCBI theory, for example, "agenda formation" is to occur repeatedly, with the agenda modified on the basis of previous experience, new information, and changing values and perceptions. It is difficult to represent this repetition and link the activity to outcomes that are different at different points in time.

ENCOURAGING SPECIFICITY

We have also struggled with urging stakeholders to be more explicit about detailed steps along the pathway of change. Even so, important links are missing between early strategies and long-term outcomes. Although stake-holders have a fairly clear vision of the changes that they want to see in their communities, they find it more difficult to see the steps that must be taken to arrive at these outcomes. Unfortunately, turning around economically distressed neighborhoods, making institutions stronger and more respon-sive, and promoting family and child health are very difficult and compli-cated challenges. The powerful strategies and know-how required to effect those changes are not revealed in the initial theories.

We anticipate that, as staff and village residents experience success with initial action projects, they will gain confidence and capacity to take bolder steps. At that stage, they will be asked to reconsider the long-term outcomes and make specific choices about the pre-conditions for change. Since expanding local capacity is a fundamental tenet of community build-ing, CCBI will need to involve consultants and advisors who can contribute to the staff's and residents' abilities. The theories can then be more fully developed to guide the ensuing evaluation.

Determining Benchmarks and Indicators

DISTINGUISHING OUTCOMES FROM STRATEGIES

Traditional evaluation has distinguished between process and outcomes. Strategies and their related activities have been considered process, while longer-term results are generally seen as outcomes. We have found the distinction between process and outcomes difficult to apply in our work with CCBI.

CCBI's early work is clearly about putting structures and processes into place that are intended to build the communities. Within the theory, however, these are pictured as strategies, the accomplishment of which are early outcomes. For example, putting into place a recruitment process for village council members contributes to village council formation and oper-ation. Having an accepted and effective method for ongoing recruitment can be seen as a short-term outcome.

Rather than getting bogged down in these distinctions, we are cur-rently using words like *benchmark* and *indicator,* which seem to be more familiar to stakeholders. We have tried to describe processes in terms of observable outcomes that can serve as signs that the processes have been accomplished well. Thus, outcomes will be the primary focus of our measurement.

Adopting an outcome focus precludes the detailed descriptions of processes that have been characteristic of many previous CCI evaluations. We are concerned, however, that the evaluation may miss important stories about individuals and the efforts they make or problems and barriers that occur in the political and social contexts. We hope that the oral histories will record these events and help portray the rich fabric of CCBI.

Establishing Standards and Thresholds

The idea of benchmarking and the interpretation of indicators on an ongoing basis implies a comparison against a definition or standard. In industry, benchmarking often takes place by comparing a company's performance with that of its competitors. In public health, the comparison may be within the same population over time. Standards also may reflect fundamental values and societal goals or be based upon scientific determinations.

In the field of CCIs, values and goals are rarely stated as clear thresholds or levels. The experience of practitioners may be a useful source for a threshold for what works, but that experience is not always codified or readily available to evaluators. Comparing communities with one another or with themselves over time may be a useful way to establish benchmarks, but there is little existing experience with these methods. The field should invest in developing its knowledge base toward this purpose.

Choosing an Appropriate Level of Detail

If we knew the one or two most powerful ingredients of any strategy, the lists of benchmarks and indicators could be greatly simplified. Regrettably, the knowledge base about community change is insufficiently developed to point to those key elements. For example, experience suggests that inclusiveness is related to the success of coalitions, but to what categories of people does that suggestion apply? Does inclusiveness demand that all geographic areas be represented at the table? At this stage, it seems wise to include as benchmarks elements that may make a difference in the initiative's success and ones that could be improved if the evaluation finds them wanting.

Making the Evidence Compelling

The evidence coming out of the CCBI evaluation must be compelling and useful for the purposes to which it will be applied. Those purposes may be different for the various stakeholder groups.

Staff and residents are most likely to need evidence in a form that will tell them how to improve what they are doing, or when something has been accomplished and it is time to move on to something else. For them, compelling evidence must distinguish between strategies that were incompletely implemented and strategies that were done according to the standards but did not produce the desired changes. They will want to know whether a correctly implemented strategy did not work because of an external force or because the theory was flawed to begin with. When outcome indicators move in the positive direction, they will want to know which strategies were most helpful and should be continued and which ones have accomplished all they can.

Board members and funders are likely to want answers that can guide future resource allocations. For them, compelling evidence should distinguish between strategies that have produced good results and those that have been less productive. They will want to know whether the invested resources have produced something of value that would not have occurred otherwise.

Our experience thus far suggests that the theory of change approach will be useful in providing the compelling evidence of improvement needed by staff and residents. Seeing their own thoughts operationalized should guarantee that the evaluation will provide findings they can act upon, and frequent feedback of findings and opportunities to make modifications should prevent the evaluation from departing from the reality of the initiative. Sensitive, well-timed measurements can help evaluators distinguish weak implementation from theory failure and fairly describe implementation problems, so they can be resolved.

It is less clear how the evaluation can build a compelling case that the theory itself is powerful and valid. The CCBI theory as it now stands is not adequate to account for competing explanations and the influence of factors not included in the model. This will not present an insurmountable problem for testing the early stages of the theory, when most of the predicted effects are internal to the initiative itself. Later predicted changes in the community and its residents, however, are less internally controlled or explained. Much greater consideration will need to go into fully specifying the model, so that the influence of external factors can be ruled out or explicitly brought into the change process. Without the detailed steps that are currently missing from the theories, it will be difficult to produce the compelling evidence stakeholders need in allocating resources among promising initiatives.

Building a Methodology That Works

The CCBI experience in implementing a theory of change approach to evaluation confirms that the method is a good fit with the way CCIs work. It allows the evaluation to be shaped by the ideas, values, and aspirations of stakeholders at all levels and at many points. The evaluation design is not imposed from without, but rather is gradually shaped through a collaborative, analytic process. This deepens stakeholders' understanding of and commitment to the evaluation plan. It also increases the likelihood that the evaluation will be used by the stakeholders to improve the initiative.

Considerable work remains to be done in specifying and refining the theory of change method. This will occur as the technique is applied in many CCIs and the experience of evaluators and practitioners is codified. Several methodological issues stand out in particular among those that need to be addressed:

- **Measurement.** Most of the benchmarks that have been identified for CCBI do not have existing, tested measures. As currently phrased, they seem to call for simple dichotomies, although more refined quantification will be needed to reveal subtle changes. It is only when more sophisticated and sensitive measures are developed that we will be able to analyze how change in one concept leads to another—the kind of evidence promised by the theory of change approach.

• **Modeling change.** Theories of change tend to be depicted as linear, although the real process of change is dynamic and reciprocal. The initiative may be moving along several pathways, and the effects of strategies may depend upon their synergy. Considerable work is needed to discover how data can be analyzed to represent these complex processes correctly.

• **Extraneous influences.** As the evaluation moves to examine interim and long-term outcomes, the problem of alternative explanations will become more apparent. Generating compelling evidence for the value of the initiative may depend on adequately taking into account social and economic processes outside the initiative that may be influencing outcomes, positively or negatively. Choosing the correct forces to include will require some type of higher order theory about the communities in which the initiative is working and how outside factors affect them.

These and other methodological challenges require serious pilot investigation within the context of multiple communities. The complexity of evaluating CCIs, combined with the considerable investment in them and a vital need to know their effectiveness, suggests that this work has some urgency. The evaluation committee of Aspen Institute's Roundtable on Comprehensive Community Initiatives for Children and Families has served the vital function of stimulating, supporting, and synthesizing this type of work, but the promise of theory of change evaluation is just beginning to unfold. Only through sustained effort can we expect to refine the methodology and achieve its practical application.

Note

Financial support for this paper was provided by the Aspen Institute's Roundtable on Comprehensive Community Initiatives for Children and Families. The assistance of the following individuals and groups is gratefully acknowledged: Anne Kubisch, James Connell, and Karen Fulbright-Anderson of the Roundtable's evaluation committee; Greg Brown, Tracy Robinson, John Ward, and Ginna Fleshood, Cleveland Community-Building Initiative (CCBI) village coordinators; members of the village councils; the CCBI board of trustees; Emma Melton, group facilitator; and Carmen Griffey, program analyst at the Center on Urban Poverty and Social Change, Mandel School of Applied Social Sciences, Case Western Reserve University.

References

Brown, Prudence. 1996. "Evaluation of Comprehensive Community Building Initiatives." In *Core Issues in Comprehensive Community-Building Initiatives,* ed. Rebecca Stone. Chicago: Chapin Hall Center for Children.

Brown, Prudence. 1995. "The Role of the Evaluator in Comprehensive Community Initiatives." In *New Approaches to Evaluating Community Initiatives: Concepts, Methods, and Contexts,* ed. James Connell et al. Washington, DC: Aspen Institute.

Connell, James P., Anne C. Kubisch, Lisbeth B. Schorr, and Carol H. Weiss, eds. 1995. *New Approaches to Evaluating Community Initiatives: Concepts, Methods, and Contexts.* Washington, DC: Aspen Institute.

Cleveland Commission on Poverty. 1992. *The Cleveland Community Building Initiative.*

Coulton, Claudia, and Jill Korbin. 1996. "Measuring Neighborhood Context for Young Children in an Urban Area." *Journal of Community Psychology* 24 (1):5-32.

Sonnichsen, R. C. 1994. "Evaluators as Change Agents." *In Handbook of Practical Evaluation,* ed. J. S. Wholey, H. P. Hatry, and K. E. Newcomer. San Francisco: Jossey-Bass.

Weiss, Carol Hirschon. 1995. "Nothing as Practical as Good Theory: Exploring Theory-based Evaluation for Comprehensive Community Initiatives for Children and Families." In *New Approaches to Evaluating Community Initiatives: Concepts, Methods, and Contexts,* ed. James Connell et al. Washington, DC: Aspen Institute.

The Virtue of Specificity in Theory of Change Evaluation: Practitioner Reflections

Susan Philliber

In the provision of human services, thinking about outcomes is still cutting edge stuff. Rooted in the tradition of "doing good," human service agencies have traditionally focused on exactly that—the "doing." Providers are often rewarded for high client counts and units of service delivered, rather than for outcomes produced. This tendency produces a mentality in human services that is very different from that of the business world. Given this tradition, the introduction of a theory of change approach evokes responses from delight to terror, from relief to bafflement.

Still, even for human service providers, producing a clear statement of the underlying theory of change for any project is a necessary prelude to evaluation. These few pages describe how my colleagues and I introduce this approach with every evaluation we do, and what happens when we introduce it, drawing on concrete illustrations from real programs. We have used the approach with programs to address teen pregnancy, HIV, school-linked services, homelessness, domestic violence, and juvenile crime and in other settings.

Although an evaluation must begin with clear theory of change—and with a process of consensus building to construct that theory—a draft theory is only a starting point: it does not make measurement decisions, select samples, or ensure good research practice. It does not guarantee faithful data collection or intelligent analysis. Similarly, when used to guide programs, a good theory of change can provide a measure of clarity and singularity of purpose, but it cannot insure that staff will deliver as promised or that the program will produce the anticipated outcomes. The theory does not ensure that the right clients will be targeted, or even that the planned intervention will occur at all. In short, the theory of change approach is necessary to good programs and good evaluation, but it is not sufficient.

A good theory of change is also not a substitute for secure causal analysis, complete with randomly selected control groups. Ascribing such power to theories of change has been attractive to researchers working in areas where traditional experimental designs are not easily applied. And indeed, when program strategies occur as outlined in the theory of change and the posited outcomes follow, causation is certainly suggested. But while seeing a theory "come true" is persuasive, a theory alone still fails to meet the strict criteria that scientists have always imposed upon themselves to ascertain cause. The possibility remains that the chain of events occurred because of factors not included in the theory of change and that any number of intervening, unmeasured variables could account for the achieved outcomes. This caution does not diminish the value of the causal reasoning that must occur to produce a theory of change. That process in and of itself is very valuable to a program.

Charting a Concrete Theory of Change

Words like "theory" or "paradigm" or "logic model" often sound academic and even a little frightening to those seeking evaluation help. Avoiding those labels, we begin evaluation planning with two questions for program, agency, or project staff:

• What do you do here exactly? Tell us what you plan to deliver, to whom, by when.

• What do you expect to happen in the short run and in the longer term as a result of what you are delivering? Tell us who it will happen to, by when.

These questions yield what evaluators call program "process" and program "outcomes." As the questions are answered, the resultant theory of change is written down in a horizontal format in causal order: processes on the left, short-term outcomes in the center, and longer-term outcomes on the right. The horizontal format is important because it enables those working on the model to see immediately the causal sequence they are suggesting.

The Trucking Company

To get program staff to understand the utility of creating a theory of change, we often assert that the average trucking company in America does better evaluation than the average human services program. We add that this is a sad state of affairs, owing to the obviously greater importance of human service work.

Imagine, we say, that Joe and Eddie own a small trucking company and plan to deliver a load of apples from upstate New York to Oshkosh. What would they do before they left to accomplish this task? Members of the group soon suggest that Joe and Eddie would load the apples, check the truck, get money for expenses, and buy a map. We agree, translating these tasks into checking on resources and making a plan to accomplish the ultimate goal—reaching Oshkosh.

Now, we ask them to imagine that Joe takes the apples and returns. Eddie asks Joe if he got the apples to Oshkosh. But instead of talking like a trucker, Joe responds like a human service provider. "Oh, I drove really hard day and night," replies Joe. Eddie looks puzzled.

"Yes, but did you get the apples to Oshkosh?" he asks.

"And," says Joe, "the apples really enjoyed the ride."

We point out that this kind of talk among human service providers seems appropriate but among truckers seems silly. Why can't we ask a program if they got their apples to Oshkosh? Of course, that would mean that the program had indeed defined the equivalent of Oshkosh—their desired longer-term outcomes—and that they had the equivalent of a map—the theory of change.

Groups are quick to say that people are not apples, an observation with which we readily agree. We hasten to add that they have volunteered, even eagerly applied, to be in the "people moving" busi-

ness. Most agree that asking them about getting their apples to Oshkosh is fair and that they do need a "map."

This analogy can be put to further use as the theory of change is developed. Process measures and short-term outcomes can be talked about as the equivalents of sign posts along the highway— ways to know that one is still on the way to Oshkosh and not off in a ditch. We suggest that Joe would not drive around with his head down for two days and then look up to ask if this is Oshkosh.

We find that program and service staff remember this analogy. They often talk to us about their "map" and how close they are to "Oshkosh" long after they have forgotten anything technical we tried to say about evaluation.

As these processes and outcomes are being described, we disallow "vague-speak." Program staff cannot tell us they intend to "develop youth to their fullest potential" without being asked how we would know a fully developed kid if we ran into him. They cannot tell us they intend to "encourage higher comfort levels" without defining exactly how they intend to do that. We always remind clients that most evaluators are arrested at the concrete stage of thinking (a principle that we actually believe is true, at least during working hours), and so they will need to use concrete language to talk to us.

In order to make things as clear as possible, we employ some simple guidelines in getting the theory of change on paper. These include:

• State one process or outcome at a time—no use of the word "and." Since we will have to measure achievements one at a time, it keeps things clearer.

• Use specific verbs like "increase" or "decrease" rather than vague words like "promote" or "encourage."

• Since this model will be the basis for a measurement plan, keep it simple and emphasize the essential elements, rather than including everything staff members might be able to think of.

At this brainstorming session, it is generally most fruitful to have line staff, executive staff, board members, funders, and other important stakeholders involved. A particularly interesting group to include is clients of the proposed program or project. Each group has a different perspective and set of needs, and each brings unique comments to the table.

Sometimes it is difficult to get anything into the model but process. Staff members want to assert that "holding 15 workshops" is their ultimate outcome. In order to shift their thinking to outcomes, we remind group participants that anything done, offered, created, or held by them (as opposed to clients or members of the target population) is by definition process, and we ask them why they are doing these things. Some agencies or programs are almost defined by their processes or strategies, and for them this can be a particularly difficult hurdle.

Getting Stuck on Process

A frantic call from a program director revealed that she was being "forced" to do an evaluation. She needed an evaluator immediately. We began our conversation in the usual way, trying to construct a theory of change. I asked what she was doing that needed to be evaluated.

"I have a contract to do short-term counseling with adjudicated juvenile delinquents," she replied.

"To what end?" I asked.

"So they won't repeat their criminal behavior," she said.

I began talking about the very real uses of short-term counseling as an intervention but expressed grave doubts about its utility for this purpose. I explained the high-risk nature of the young people she was going to deal with, the many approaches to juvenile delinquency prevention that had been tried over time, how difficult this work was. Did she really think counseling would work?

"We're a counseling agency," she asserted impatiently. "Counseling is what we do!"

Here is a strategy in search of an outcome, not an outcome in search of a strategy. The agency is defined by what it does as an intervention, not by the outcomes it works toward.

Who said that if all you have is a hammer, every problem looks like a nail?

As a theory of change develops, the participants often produce a long list of outcomes that they believe will occur. Some of these are more important or compelling than others. For example, a group may say that, as a result of some planned intervention, young people in their program will "develop more comfort with their teachers," and thus "will attend school more." The second outcome, improved school attendance, is the more compelling outcome in many ways. While both variables can be measured, a program that increases school attendance is more important and more fundable than one that increases student comfort levels. Moreover, the more compelling outcome in this particular model is also easier to measure.

In a situation like this, an evaluator can look ahead to the measurement implications of each suggested process and help programs sort through the outcomes to be included in the model. Although important logical steps should not be excluded, it is not essential to measure every potential interim outcome. Thus, although improving student comfort may well be an important interim outcome, especially if it gives participants encouragement that they are making progress toward their ultimate goal, the emphasis needs to be on measuring progress toward the program's compelling, long-term aim.

Once the theory of change becomes visible, the working group may recognize that the theory is flawed. Generally, the flaw can be traced to an intervention plan that is not strong enough, intense enough, or well enough targeted to produce the hoped-for outcomes. When there is a very wide gap between the interventions and their desired results, we call these "Grand Canyon models" and encourage the group to talk about the problem.

But Can This Work?

An agency had accepted a grant to "reduce the county's teen pregnancy rate by 10 percent in three years." Those familiar with the history of teen pregnancy prevention programs know that this is an ambitious goal, one that has eluded the most dedicated efforts for three decades.

In order to create a theory of change for the project, we asked, "How do you plan to do that?" The program director offered four interventions:

- *parent-child communication workshops for some 40 parents and their children*

- *a media campaign, including radio spots and posters*

- *a contraceptive educator at the local health clinic to talk to all girls who come into the clinic for service*

- *a series of speakers in the community for groups like the PTA and Kiwanis*

Clearly the likelihood that this would work was slim. The parent-child communication workshops and the contraceptive educator would reach too few people in a fairly large county. The media campaign was not a sufficiently intensive intervention to produce the goal, nor was the speakers' program. The plan had coverage, targeting, and intensity problems.

When these interventions and their desired outcomes were written down into a theory of change, the program director realized that her model was flawed. In her original proposal, the exact interventions and their desired outcome were not this clear. The program director had inadvertently and successfully hidden this problem from both herself and the funder.

What were her choices at this point? She could revise the intervention so that it might be able to produce the desired outcome, or she could revise the outcome to make it match what the interventions were likely to produce. She chose the latter option, and the funder, although disappointed, continued to support her.

Draft theories of change sometimes show confusion about targets, revealing a plan to work with one group while expecting outcomes in another. For example, a plan may include a program to offer health services to a school population and an expectation that community rates of some health problem will decrease. This is not an impossible outcome, but it is an unlikely one in most communities, since not all school families will use the health services and many community families have no members at the school. In other words, it is not at all clear that serving a portion of the school population, even very successfully, can produce community-level improvements. By carefully specifying expected target groups in every process and outcome statement, an evaluator can help reveal these potential pitfalls.

Because theories of change are only that—theories—they need to be created with an eye to change. Replaceable, disposable paper, not stone tablets, is the appropriate medium on which to record them. We counsel programs to reexamine their theories regularly, and certainly to reexamine them every time they have data in hand against which to check. Thus, creation of a theory of change does not end with the first draft, particularly for initiatives that have the luxury of interactive evaluations, which ideally function more like smoke detectors than like autopsies.

Promoting Good Management with a Theory of Change

Administrators and funders are often the first to see the management potential of a theory of change. They recognize the value of a concise statement of what an organization does and what it expects to produce. They see that such a statement could be used to orient new staff members, educate potential funders, and maintain clarity day to day about what is important. As this potential becomes evident, groups sometimes want to refine and embellish their models, adding specific processes and outcomes for various departments or divisions. The resultant theories of change can come to read like job descriptions, with expected outcomes attached. This is all to the good, allowing staff to see the utility of a theory of change quite apart from its function in guiding an evaluation.

This process becomes especially interesting when staff members who have been working together for some time find themselves in disagreement about what the theory of change should include. Although people rarely disagree about process or what the program is doing, they often disagree about what those activities are supposed to produce. When this occurs, we suggest that they may not have been coordinating their work in an ideal way, and indeed all assembled generally see the implications of their failure to agree.

When Staff Disagree

In the midst of a spirited discussion to create a theory of change, the agency health educator began naming the outcomes of her work. "Knowledge should increase among those people I reach," she suggested.

"Well, maybe," said the agency executive director, "but the real outcome of your work in the community should be how many clients you recruit for this agency."

The educator was obviously stunned. "Well, no," she began to stammer. "That's not my job."

"It certainly is," asserted the director.

"But I have just spent two weeks in a juvenile detention facility doing education work," protested the educator. "They can't come here for service."

This exchange made it readily apparent to this group that they needed a clear theory of change so they could all pull the sled in the same direction.

Here is another example:

A group working on support for families who have been the victims of fires or other disasters was trying to reach agreement on their desired long-term outcomes for clients. One staff member suggested that clients "should improve their previous level of living" as a result of their work. Others objected vehemently, arguing that getting clients back to their pre-disaster standard of living was enough. Still other staff members asserted that they could not be held accountable for any of these outcomes. Instead, they argued that they could only work with a family through the point of creating a plan to recover from the disaster. Others backed off even further, wanting only to measure whether they could provide families with two days of emergency assistance in housing, food, and clothing.

As this argument continued, it became clear to staff that they were handling their workloads very differently, carrying their clients to different endpoints, and in general deciding individually what the program was about. This point was not lost on managers, who saw that the discussion around outcome had revealed some very real work issues, quite apart from evaluation.

Making the theory of change this clear also makes it plain that measurement is possible and about to occur. While some greet this step with positive emotions, others who are less accustomed to being accountable for outcomes become fearful. Since the process of letting participants create the theory of change has taken away their defense that the evaluation is about to measure things that are irrelevant, their fear may be expressed through other objections.

Some may argue that it is not fair to hold them accountable for client outcomes because there are so many other influences in a client's life. This is tantamount to arguing that their intervention is not strong enough to produce the planned outcomes, so more discussion is sometimes needed to deal with this issue. "You can't measure what I do" is another argument that can arise, usually generated by fear that an evaluator might indeed be able to measure exactly what is being done and what it produces. This objection is most easily countered by refining the theory of change to be more specific about "what I do." Then measurement alternatives can be discussed.

Sometimes project staff want to adjust the theory of change when they see that the theory will be the basis for evaluation. They may back away from outcomes, scale down their hopes, and otherwise react to what they see as an approaching trap. All of this must be dealt with as gently as possible, understanding that outcome and causal thinking may be new and legitimately frightening. But these kinds of reactions make it particularly clear how valuable the approach is. The resultant clarity, even if the project does not progress to evaluation, has distinct benefits in its own right.

Promoting "Buy-In" by Program Staff

It is a luxury when this process can take place before a new program begins. More often, however, programs decide (or are forced) to evaluate well after a program has begun. Even so, an evaluator is needed to help "surface" the theory of change. What to measure, and how and when to measure it, becomes much clearer once the theory is on paper. Moreover, the process of surfacing the theory encourages "buy-in" by the program staff. They are the ones committed to the outcomes to be measured, rather than having those outcomes suggested to them or, worse, imposed by outsiders.

Sometimes the theory of change can be made explicit very quickly, taking no more than two hours or so of facilitated dialogue. To accomplish this, it is most useful to convene a broad-based group and ask them to begin by defining what their "ultimate" or "longer-term outcomes" are supposed to be. The discussion can then move to interim outcomes, or "signs that you are getting there," and then to a description of process, or "services or techniques you use to reach these outcomes." When the discussion proceeds in this order, program staff often pick up the project's logic, or lack thereof, rather quickly.

It is also often helpful to have everyone in the room write out the theory of change on a worksheet before group discussion begins. This process allows individuals to assess their own clarity about process and outcome and makes underlying disagreements among staff clearer. The facilitator can collect these worksheets or can ask groups to contribute from them verbally when the overall discussion begins.

The role of the evaluator is not to impose, direct, or do anything in isolation from program partners. Instead, the evaluator becomes the facilitator, listener, educator, and partner in using data to improve the program. These roles need not mean that the evaluator becomes less "objective." The rules of evidence for program success do not change. Rather, the evaluator comes to recognize that the knowledge and perspectives of evaluator and program personnel are necessary to create a good evaluation.

This more cooperative role is also helpful at the stage of evaluating results, when the tendency to "kill the messenger" becomes a distinct occupational hazard. This danger is heightened in evaluations that are imposed or created by outsiders, without participation and buy-in from within the program itself. Charting the theory of change together dispels the argument that the evaluator measured the wrong things or did not understand the program in the first place.

Sometimes flaws in a theory of change are not as apparent to program staff as they are to evaluators. As researchers, they may have direct experience with similar programs or be knowledgeable about the issues facing the program through literature. If so, the evaluator can bring information to the group to use in creating and assessing the proposed theory of change. For example, we would not move ahead to evaluate a model that depended on short-term, information-giving activities to produce changes in contraceptive behavior and reduce teen pregnancy rates. Instead, we would attempt to educate program staff about strategies that have proven effective or ineffective in producing those outcomes, asking them to reconsider their theory of change. In such situations, the evaluator becomes an educator and partner in program design.

Some human service programs and projects approach evaluation with dread, but almost all come to the process with confusion about how to capture what they are doing. As the theory of change emerges, they usually see a line of attack, where before they saw only a complex and vague problem. The next step, then, is for the evaluation team to suggest alternative measurement strategies for each outcome, from which the program and evaluation teams can together choose the most appropriate measures.

By bringing program staff into the design process, evaluators can enhance staff members' comfort and demystify what they may have believed would be a complex, statistical, impersonal endeavor. It puts program staff in control of how the evaluation will be done and nicely avoids many of the complaints made of evaluations and evaluators, including the imposition of outcomes and measures by outsiders.

Shaping the Evaluator's Role in a Theory of Change Evaluation: Practitioner Reflections

Prudence Brown

Introduction

This essay describes efforts to implement a modified theory of change approach in two comprehensive community initiatives (CCIs) and one education reform initiative. Although the initiatives are at different stages of development, this discussion focuses on the initial phase, the period during which our evaluation team worked with each site to help articulate a theory of change and specify goals, outcomes, and benchmarks. During this phase, we typically confront interesting questions about the role of the evaluator.

We call our evaluation method a modified theory of change approach because we had neither the charge from our funders nor the resources to implement the approach in its full depth and detail. For example, knowing that our subsequent ability to collect data would be limited, we did not specify and benchmark alternative theories of change at each site, nor did we spend much time identifying an extensive list of indicators for each outcome. Further, for one initiative, the funder was more interested in the theory of change approach as a way to help sites make linkages between their strategies and outcomes during the planning period than as the primary vehicle for evaluating the initiative later. As a consequence, we are not well positioned to comment on the utility of the approach as a method of evaluation. Rather, we focus here on early implementation, sensing that some of the issues we have confronted will resonate with the real world experiences of others. The examples we cite have been modified in some cases to preserve the anonymity of an initiative or its sites.

The Evaluator's Role:
Four Examples

Like the Cleveland Community-Building Initiative evaluation described in this volume by Sharon Milligan and colleagues, our evaluations began at each site by helping participants to "articulate the theories of change as viewed by multiple stakeholders" and "identify important concepts and key benchmarks along the change pathway." Confirming the experiences of other evaluators, we found during this early planning period that engaging with sites requires broad participation and has significant implications for relations among stakeholders, including the evaluator. Every stakeholder's voice must be heard, divergent needs addressed, and different agendas surfaced. All theories have equal weight at this stage of an initiative's development.

During this process, the role of the evaluator undergoes an important shift, from that of an outside appraiser to that of a collaborator. As the theories of the various stakeholders are clarified, the initial balance of power is altered, as well. Participants gain new understanding of their own goals and those of others, while important issues such as the proper locus of authority and responsibility for implementing the work become clarified. This understanding often comes through the efforts of the evaluator, whose task is to foster open and clear communication among stakeholders and surface underlying assumptions and cherished beliefs. Having permission to ask certain questions at a certain level of specificity allows the evaluator to stimulate sharper, more defined thinking by all stakeholders. The following example illustrates this dynamic.

The Evaluator and an Initiative with an
Emerging Theory of Change

In an initiative aimed at public education reform, the evaluator worked with one of the sites to help participants identify the pathways between their advocacy activities and the systemic changes they hoped to achieve. At first this was a very difficult conversation. The group had for many years used a political framework through which it explained its actions to its current membership and to the parents it was trying to recruit. Developing the specifics of a theory of change approach required the group's leadership to make explicit certain assumptions about the links between actions and desired outcomes. This involved the group in actual debate about those links and uncovered some conflicting views about future strategy. For example, the group often sponsored "actions" to bring attention to its cause, such as making a surprise visit with a busload of parents to an important official's home. The debate involved several key questions. How would such a strategy lead to the desired outcome—by threatening damage to the official's public image, influencing a school board vote on a particular issue, communicating widespread parent opposition to the official? What other strategies might accomplish the same ends? What benchmarks are fair indicators of progress? Resolving these questions entailed a great deal of time and not a little conflict, but the group was strong enough to try to use the debate to become more effective. As a positive secondary consequence, one of the funders reported that the written evaluation framework (developed collaboratively by the site and the evaluator) allowed her to see clearly for the first time what the group actually did and how the impact of its work could be assessed. In this case, this new understanding strengthened her commitment to the group and her ability to speak to other funders on its behalf.

A second example demonstrates the shifting relations among stakeholders that often result from engagement in a theory of change approach. It also signals the multiple roles the evaluator can assume in this process.

The Evaluator and an Initiative with Diverse Constituencies

One CCI site involved a collaboration among partners from four different ethnic groups and geographic areas of the community. Although each partner had theoretically affirmed the notion of collaboration, they struggled constantly about focus and methods, their misunderstandings exacerbated by language, religious, and economic differences. The work of the evaluator was among the factors that brought them together and helped them produce a strategic plan and a related evaluation framework. The evaluator presented the theory of change approach in a series of brainstorming sessions, inviting each group to be explicit about its interests while not guaranteeing that all those interests could be addressed. At first the partners were hesitant to put their agendas on the table, but they became more forthcoming as they realized that the strategic plan would drive decisions about resource allocation and that the evaluation framework would define interim and long-term success. The evaluator played an active role in this process: she met with each party alone on a regular basis, helping to identify and frame priorities; she challenged members when they moved away from the agreed-upon goals of the group; and she helped provide focus and momentum when local political differences seemed to overwhelm the conversation.

The next two case examples illustrate some of the complexities for evaluators of assuming new roles. They also raise questions about how to implement theory of change evaluations in less than ideal circumstances.

The Evaluator and an Initiative with Competing Political Agendas

The evaluator at one CCI site tried to engage members of the governance committee individually and collectively in developing an evaluation framework. At this site, a strong political agenda worked against achieving specificity about outcomes and benchmarks. Appointments with the evaluator were often canceled; partners expressed one view when alone with the evaluator and another in governance committee meetings; emergency issues were allowed to bump the evaluator's work from meeting agendas. Further, the initiative's staff director lacked the leadership skills and support to move ahead with developing a framework independently. With much persistence, the evaluator assembled a draft framework, which was discussed and approved at a gover-

nance committee meeting. Although all parties agreed about the major outcomes and strategies, the resulting framework risked being mechanistic or irrelevant to what was driving the site as full-scale implementation began.

The Evaluator and an Initiative with a Weak Theory of Change

In one CCI, a foundation put forth the beginning parameters of a theory of change, then selected seven sites that responded positively to the opportunity to participate. Partly because the foundation's theory was not developed or communicated clearly, the sites were drawn to the initiative as much by the promise of resources for their neighborhoods as by the initiative's ideas and goals. Further, the funder did not direct the technical assistance provider to reinforce the theory of change approach or to integrate it into his strategic planning assistance. After the sites received a weak directive from the funder to participate in the development of an evaluation framework, the evaluator was left to champion theory development and the theory of change approach with the sites. Over time, the evaluator was able to establish collaborative relationships and produce, with input from the sites, an evaluation framework for the implementation phase. Yet without a well-articulated, initiative-wide theory of change that was owned by the funder and technical assistance providers, the individual site frameworks were too diverse to form the basis for significant cross-site testing and analysis.

Lessons for Establishing an Effective Role

These examples illustrate some of the complexities of the evaluator's role during the planning process. They are derived from a limited number of quite different initiatives, none of which has been in existence for more than two years. Despite these limitations, we suggest some initial lessons about using a modified theory of change approach to help develop an evaluation framework during the CCI planning process.

Establishing a theory of change framework in the planning period involves multiple tasks and can be very time consuming. This conclusion may be obvious but needs to be underscored. The evaluator charged with helping participants articulate their theories of change and establish appropriate outcomes and benchmarks takes on a wide variety of tasks that tend to be evolutionary, iterative, and diverse in their requirements. The process demands that the evaluator learn enough about the participants and establish strong enough relationships that he or she can help construct the framework collaboratively. This involves such tasks as:

• understanding and then incorporating into the framework the language and perspective of the sites, so that the framework has a meaningful connection to their day-to-day implementation experiences

• establishing sufficient trust so that the evaluator can assume the role of friendly critic and challenge the site's thinking without threatening the relationship

• interacting repeatedly with sites to capture their current thinking and reflect it back to them, with the expectation that this feedback will contribute to the evolution of their thinking and to a modified or elaborated framework

• ensuring that all the key stakeholders are involved in the process

If these tasks are to be accomplished within a reasonable amount of time, the evaluator needs the full engagement and support of the sites and the funder. In two of the examples described earlier, the process turned out to take much longer than expected because the sites needed to spend time on tasks that had little to do with their theories of change. In one initiative, the planning process was extended from 12 to 18 months after the first 6 months were spent building an effective collaborative body to guide the initiative. Although the evaluation team was present from the beginning, the sites were not ready to engage either with the team or with the substantive aspects of the planning process until certain organizational issues had been resolved. Early work had to be discarded once the sites turned to strategic planning in earnest, since they had developed quite different ideas and assumptions about how change could be stimulated. In another site, unanticipated political disputes had to be resolved before effective strategic planning could begin.

An evaluator using a theory of change approach needs to draw upon a wide variety of skills during the planning period. As the examples illustrate, establishing a theory of change approach is a process that is substantive, political, and methodological. In helping the sites articulate their assumptions about change or identify benchmarks to assess progress, an evaluator well versed in the substance of the initiative is better able to stimulate participants' thinking and challenge it constructively. If participants select a strategy and specify interim outcome measures that seem unrealistic, a knowledgeable evaluator can refer them to existing findings or programs that might inform their decisions. If we imagine evaluators distributed along a continuum of substantive expertise, evaluators who consider themselves experts in the particular field of the initiative are at one end, while at the other end are evaluators who see themselves as facilitators who translate the site's goals and strategies into an agreed-upon format, regardless of content. Our experience suggests that simply being knowledgeable about a field can help the evaluator probe assumptions and benchmarks more deeply, build credibility with the sites, and accelerate the process of creating a framework that receives the support of all stakeholders.

Group process and political skills are also valuable assets for the evaluator. Developing a framework that reflects the investment and approval of multiple and diverse groups of stakeholders requires the evaluator to work closely with all parties, appreciate the dynamics among them, identify common ground, and address differences in perspective. The example of the initiative with diverse constituencies illustrates the need for these tasks and skills. In a collaborative venture like a CCI, it is especially important for the evaluator to surface disagreements or differences in perspective among participants early in the planning process so that these differences do not undermine the ability of the site to work as a unified force.

Finally, to resolve the methodological issues that arise in constructing an evaluation framework, an evaluator should be knowledgeable about quantitative and qualitative sources of data and the use of administrative data records. Because well-established measures do not exist for many of the relevant indicators, an evaluator may need to combine an appreciation for the value of psychometrically established measures with a creative sense of how to develop new ones. In the example of the initiative with an emerging theory of change, the long-term outcomes are changes in policy. As the group worked to develop its theory of change framework, the pathways they articulated included a variety of measurement points—fear of negative media attention, increased public awareness of the grantee's agenda, increased parental leadership—that were difficult to assess reliably, especially within the evaluation's limited resources.

As an active participant during the planning period, an evaluator can improve the quality of the process and its product. This is not a traditional evaluation role; rather, it requires the evaluator to engage in an often messy process and become part of the action. Simply helping sites identify and specify in measurable terms their outcomes and benchmarks can be viewed as a technical assistance activity. Once the line between evaluation and technical assistance is crossed, however, an evaluator may face a range of dilemmas associated with the new role for which there are few models or agreed-upon standards.

Theoretically, the evaluator's technical assistance can be limited to helping the site construct the evaluation framework. For example, if the site has trouble expressing the precise pathways it anticipates between a particular strategy and set of outcomes, the evaluator can draft possible scenarios and use them as the basis for discussion with the group. For some groups, much of the work gets done in this iterative fashion, with the evaluator taking the lead in constructing aspects of the framework and then getting feedback from the site. This is clearly a delicate process, one into which the evaluator's knowledge and biases cannot help but enter, ideally in a constructive fashion. Yet there are also dangers in being too passive, especially if the stakeholders have an interest in distancing themselves from the framework (as in the initiative with competing political agendas), the theory of change approach plays a marginal role (as in the initiative with a weak theory of change), or the site's capacity is very weak. Either way, the framework can end up belonging more to the evaluator than to the site, or it can prove to be inadequate as the evaluation moves into full-scale implementation. Although updating the frameworks along the way will be normative in most CCI evaluations, the frameworks need to be sufficiently well constructed at the outset to require only updating, not wholesale transformation.

The evaluator's substantive influence might be reduced by separating the development of the evaluation framework in the first phase from the subsequent use of that framework to evaluate CCI implementation. Two different individuals or teams could carry out these functions. The first might be considered responsible for the "pre-evaluation" phase; the second for the actual evaluation. While such an arrangement may present some advantages in terms of bounding the role of the evaluator, it could also create an artificial discontinuity between planning and implementation and reduce the evaluator's overall understanding of and ability to provide informed feedback to the CCI. Much more experience with these roles is needed before such questions can be resolved.

Conditions for a
Productive Evaluation

In thinking through the dilemmas of the theory of change approach, we have identified at least three conditions that enable an evaluator to work most successfully. Although not necessarily prerequisites for successful engagement between evaluator and initiative, these conditions may contribute to such engagement.

An overall theory of change should be both strong and responsive to input from the participating sites. An initiative needs a strong overall theory, able to encompass the contributions of different sites, funders, and other stakeholder groups. Without such a theory, each site may develop a theory and evaluation framework that works locally but does not fit within a larger, multisite framework. Under these circumstances, evaluators may feel as if they are working on a set of case studies, not a single initiative. In one collaboratively supported initiative, the funders shared some overall goals and principles but chose not to develop these further, partly in recognition that doing so would surface significant disagreements among them. Their view that keeping the collaboration of funders together was more important than elaborating and testing a particular theory was a legitimate determination of priorities, but it limited the potential learning yield of the approach. Even in a single-site initiative, it helps to begin with the strongest possible theory about how the initiative expects to achieve its goals, while recognizing that this theory will evolve over time and in response to local factors and experience.

A support structure can reinforce the theory of change approach and the evaluation framework. Funders are increasingly recognizing the importance of effective technical assistance or coaching to help CCIs with a range of tasks at the outset of an initiative. When funders and technical assistance providers communicate the value of a theory of change approach from the very beginning of an initiative, the evaluation is likely to become an effective means for maintaining focus and momentum. The opposite is also the case. If the technical assistance provider portrays the theory of change approach as irrelevant or marginal, participants at the sites will not feel committed to the evaluation. It should be relatively easy, however, to demonstrate the value of the evaluation perspective to CCI technical assistance providers, whose emphasis on strategic planning and capacity building connects well with the principles of the theory of change approach.

Cultivating good working relations between the funder and the sites is essential. The relationship between the funder and the CCI sites provides an important context for the development of an initiative's theory of change. The funder and the sites must engage in honest dialogue about their own theories of change and agree about how those theories should inform the evaluation strategy. Such a discussion can also clarify roles, responsibilities, and locus of authority. In one case, the funder's theory of change was not well developed at the beginning of the initiative. Later, the funder did not hesitate to make its theory more explicit when the site's developing theory was seen to be inconsistent with the funder's evolving understanding of the initiative. Such differences in perspective can become problematic if the relationship between the funder and the site is characterized by lack of trust or struggles over expectations and accountability.

Under the right conditions, an evaluator using a modified theory of change approach can play a constructive role that strengthens the planning process of an initiative. Over the next few years, experience should begin to yield specific lessons about whether and how such an approach can shape an evaluation framework that retains its effectiveness throughout the life of an initiative.

Using a Theory of Change Approach in a National Evaluation of Family Support Programs: Practitioner Reflections

Sharon L. Kagan

Introduction

Family support programs have emerged as a comparatively recent phenomenon, gaining operational currency in the last two decades (Weissbourd, 1987). Designed originally as community-based entities, these programs defined themselves as antidotes to, and mediators of, more formal and highly bureaucratized social services. Rather than rigidly adhering to structured rules and regulations, family support programs sought to be flexible, contouring their activities to respond to parent and family needs. Rather than meeting the needs of one family member, family support programs sought to meet the needs of entire families and communities. Rather than focusing on interventions once problems were identified, family support programs sought not only to prevent the onset of problems, but to optimize human development and capacity. Rather than relying primarily on the expertise of professionals, family support programs sought to recognize and maximize the talents and competencies of involved families. In short, family support programs were established to be "of," "by," and "for" the families and communities in which they were enmeshed.

Not surprisingly, these family support programs raised considerable challenges for evaluators. Small, highly idiosyncratic, and designed to modify their activities continually, family support programs did not offer large populations or uniform and stable treatments to evaluate. As programs that serve all members of the family, interventions are multifocused and diffuse, often changing with family needs. As programs that are, by design, voluntary and often serve highly transient populations, they do not afford optimum settings for randomly assigning participants or for sustaining durable participant involvement. Indeed, random assignment to non-treatment groups violates a fundamental principle of family support—notably that all who need and want services are eligible for them. Moreover, identifying valid comparison groups—so necessary for quasi-experimental design—is difficult, as the environments in which family support programs exist are often contaminated by myriad other interventions. Indeed, researchers contend for good reason that using conventional approaches to evaluate family support programs is extremely problematic (Powell, 1989, 1994; Weiss and Jacobs, 1988).

Despite these caveats, the growth of family support programs and the press for public support to fund them has created a demand for a more systematic understanding of their efficacy. Do these efforts really work? For whom? Under what conditions? How do and can they mesh with conventional services? What are the factors that help them to effect community engagement and community change? How do we know that these programs are worth the investment? Indeed, policymakers and analysts alike have asked whether the family support "emperor" really has new clothes.

A National Evaluation of Family Support Programs

To seek answers to such questions, and in conjunction with the passage of the Family Preservation and Support Services Program (PL 103-66), a national evaluation of family support was authorized for the five-year period from 1996 to 2001. Conducted by Abt Associates and Yale University, the National Evaluation of Family Support Programs was intended to "document, describe and assess the relative impact and effectiveness of family support programs funded under Title IV-B of the Social Security Act Subpart 2, and any other Federal or non-Federal programs that are designed to achieve the same purposes." Inherent in such a charge are three allied goals:

• to provide a state-of-the art knowledge base on family support by gathering and synthesizing existing descriptive information on current family support programmatic and research efforts

- to enhance that knowledge base by designing a research/evaluation strategy to fill important gaps in understanding of the effects of family support

- to synthesize and analyze data in order to advance understanding of the effectiveness of different approaches to family support

After reviewing the evaluations of many family support programs (Barnes, Goodson, and Layzer, 1995) and creating a typology to categorize them (Kagan, Cohen, Hailey, Pritchard, and Colen, 1995), it became clear that conducting a national evaluation of so diffuse a treatment demanded innovation. Standard random assignment would not work, nor would the use of conventional evaluation strategies. In searching for an approach that would lend fidelity to the process while also respecting the variation inherent in family support, a "theory of change" strategy was sought.

On first review, the theory of change approach seemed ideally suited to an evaluation of family support because it sought to discern "how and why an initiative works" (Weiss, 1995) by making pathways of change explicit. Moreover, and consonant with family support, it includes key participants in the design process and gives voice to those participants' views in ways that conventional evaluation approaches do not. In so doing, it also realigns the balance of power between researchers and practitioners, according weight to each.

The theory of change process begins with program staff identifying the outcomes they hope their programs will achieve. Participants—with evaluators—then discern the nature of activities offered by the initiative, linking them through interim accomplishments to ultimate goals. Through a series of iterative discussions, the lifeline of the program is plotted so that the paths from activities to outcomes are graphically portrayed to form a map of the program's theory of change. Inherent in the process of creating the map, participants' ideas about how change occurs are manifest. Clarity is often achieved regarding the precise nature of the goals to be achieved, as well as regarding which frameworks will guide the evaluation.

The rationale for using the theory of change approach in the National Evaluation of Family Support Programs had several facets. First, the approach is aligned with family support in that it captures the non-linearity and iterative nature of the programs. Rather than expecting defined and static interventions, the theory of change approach welcomes the diversity and changeable nature of interventions. It regards critical contextual factors not as theoretical nuisances, but as important variables to be understood and examined. In respecting the role of context, the approach appreciates, rather than tolerates, variation within and across sites—a critical element in family support programs. The approach is responsive to interventions that are multi-, not uni-, dimensional—precisely the kinds of interventions that are found in most family support programs.

But perhaps the most appealing aspect of the theory of change approach is that it is as helpful to program personnel as it is to evaluators. By demanding precise thinking about the purpose and outcomes of various activities, the process of building a theory of change forces program staff to examine their own assumptions and beliefs about what works, for whom, and under what conditions. With the evaluators and participants present, activities that are and are not likely to yield the desired outcomes can be identified and the program refined accordingly. In this respect, the process is valued by providers.

From the perspective of the evaluators, the approach evokes both a new and valuable role and a new set of responsibilities. Evaluators become collaborators with program personnel; the hierarchical relationship that often elevates the evaluators' status is minimized. Indeed, the theory of change process engages evaluators as co-explicators in reaching consensus regarding the language attached to the program's intentions. For the most part, theory of change evaluators are not the shapers of intentions, but thoughtful allies in explicating them. Their role is less to pass judgment on the validity of the theory than to identify it.

It should be noted, however, that the collaborative relationship developed between program personnel and evaluators—and the way theory of change information is used—may vary significantly, framed by the interests and experiences of the evaluators and program participants, the stated purpose of the exchange, and the maturity and nature of the programs involved. If, for example, the evaluators are using the process to help distinguish and select among programs for further evaluation, then the potential for program improvement may be limited, as might the duration of the involvement of the evaluator. If, however, the purpose of conducting the theory of change process is to engage the evaluator in a more sustained or consultative relationship, then the programmatic implications of the process might be more intense.

Allied with these issues are considerations regarding whether the evaluation is more formative or summative. It may be that in more formative evaluations the role of the evaluator has greater programmatic impact than in more summative evaluations. Moreover, more mature programs may be less willing or able to alter their efforts, while those at earlier stages of development may have more flexibility, and hence may be better able to use the results for programmatic purposes. The point is that the dynamic theory of change process can be adapted for a variety of evaluative and programmatic purposes.

The Theory of Change Approach: The Process

Once it was determined that the theory of change process made sense for the evaluation, we clarified our intention to use it to improve our understanding of the 16 programs that were candidates for the final evaluation. Clearly, the theory of change process could not be the only criterion used to determine a program's appropriateness as a subject for evaluation, but we decided that it would be helpful in discerning which programs would best qualify for first-round inclusion in the study.

Then we embarked on the process: site visits were made to the candidate programs by teams of workers, typically a researcher and a program specialist. Prior to visiting each site, written materials were extensively reviewed by the site visitors. On site, the visitors held entry interviews with the directors and key staff, followed typically by program observations. Initial meetings were held to discuss the theory of change process with key staff; and then at least two and sometimes as many as five follow-up sessions were held to come up with a theory of change map for each program.

To assure the fidelity and accuracy of the map, the evaluators finalized the map and sent it back to the program for approval or refinement,
if necessary. For each program visited, an individual map portraying the
program's theory of change was created. Similarities and differences
among programs were discerned, as were similarities and differences in the
outcomes desired. Ultimately, a "generic" family support theory of change
was created, and from it, "generic" instruments were identified. In addition, individual instruments were also selected, tailored to site-specific
needs.

The theory of change process, then, served to illuminate what was to
be evaluated; it did not provide specific answers regarding how to conduct
the evaluation. Having said that, however, using a theory of change
approach—because it uncovers such richness of program detail—cannot
help but underscore the necessity of getting beneath the numbers to reveal
the nuances of a program's impact. As such, the theories of change process
points toward increased use of qualitative information, typically in combination with more quantitative data.

In discerning the "what" of the evaluation, the process was also
extremely useful in guiding the thinking and collaborative process between
evaluators and program personnel that was to ensue as the precise methodology of the evaluation unfolded. The process was highly regarded by both
program staff and evaluators. Program personnel—including many who
were not selected to participate in the first round of the evaluation—indicated that the work had been beneficial to their long-term planning.
Although many expressed appreciation for the maps as blueprints for
action, they were even more grateful for the opportunity to learn a valuable
process for strategic planning. From the perspective of the evaluators, the
theory of change maps provided an informative operational overview of
the family support field.

Although it is still too early to comment on the actual impact of
the theory of change process on the outcome of the evaluation, it may
be helpful to speculate on several points. First, it appears that the
process heightens the awareness and intentionality of program efforts.

Because efforts are more closely aligned with the ends that are being sought, program results may increase. Second, for programs that are designed to have flexible interventions—including family support programs—the theory of change approach may need constant updating. As such, evaluators will need to consider how much adaptiveness they can incorporate into their evaluation methods and tools, as programs change and become far more explicit about those changes. Third, the process beckons evaluators to examine how inventive evaluation methodologies can be developed and/or used. The process strongly reaffirms the challenge of using conventional methods for unconventional programs and services.

Critical Questions

As productive as the theory of change approach has proven to be, its innovative nature raises many important, but unresolved, theoretical and practical issues. Dialogue on these knotty issues may help evaluators refine the process based on experience and thoughtful consideration. Several theoretical issues deserve focused attention:

• Is there only one theory of change per program or do many theories coexist? What are the benefits and liabilities of each?

• Do theory of change models change over the lifespan of a particular program?

• Does the approach work better with some kinds of initiatives than with others (for example, those that are more circumscribed and less global)?

• What constitutes the unit of analysis for the theory of change approach? Is it the whole comprehensive program or its sub-parts? Who decides, and by what process?

• What is the appropriate level of detail for the outcomes? How specific should the theory be?

At the same time, several key practical questions demand further discussion:

• How do we capture the synergy among the efforts described in the map?

• How much should the evaluator know about the program before embarking on the theory of change process?

• What kind of training, experience, and knowledge do evaluators need to do their work successfully?

• What is the optimal nature of the relationship between evaluators and program staff? Does too close a relationship limit objectivity? Does too little impair understanding?

• When interviewing groups about their theories of change, is it preferable to have cross-sections of program participants or to have role-alike groups (for example, parents, staff, or board members)? If role-alike groups, is there a preferred order?

Using the theories of change approach has been rewarding because it fits so well with the intentions of family support. It has served program and evaluation personnel by establishing the basis for egalitarian relationships, providing conceptual cogency to an array of efforts, and, perhaps most important, creating a viable template for mounting an evaluation of extremely complex phenomena.

References

Barnes, Helen V., Barbara D. Goodson, and Jean I. Layzer. 1995. *Review of the Research on Supportive Interventions for Children and Families.* Volume 1. Cambridge, MA: Abt Associates.

Kagan, Sharon L., Nancy Cohen, Linda Hailey, Eliza Pritchard, and Hope Colen. 1995. *Toward a New Understanding of Family Support: A Review of Programs and a Suggested Typology.* Cambridge, MA: Abt Associates.

Powell, Douglas R. 1994. "Evaluating Family Support Programs: Are We Making Progress?" *In Putting Families First,* eds. Sharon L. Kagan and Bernice Weissbourd. San Francisco: Jossey-Bass.

Powell, Douglas R. 1989. *Families and Early Childhood Programs.* Washington, DC: National Association for the Education of Young Children.

Weiss, Carol Hirschon. 1995. "Nothing as Practical as Good Theory: Exploring Theory-based Evaluation for Comprehensive Community Initiatives for Children and Families." In *New Approaches to Evaluating Community Initiatives: Concepts, Methods, and Contexts,* ed. James Connell et al. Washington, DC: Aspen Institute.

Weiss, Heather B., and Francine Jacobs. 1988. *Evaluating Family Programs.* Hawthorne, NY: Aldine.

Weissbourd, Bernice. 1987. "A Brief History of Family Support Programs." In *America's Family Support Programs,* ed. Sharon L. Kagan, Douglas Powell, Bernice Weissbourd, and Edward Zigler. New Haven: Yale University Press.

Applying a Theory of Change Approach to Two National, Multisite Comprehensive Community Initiatives: Practitioner Reflections

Scott Hebert and Andrea Anderson

Introduction

In recent years, several very significant national initiatives have aimed to address the chronic poverty afflicting some of our nation's communities, particularly inner-city neighborhoods with high concentrations of people of color. Among the most ambitious of these are the Annie E. Casey Foundation's Jobs Initiative, originally funded in 1995, and the Empowerment Zones and Enterprise Communities Program, launched by the U. S. Department of Housing and Urban Development in 1994.

The Annie E. Casey Foundation's Jobs Initiative is an eight-year, six-site demonstration designed to improve access to family-supporting jobs for disadvantaged young adults residing in inner cities. The selected sites are Denver, Milwaukee, New Orleans, Philadelphia, Seattle, and Saint Louis. Seed money is being provided by the Annie E. Casey Foundation in annual increments to help groups of local actors in these communities pursue systems reform agendas to promote better connections between disadvantaged job seekers and good jobs in the regional economy. In each site, a "development intermediary" is responsible for mobilizing the civic infrastructure, facilitating the process of defining regional strategies, making investment decisions regarding prototype jobs projects that will be used to test job access mechanisms, establishing a jobs policy network, and initiating a systems reform agenda. In addition, an "impact community" of 50,000-100,000 residents within the inner city has been designated at each site. The impact community is expected to provide a framework for the regional Jobs

Initiative to understand the barriers faced by disadvantaged job seekers, as well as to contribute at least half the participants in the jobs projects.

The Empowerment Zones and Enterprise Communities (EZ/EC) Program of the U.S. Department of Housing and Urban Development (HUD) is designed to encourage comprehensive planning and investment aimed at the economic, physical, and social development of the neediest urban and rural areas in the United States. As such, the HUD initiative represents a major element in the federal government's community revitalization strategy. Thus far, HUD has made EZ/EC program awards to a total of 72 urban communities. Individual communities design their own strategies, but each local effort is expected to incorporate four key principles in its strategic plan: economic opportunity, sustainable community development, community-based partnerships, and a strategic vision for change. In addition, the target community and its residents are expected to be full partners in the process of developing and implementing the strategic plan. Federal financial assistance and support for the local EZ/EC efforts are provided in a variety of forms, including flexible social services funds, wage tax credits and tax deductions for participating businesses, tax-exempt bond financing, and special Economic Development Initiative (EDI) grants. The EZ/EC program also recognizes that communities cannot succeed with public resources alone, and therefore emphasizes the leveraging of additional private and nonprofit support.

Like many other CCIs, both the Jobs Initiative and the EZ/EC program are intended to improve the conditions and outcomes of disadvantaged residents, largely by expanding economic opportunities. The Jobs Initiative clearly reflects a targeted approach to economic development through activities to improve employment connections for disadvantaged job seekers.[1] The EZ/EC program aims for more general transformation of economic conditions in the specified zone areas. All EZ/EC activities are concentrated within the specified zones, while Jobs Initiative sites attempt to improve employment connections throughout the region.

Within the general guidelines established by their funders, both the Jobs Initiative and the EZ/EC program exhibit broad variations among sites in the strategies and activities being pursued. In all cases, however, the local efforts represent complex, multifaceted interventions. All sites are pursuing saturation models, in that all residents of a zone (in case of the EZ/EC program) or all disadvantaged job seekers in the region (in the Jobs Initiative sites) are expected to realize benefits from the initiative activities over the course of the interventions.

Abt Associates was selected as the prime evaluation contractor by the Annie E. Casey Foundation for the Jobs Initiative evaluation and by HUD for the EZ/EC assessment; Scott Hebert is serving as project director for both studies.[2] For the Jobs Initiative evaluation, Abt is teaming with the New School for Social Research. For both evaluations, Abt has also contracted with local research affiliates in each of the intensive study sites to provide ongoing data collection capacity and local insight.

The Jobs Initiative evaluation, scheduled to run for the duration of the eight-year initiative, is intended to assess the Jobs Initiative's effects at each site and across sites in the following areas:

• institutional change and systems reform, in terms of how the regional labor market and workforce development system function for disadvantaged job seekers

• earnings, employment, and family outcomes for participants in the Jobs Initiative projects

• community outcomes, where relevant

The EZ/EC study, more formally known as the Interim Outcomes Assessment, is scheduled to take place over five years and has three principal objectives:

• establish measurements of key zone characteristics at baseline

• identify local outcome measures, as well as common national measures toward which a long-term (ten-year) evaluation will be directed

• assess progress toward community transformation after the first five years of program operations

The two national initiatives pose complex challenges to evaluators. As saturation models whose strategies cut across multiple systems, they do not lend themselves to traditional evaluation methods involving randomized control groups or comparison groups to establish counterfactuals. In addition, although funded within national initiatives, all sites have used a bottom-up approach to program design, producing agendas of activities and objectives that are dependent on unique local conditions. Designing an appropriate cross-site evaluation framework with rigorously specified and consistent outcome measures is therefore very difficult (Hollister and Hill, 1995; Giloth, 1996). Recognizing these challenges, the funders sought evaluation frameworks that would blend traditional and nontraditional research methods, with significant evaluation resources devoted to applying a theory of change approach.

This paper discusses the experiences to date of the Abt Associates evaluation teams in their application of the theory of change approach in assessing these two national initiatives. Although the results are preliminary, we believe they highlight a number of key methodological issues and offer some insights into addressing the particular challenges of CCI evaluation.

Challenges in Conducting a Multisite CCI Evaluation

Unlike evaluations that apply the theory of change approach to a single site, the national evaluations of the Jobs Initiative and the EZ/EC program are using this approach on a cross-site, multiple-community basis. Specifically, these evaluations are employing theory of change methods in all 6 Jobs Initiative sites and 18 of the 72 EZ/EC program sites to produce both site-specific and cross-site findings. Working across so many sites raises important issues regarding staffing and allocation of resources, articulating local theories of change, and reconciling discrepancies within the evaluation framework.

Staffing and Allocating Resources

A theory of change approach typically requires detailed articulation and tracking of micro-stages in the intervention, entailing the commitment of fairly substantial research staff resources. Our mandate to study a large number of sites geographically distant from one another limits the amount of time that the core national evaluation team can spend on-site. Accordingly, the Abt national evaluation teams have recruited local research affiliates to conduct many of the data collection activities at each site. These researchers reflect a broad range of academic disciplines and provide the national evaluators with invaluable local expertise regarding the political, economic, and social contexts of the interventions. Their proximity to the sites also extends the evaluation's on-site presence, essential for a theory of change approach.

For the most part, the local research affiliates have been recruited from the faculty of local universities, although independent consultants are being utilized at some sites. Typically, the local research team consists of one or two individuals, sometimes supported (where the affiliates are faculty members) by graduate students acting as research assistants. In all cases, the individuals selected to serve as local research affiliates had demonstrated interest in and experience with the issues being addressed by the local initiative. In general, however, the local research affiliates had little or no previous experience in applying the theory of change approach. Consequently, at the commencement of each study the local affiliates were brought together for a two-day training conference on the theory of change approach. In addition to ongoing guidance provided through memoranda, internet list servers, and conference calls, periodic cross-site meetings are held to identify and respond to issues that arise in the application of the theory of change approach.

Perhaps the most significant ongoing research issue, however, is the limited amount of resources available for local research affiliates. Budget constraints have allowed the national evaluations to allocate an average of less than eight staff hours per week per site to local research affiliates. Although several local teams have been able to supplement their budgets with funding from other sources, all teams constantly face hard choices in setting priorities for data collection activities.

In addition, using a large group of affiliates has brought to light some difficulties that traditionally trained research professionals may experience in understanding and accepting the theory of change approach. Some local affiliates have raised issues about the "hybrid" nature of the approach and its failure to separate process and impact analyses. Others have been concerned about the lack of a clear counterfactual. Most important, many of the researchers have had to overcome their belief that they must maintain an "arm's-length relationship" with local stakeholders.

On the other hand, it is important to acknowledge that, while many of its features are nontraditional, the theory of change approach relies heavily on traditional data collection methods. Moreover, the findings it yields can be buttressed by more traditional analysis frameworks. For example, in the national evaluation of the Jobs Initiative, we will be conducting pre and post surveys of project participants and assessing longitudinal data from administrative databases, in addition to interviewing key stakeholders, observing governance meetings and other project activities, and conducting focus groups with community leaders. Similarly, in the EZ/EC national evaluation, we will supplement the data collected through interviews and focus groups with interrupted time series analyses of business activities in the zone, neighborhoods contiguous to the zone, and comparison areas in the city, and with pre and post surveys of a random sample of business firms.

Articulating Local Theories of Change

Both evaluations are currently at the stage of articulating theories of change with the individual sites. Working with stakeholders in 24 separate sites provides a unique opportunity to explore common patterns and variations in the theory articulation process and to identify techniques that may be useful in facilitating that process.

Introducing the Approach and Its Terminology

In both evaluations, we are working with sites that have either completed a formal planning process or are currently engaged in a process independent of the theory of change exercises. This situation has both advantages and disadvantages. On the positive side, the existing planning documents give the evaluation team a good place to start. Moreover, to the extent that the documents have been formally approved by governing boards, they present "official" consensus positions of influential stakeholders, at least in the short term. The planning documents specify in some detail the key problems to be addressed and the ultimate objectives the sites are trying to achieve; some also describe the major strategies to be implemented in pursuit of those objectives.

Yet applying a theory of change approach after substantial planning has already taken place has a negative side. First, co-constructing the theories may be perceived by stakeholders as duplicating the earlier planning process and adding unnecessary burdens on the local implementers. Alternatively, the theory of change exercise may be viewed as a critique of the existing planning process and documents, causing resentment or frustration among the stakeholders. Our experience suggests that existing planning documents vary widely in completeness and quality and that stakeholders may need to define expected performance milestones more precisely for the purposes of the evaluation. Stakeholders may not acknowledge the limitations of the previous planning activities and may resist the added accountability implied by the further specification of performance measures.

Although they are by no means guarantees of success, we have found several techniques to be reasonably effective at reducing stakeholder resistance. First, we believe it is best to avoid using jargon, including the term "theory of change," when discussing the approach with stakeholders. Specifically, "theory of change" seems to imply a level of abstraction that many stakeholders find objectionable. Rather, we use the term "pathway of change," which clarifies the importance of articulating elements along the pathway, specifying their sequence and timing, and tracking the actual evolution of the intervention. We also emphasize that stakeholders will help define the assessment measures. We explain to local stakeholders, for example, that "the evaluation will be based on the goals and activities that you feel are most important," and that evaluators will work with them closely to identify "a step-by-step description of what you hope to accomplish and how you hope to accomplish it."

WORKING WITH STAKEHOLDERS

Because of the importance of stakeholders as partners in specifying the evaluation framework, a fundamental question for any theory of change evaluation is how broadly to define the term "local stakeholders." Resource constraints play a major role in setting limits on how broadly to cast the net. Further, although a core group of individuals generally emerge as key stakeholders, members of that group may want to specify who the additional stakeholders will be and the sequence and venues in which the evaluation team will talk to them. In cases where there has been a change in the leadership or a struggle over conflicting visions for the initiative, the core group may express very strong opinions about individuals who should not be considered stakeholders. In a traditional evaluation framework, where the independence of the evaluator is emphasized, these issues are somewhat easier to resolve than in a theory of change approach, in which the evaluator must establish a close working relationship with the stakeholders. The process of identifying stakeholders will need to be approached thoughtfully, in order to avoid alienating key local actors. At the same time, the evaluator must take pains to ensure that the final specification of stakeholders is broad enough to include all significant stakeholder groups, including some individuals who may express a theory of change that differs appreciably from that articulated by the local "establishment."

In initiatives that have already gone through a formal planning process, the evaluator may not be able to reach all the key stakeholders who shaped the initial plan. Moreover, as the composition of key stakeholders changes over time, there may also be changes in the consensus concerning the intervention's purposes and activities; therefore, the current theory of change may be substantially different from the theory presented in the formal planning documents. This situation is especially common in initiatives that have experienced a turnover in leadership.

Some changes in the composition of stakeholders are probably inevitable over the course of most initiatives. Consequently, the evaluator must recognize the potentially tentative nature of the articulated theory, especially if it was surfaced during the early stages of the initiative.

Evaluators need to document shifts in leadership and initiative design and attempt to assess the reasons for these changes. In cases where new leadership has abandoned an initial "formal" plan that was developed prior to the introduction of the theory of change approach, it seems logical for the evaluator to base the progress measurement plan on the theory that is actually being implemented. However, to the extent that a competing theory of change has significant support among stakeholders, the measurement plan should ideally seek to assess progress relative to this alternate pathway as well.

DESCRIBING THE THEORY OF CHANGE

The process of surfacing the local theory of change can occur in a number of different ways, including individual interviews or focus groups with stakeholders. As the basic theory begins to emerge, the evaluator can prepare a written, schematic description of the theory to be shared with stakeholders for confirmation. The evaluator can then work with stakeholders to refine the theory by filling in gaps or addressing apparent inconsistencies. Alternatively, the evaluator can prepare a general description of what the local theory might look like, based on written materials from a pre-existing planning process or the evaluator's prior experience with similar efforts. The stakeholders can review this initial description and provide detailed feedback that the evaluator can use to correct and refine the description. The revised theory is then reviewed again by stakeholders for acceptance or further refinements.

A benefit of the first approach is that starting with a clean slate reduces the risk that evaluators will impose their own biases in theory formulation. This approach, however, can be a very time-consuming, iterative process for both evaluators and stakeholders. The second approach can be much more efficient, but the evaluator must be sensitive to the potential for unduly influencing how the stakeholders frame the local theory.

Because of limited on-site research resources and a desire to minimize the demands on stakeholders, the Jobs Initiative and EZ/EC program evaluations have taken the second, less staff-intensive approach to the articulation of local theories of change. To help offset stakeholder resistance to what might be perceived as duplication of the prior planning activities, we have been very explicit about using the existing planning documents to frame the initial articulation of the theory of change. If these documents are based on a sound planning process, they can supply a good portion of the information needed to complete a preliminary description of the underlying theory of change. In fact, even incomplete, illogical, or otherwise problematic documents should be prominently reflected, as a means of demonstrating that the evaluator sees value in the previous planning efforts and to start the process from a vantage point familiar to the stakeholders.

In cases where the planning documents are problematic, the next step—and potentially a very difficult one—is getting the stakeholders to acknowledge the limitations of the existing plans and accept the theory of change approach as a potentially effective way to move beyond those limitations. The evaluator can stress the value of the theory of change approach as a strategic planning tool to review, extend, or make more explicit the existing plans. The evaluator can also explain that the evaluation will provide the site with timely data for self-assessment and mid-course corrections. In this way, stakeholders can begin to appreciate the potential of the approach to add value to their endeavors, rather than viewing the exercise as redundant or threatening.

PICTURING THE THEORY OF CHANGE

The choice of how best to summarize the intervention pathway visually depends on the complexity of the underlying relationships in the theory and, more important, the compatibility of the representation with the learning styles of the stakeholders: some individuals find flowcharts easy to interpret, and others do not. In general, schematic representations have proven useful in summarizing the theory elements and their temporal relationships, especially when supplemented with narrative descriptions.

The underlying assumptions and hypotheses about the logical relationships among theory elements should be stated explicitly, since these relationships are at the heart of what the evaluation will be testing. (For example, do improved cognitive and interpersonal communication skills help new employees to adapt better in the workplace, and therefore lead to increased retention?) In a flowchart, these hypotheses are often reduced to arrows connecting the various elements. To avoid this problem, we number the arrows to correspond with narrative descriptions of the assumptions or hypotheses they represent.

ENCOURAGING A BROAD AND STRATEGIC APPROACH

Stakeholders have a tendency, perhaps reinforced by the use of existing planning documents, to focus on specific projects or activities when defining the initiative pathway rather than on the strategies underlying the action steps. This tendency produces several undesirable effects. First, if the initiative involves a large number of distinct projects or activities (an EZ site, for example, can have as many as 100 separate projects), the theory description frequently gets bogged down in excessive detail. Moreover, by concentrating on projects or activities at the expense of broader strategic questions, the key milestones along the pathway often end up being defined largely in terms of inputs, events, and outputs rather than outcomes.

In addition, many of the local interventions are taking place in communities where other initiatives are already addressing similar problems and may even share common strategies and objectives. For example, in several study sites, the EZ/EC program is seen as one element in a larger movement to address decline in the target neighborhoods. In Seattle, the Jobs Initiative strategies have been adopted by the city's welfare-to-work effort. In such cases, the intervention must be examined in the larger context if its contribution is to be properly understood. This larger context can easily be overlooked if stakeholders and researchers become too narrowly focused on specific program activities and projects when attempting to articulate the local theory of change.

It is very important that researchers urge local stakeholders to think strategically in articulating their theories. For example, an official in one community explained that the local program was implementing a one-stop shop as part of its initiative because it represented the current "state of the art" thinking about promoting economic development in a distressed area. This view suggests that the site had simply looked at what other communities were doing for the latest "in vogue" approaches, rather than examining the underlying problems facing the community. In such a case, even extensive probing by the evaluator may fail to uncover a detailed theory of change. In most instances, however, the intervention design will be found to be based on a complex if unstated set of assumptions regarding problems, approaches, action steps, outcomes, and the relationships among these elements. The challenge to the evaluator is how to tease out these implicit hypotheses through discussion with the stakeholders so that the assumptions can be examined and used to frame the overall theory or pathway of change.

SPECIFYING INTERIM ACTIVITIES AND OUTCOMES

We have found it helpful to begin the process of articulating interim steps by getting local stakeholders first to confirm the ultimate objectives they hope the intervention will achieve. This can be done either by asking the stakeholders to describe those ultimate objectives or by presenting the stakeholders with the evaluator's impressions regarding the ultimate objectives and having the stakeholders corroborate or revise them. In most cases, stakeholders can articulate the long-term goals of the local initiative, at least in qualitative terms, and specify the initial steps they feel the initiative should take. Once those beginning and end points have been made explicit, the evaluator and stakeholders can specify in reasonable detail the middle stages of the pathway. This middle period is by far the most challenging aspect of the articulation process, as it focuses on the period about which stakeholders' views are most vague.

In some cases, it has proven useful to ask the stakeholders to work backwards from the long-range objectives, specifying the interim outcomes they would expect to see and describing the types of activities (and their sequence) to achieve those outcomes. In other cases, stakeholders may find it easier to speculate on what activities should follow the initial action steps, and then to try to make explicit the interim outcomes they would expect to see along the process. Accordingly, it is crucial that the evaluator remain flexible regarding moving from activities forward to outcomes, or from outcomes backwards to activities, depending on which approach the stakeholders find most helpful.

It should be acknowledged that, even if the evaluator and stakeholders go through this exercise very systematically, few sites will be able to provide much detail regarding the expected pathway over the next year or two.
Thus, for a long-term intervention such as the Jobs Initiative (with a projected duration of at least eight years) or the EZ/EC program (where major
outcomes may not be discernible until the ten-year point), the evaluator
must recognize that it is unrealistic to believe that stakeholders can articulate the entire theoretical pathway. In all likelihood, the particulars of the
overall theory or pathway of change will need to be articulated in waves
over time.

Reconciling Practical and Theoretical Differences

As the theories or pathways of change are being articulated, the evaluator
may need to reconcile important differences in the theories themselves and
in practical aspects of the evaluation. In the two national evaluations, we
have made several strategic choices to establish consistency within sites,
among sites, between sites and funders, and over time.

ESTABLISHING A CONSISTENT LEVEL OF DETAIL

Defining the level of data to collect, both to describe the theories fully
and to track the actual experience of the interventions, is a difficult task
in a multisite evaluation. Resource constraints play a large role in determining how much and what kinds of data can be collected, as does the
tolerance of stakeholders for the data collection process. For example,
even if the evaluator manages to collect minutely detailed information in
the theory articulation process, stakeholders can be alienated from
future cooperation if they see the resulting theory description as too
complicated and difficult to understand. To minimize the data collection
burden and make the process meaningful for stakeholders, we believe
the evaluator should work with stakeholders to capture the essence of the
local theory of change through the initiative's key underlying assumptions and principles, implementation steps, and expected outcomes.

When applying the theory of change approach in a multisite context, the evaluator faces an added degree of difficulty, in that the complex process of theory articulation must follow a common framework to permit cross-site comparisons. Both to facilitate discussions with stakeholders and to promote comparability, we are using such a framework for initial exploration of the theories underlying the interventions. For each site, we are working with stakeholders to explicate the following elements:

• key client groups or customers that the initiative will serve

• principal problems faced by those client groups or customers, and the unique opportunities that may exist to address those problems

• major strategies that have been adopted to address the specified problems and take advantage of the identified opportunities

• key actions steps and resources necessary to implement the strategies

• intermediate, interim, and long-term outcomes by which progress and results can be measured

• hypotheses or assumptions regarding relationships among the various elements

ADDRESSING MULTIPLE THEORIES, ILLOGICAL ASSUMPTIONS,
AND "NO THEORY" SITUATIONS

As we suggested above, the process of working with stakeholders to articulate the theory of change may sometimes reveal that the stakeholders collectively reflect multiple theories regarding what the initiative is about and how it should proceed. When this situation arises, the evaluator must consider when to try to facilitate a consensus among stakeholders and when to track multiple theories.

When differences among theories seem relatively minor, we feel it is helpful to bring these to the attention of the stakeholders, who can then directly consider the differences and their implications. This process can clarify distinctions in how various stakeholders perceive facets of the initiative and, by sensitizing members of the stakeholder group to differing viewpoints, improve communications among them. When differences are made

explicit, the stakeholders can also collectively decide whether it is important to reach an "official" consensus position or, alternatively, to accept a
degree of variation in their views regarding certain aspects of the initiative.

When distinctions between the theories are significant, the clarification and resolution process can be much more difficult. In some instances,
the stakeholders may be resistant to making the conflicting theories explicit, fearing that the process will threaten fragile relationships. In other cases,
the stakeholders may be willing to examine explicitly the conflicting theories but unable to decide among them. As Weiss (1995) has argued:

> [A] community initiative may work through a variety of different
> routes. There is no need to settle on one theory. In fact, until bet-
> ter evidence accumulates, it would probably be counterproductive
> to limit inquiry to a single set of assumptions. Evaluation should
> probably seek to follow the unfolding of several different theories
> about how the program leads to desired ends. It should collect
> data on the intermediate steps along the several chains of assump-
> tions and abandon one route only when evidence indicates that
> effects along that chain have petered out.

In addition to deciding how to reconcile multiple theories among
stakeholders, our experience suggests that the evaluator must also be atten-
tive to distinctions between local stakeholders' theories and the theories
held by funders. Program guidelines and contractual conditions associated
with the initiative's funding may guide early stakeholder descriptions of the
intervention, especially those presented in proposals, planning documents,
and other reports to the grantor.[3] As a result, the evaluator may be tempted to superimpose the grantor's theory on the local initiative. Despite
superficial appearances of consistency between stakeholders' and grantor's
theories, however, the evaluator must be careful to test whether such apparent correspondence is real; once the elements of the initiative have been
specified more precisely, the evaluator may discern fundamental differences
between the local stakeholders' and the grantor's assumptions. Also, the
stakeholders' and grantor's theories are likely to diverge over time, as the

site deals with unique local circumstances in the process of implementation and refines its theory accordingly.

The evaluator may also be required to decide how to handle apparently illogical assumptions embedded in the stakeholders' theory. Although the theory of change approach as defined by Weiss (1995) and Connell (1997) is predicated on testing the stakeholders' vision of how the initiative is expected to work, the value of the approach depends on the theory being plausible, measurable, and testable. If stakeholders' hypotheses regarding the relationships between initiative elements—and particularly between planned actions and expected outcomes—are wholly without logical basis, it can be argued that the approach will have little merit as part of an impact evaluation since the outcome is largely preordained. On the other hand, there may be situations where, although the logical connections between elements are not immediately obvious, an evaluator's probing can help stakeholders articulate a stronger case for the potential of the planned strategy. Accordingly, in the theory articulation process, the evaluator should examine even highly speculative hypotheses carefully: these are the situations where the most unexpected, and therefore perhaps the most important, lessons may emerge.

A final possible dilemma for the evaluator is the initiative that appears to have no underlying theory to guide the intervention. This situation may arise when the intervention design consists of a "shopping list" of activities with no apparently unifying strategic elements. However, our experience suggests that, even in these situations, careful discussion with the stakeholders often reveals key assumptions that have framed the initiative design and form a rudimentary theory of change, albeit a poorly developed one. When the intervention consists of disparate activities conducted in different neighborhoods, for instance, the evaluator may uncover a local theory of change governing how the activities were selected rather than a programmatic focus of the activities themselves: that is, the community is pursuing an empowerment strategy that allows each neighborhood to select activities that its own local residents see as most needed.

Applying Consistent Standards over Time

Revisiting the theory of change over time raises two questions that the evaluator must answer. First, how far should the evaluator go in pressing stakeholders to articulate details of the pathway beyond the next year or two, since at some point such conjecture becomes highly speculative? Second, what limits, if any, does the evaluator need to impose on stakeholders over time for revising their theory or pathway to reflect the actual experience of the intervention? The latter question reflects what appears to be a basic tension regarding the use of a theory of change approach for formative evaluations versus its potential value in performing impact assessments (Patton, 1980).[4]

Some proponents of theory-based evaluation, such as Weiss (1995), have described the provisional nature of the underlying hypotheses that stakeholders put forward. Inherent in this view, it seems, is a recognition that stakeholders will refine their theory on the basis of the intervention experience. In fact, under this conceptualization, the explicit revisiting and revision of the theory appears be one of the basic methods through which stakeholders derive lessons regarding possible improvements and the evaluator learns about community change processes. Therefore, for evaluators who want to use the theory of change approach for formative or process evaluation purposes, the repeated reshaping of the theory or pathway over the course of the intervention may not necessarily represent a methodological concern.

On the other hand, evaluators who wish to use the approach to conduct impact assessments may find that revisions to the theory raise a very thorny methodological issue. Although the theory of change approach does not purport to solve the problem of the counterfactual, it can be argued that, in order to build a case for causation between intervention and outcomes, the key hypothesis must be identified as clearly as possible at the beginning of the initiative and tested to determine the effect of the intervention. According to this view, the ability to infer attribution will be directly dependent on the degree of consistency found between the original hypothesis and reality as the intervention unfolds. Accordingly, while the stakeholders may revise their theory over time, the evaluator is primarily interested in the original hypothesis.

In the Jobs Initiative and EZ/EC evaluations, because we are trying to use the theory-based approach to assess both process and impacts, we have attempted to reconcile these two schools of thought. Consequently, while recognizing the limits to which the stakeholders can meaningfully specify details far into the future, we have attempted to get them to articulate the basic elements of their overall theory of change as early as possible in the intervention. The basic elements that we are working to delineate at or near the beginning of the local initiatives include the major hypotheses underlying their pathways and the key interim outcomes expected at each stage of the intervention; together, these elements represent a very abridged description of the entire theoretical pathway. In addition, we have asked them to specify in as much detail as possible the key resources, activities, and events expected for the upcoming year.

On an annual basis, we intend to revisit the theory with the stakeholders at each site to obtain specific details regarding resources, activities, and events for the successive year. In addition, we will ask stakeholders annually to identify refinements that they wish to make in the basic pathway elements, both those that have already been encountered and those anticipated in the future. In this way, our theory articulation approach will provide us with the "original" theory or pathway, as well as detailed data on how and why the pathway has been refined over time.

Developing a Data Collection and Measurement Plan

As part of the national evaluations, we have been developing research designs for each site. We have approached the development of these designs as two related steps: articulating the basic theory of change for the site and developing a data collection and measurement plan. The purpose of this plan is to identify methods for collecting and analyzing data that can help the evaluator and stakeholders determine the progress achieved by an intervention relative to the ultimate outcomes desired for individuals, institutions, and the community and how actual experience compares with the theory held by stakeholders. Given this purpose, data to be collected in tracking an initiative might include the following categories:

- the nature of the initiative's events and activities

- the sequence and timing of those events and activities

- the resources applied to carry out the events and activities, and the roles played by various partners in the initiative

- descriptions of any significant external events that were not anticipated by theory

- indicators of interim and long-term outcomes

The first three items permit the evaluator to determine whether the initiative activities were implemented consistently with the stakeholders' initial assumptions. The fourth item identifies new external factors that may affect the continuing validity of the assumptions underlying the theory of change. The outcome indicators—the last category—may be most challenging to identify and collect, but they are also the most essential for determining whether the activities and strategies are having the desired results.

AGGREGATING ACTIVITIES AND OUTCOMES

While the general categories of data to be collected may be expected to be fairly consistent across theory of change assessments, the evaluator will need to grapple with determining the appropriate level of detail and units of measurement to be used with each application. In developing a local research design, the evaluator will need to work with stakeholders to determine the parameters for appropriate generalizations. For example, few evaluations will have the resources to track all aspects of an intervention with many distinct activities or projects. Under such circumstances, the evaluator and stakeholders should agree on suitable interim outcome measures for groupings of related projects or activities. The evaluator and stakeholders must therefore work together to articulate both a theory of change and a measurement plan. A principal challenge in this process is finding a framework for generalizing the measurement process without losing the unique characteristics of the local intervention or excluding factors that may ultimately determine success or failure.

When confronted with a vast array of planned activities, the evalua-tor and stakeholders may have considerable difficulty in establishing prior-ities. In the national evaluation of the EZ/EC program, it has sometimes been useful to encourage local research affiliates and stakeholders to "fol-low the money" as a way to sort through the complexity. Even when an ini-tiative encompasses a diverse assortment of strategies and activities, its fun-damental priorities are usually reflected in the allocation of funds and other resources among the components. By looking at how resources have been assigned, it is often possible to identify the major initiative strategies, group the activities that relate to those strategies, and define a limited set of meaningful outcome measures.

In using this example, however, we do not mean to imply that the allo-cation of resources is always an effective indicator of key strategies and out-comes in a complex initiative. It is offered merely as an illustration of one approach for aggregating activities. It would not work well for an initiative whose major strategies concerned forming partnerships, for example.

SPECIFYING PERFORMANCE MEASURES

Once the key outcomes have been identified, the evaluator must specify the anticipated outcomes in measurable, and preferably quantifiable, terms. It is not enough to say that crime will decrease in the zone; rather, the theory and research design must also specify by how much, over what period, and how those changes are to be measured. The assessment is more likely to be viewed as relevant and meaningful when stakeholders are involved in this process, but their participation is not without potential shortcomings.

Under the theory of change approach, there is tacit acknowledgment that stakeholders can and should revise their theory and actions over the course of an intervention in light of the implementation experience and changing conditions. Embodied in this principle is a recognition that most interventions will involve some missteps, and that the important thing is not that such mistakes occur but how the initiative learns from its mistakes. Accordingly, from the stakeholders' perspective, the theory of change approach is far less judgmental than many other evaluation frameworks. Even so, some stakeholders will still be tempted to define the evaluation framework to ensure that the initiative will not be seen as "failing." For example, some stakeholders may want to set performance goals at a low level or frame milestones in terms of inputs, activities, or outputs rather than outcomes.

In such situations, what is the evaluator expected to do? One technique for addressing unreasonably low performance measures is to walk the stakeholders through the articulated pathway, questioning explicitly whether the milestones being proposed can reasonably be expected to lead to the long-term objectives. Ideally, this exercise will encourage the stakeholders to establish more appropriate measures of progress. Ultimately, however, despite the inherently collaborative nature of the theory of change, the evaluator may need to maintain some independence to set performance measures, even if some stakeholders do not feel completely comfortable with them.

Related to the task of specifying performance measures is the question of determining the initiative's expected differential impact: that is, sorting out the effects from the outcomes. In addition to the initiative-related activities, other local efforts and factors will inevitably influence the indicators that the evaluation is monitoring. Consequently, the evaluator will need to separate the potential impact of the initiative from those other factors. Therefore, in working with the stakeholders to establish clear performance measures, the evaluator will need to get them to address the question of how much difference the intervention is expected to make. To do this, they will need to speculate on the magnitude of change, if any, they would expect to see in the absence of the intervention, and then estimate the differential amount of change they anticipate will result from the intervention.

ORGANIZING DATA COLLECTION

When the data to be collected have been sufficiently delineated, including the measures for performance indicators, the evaluator must determine appropriate methods for collecting those data. Data collection methods vary according to the nature of the initiative being studied. For our evaluations of the EZ/EC program and the Jobs Initiative, for example, we are using several methods:

• observation of key initiative meetings or events

• interviews with stakeholders and other local actors

• focus groups with residents, community leaders, and businesspeople

• review of existing written materials and other secondary data, including administrative records and data bases

• primary data collection through surveys of participants in jobs projects and business establishments

Because the resources of the national evaluations are limited, the cooperation of local initiative staff has been essential to the data collection effort. All sites are conducting some form of self-assessment independent of the national evaluation. By familiarizing local initiative staff with the theory of change approach, we have been able to demonstrate that the national evaluation data are potentially valuable to their ongoing monitoring and self-assessment activities. This recognition has led the sites to agree to coordinate some data collection activities, thus allowing the national evaluations and the local staffs to benefit from both sets of data.

REVISING THE DESIGN

A final point regarding development of the data collection and measurement plan relates to the revision of the research design. Under most traditional evaluation methods, the design is fixed at the beginning of the research effort and generally undergoes little revision over the course of the evaluation. With the theory of change approach, however, the stakeholders' theory can change over time. Therefore, to give the evaluation the capacity to track revisions in the theory and new outcome measures that result from such changes, the evaluator must be prepared to make appropriate adjustments in the research design.

In the national evaluations, as noted above, we have found that local stakeholders can describe their theories in detail only a year in advance. As a result, we are planning to meet with the stakeholders on an annual basis to fill in details of the sequence and timing of activities planned for the upcoming year and identify changes in the long-term pathway of change. Accordingly, we will need to update the research design annually to ensure that the research effort continues to be directed toward the most appropriate measures.

Challenges in Completing the Analysis

The two national evaluations are in relatively early stages, and therefore our focus to date has been primarily on theory articulation and data collection, rather than on analysis functions. Nonetheless, we can anticipate some challenges we are likely to encounter as we begin to conduct the analysis. The large number of sites will produce some challenges, while other challenges may be more generally characteristic of theory-based evaluation.

Identifying Common Patterns from Multiple Data Sources

Both evaluations are designed to glean cross-site lessons from site-specific theories and interventions. In each, we hope to identify common patterns and lessons that can be discerned from the local initiatives and applied to similar efforts in the future. At first glance, the idea of cross-site analysis may seem antithetical to the theory of change approach, which emphasizes an evaluation framework unique to each site. What we hope to accomplish is a balance of site-specific findings, based on the unique character of each site, with cross-site findings, based on appropriate generalizations. The crux of the analytic challenge, then, is to accomplish generalizations that are true to each site's experience. In fact, inherent in the theory of change approach is a mechanism that we hope can serve as an effective check to prevent distortion in the cross-site analysis. We believe that the evaluator's periodic interactions with stakeholders to articulate and update the local theory can also be used to confirm the evaluator's impressions regarding experiences that may be generalizable to other initiatives or communities.

Another analytic issue, and one that may be common to a variety of theory of change evaluations, is the task of bringing together information derived from multiple data collection methods to create a unified, coherent picture of the initiative's unfolding. In principle, the triangulation that multiple data methods and sources makes possible can result in a more complete and accurate analysis of the intervention. However, determining how much weight to assign to the respective data sources is often difficult. This may be a particularly thorny issue if the stakeholders' interpretation of events is not supported by other data sources.

Attributing Cause

Perhaps the most difficult analytic problem for the theory of change approach relates to the issue of causal attribution. For purposes of impact attribution, the ideal is that the local theory is surfaced completely at the beginning of the initiative and the actual intervention experience matches the theory in all appreciable respects. It seems reasonable to assume, however, that very few applications are likely to resemble this ideal. Instead, most initiatives will likely show some congruence between initial theory and actual experience, but also some divergence.

To the extent that the theory is articulated in waves, where stakeholders' experience can inform their theory specification for subsequent phases, the congruence between theory and reality is likely to improve. Practitioners of more traditional impact evaluation methods are likely to argue, however, that this "theory in waves" approach may be appropriate for framing hypotheses that relate solely to a future period but would invalidate any impact analysis if used to reframe the overall intervention pathway.

Other challenges in dealing with the issue of attribution include the need to examine alternative plausible explanations for the results that have been observed and, as previously noted, the need to attribute differential contributions when the initiative is occurring in an environment where other changes are also taking place. The sites in both evaluations, for example, are facing a major external factor in the form of welfare reform.

These attribution issues have traditionally been addressed most successfully through the use of experimental or quasi-experimental research designs that permit statistical tests to determine confidence levels. These methods cannot be applied readily to the interventions being studied, and thus we come full circle to our purpose in using a theory of change approach for these assessments. The theory of change approach cannot provide statistically generated confidence levels, but it can provide compelling, detailed descriptions of the unfolding of the interventions and an argument regarding the apparently logical connections among theories, activities, and outcomes. The approach can provide insights about which kinds of interventions appear to work under particular conditions, which do not, and—unlike many experimental designs—the likely reasons why.

Such descriptive arguments may not be convincing to researchers who see experimental or quasi-experimental methods as the only reliable approaches to impact analysis, but we believe they will be welcomed by staff of community organizations and other practitioners who are looking for guidance on potentially effective strategies. To the extent that our theory of change research designs use traditional methods, such as pre and post surveys, those elements may enhance the credibility of the observations offered. At the very least, the theory of change approach will generate useful topics of inquiry, which can perhaps be tested later in a more controlled experimental framework.

Notes

1   Not all Jobs Initiative activities are necessarily expected to result directly in benefits for job seekers. In fact, the jobs projects are largely seen as "vehicles for discovering the nature of reforms needed in existing public and private systems" (Annie E. Casey Foundation, 1995).

2   Andrea Anderson also served on the Abt evaluation team for both studies through January 1998, when she left Abt to accept a position at Aspen Institute in New York City.

3   In multisite initiatives (like the EZ/EC program and the Jobs Initiative) whose sites are selected through a competitive process, the key principles underlying the grantor's theory of change will normally be reflected in the application guidelines. Yet even a local foundation responding to an unsolicited proposal from a community group will generally have its own theory about how the process of

change is expected to occur, which in turn will influence the unfolding of the initiative. Accordingly, it is essential for the evaluator be aware of the grantor's theory of change.

4 Patton, citing Sanders and Cunningham (1974), explains that formative evaluations are "conducted for the purpose of improving programs in contrast to those evaluations which are done for the purpose of making basic decisions about whether or not the program is effective, and whether or not the program should be continued or terminated."

References

Annie E. Casey Foundation. 1995. *Jobs Initiative: National Investor's Outcome Outline.*

Connell, James. 1997. "From Collaboration to Commitment: Rights and Responsibilities of Partners in Community-Change Initiatives." Paper presented at the Annie E. Casey Foundation Conference on Evaluation Community Change Research and Evaluation.

Hollister, Robinson G., and Jennifer Hill. 1995. "Problems in the Evaluation of Community-Wide Initiatives." In *New Approaches to Evaluating Community Initiatives: Concepts, Methods, and Contexts,* ed. James Connell et al. Washington, DC: Aspen Institute.

Giloth, Robert. 1996. "Mapping Social Interventions: Theory of Change and the Jobs Initiative." Draft report.

Patton, Michael Quinn. 1980. *Qualitative Evaluation Methods.* Beverly Hills, CA: Sage Publications.

Sanders, J., and D. Cunningham. 1974. *Techniques and Procedures for Formative Evaluation.* Research Evaluation Development Paper Series No. 2. Portland, OR: Northwest Regional Educational Laboratory.

Weiss, Carol Hirschon. 1995. "Nothing as Practical as Good Theory: Exploring Theory-based Evaluation for Comprehensive Community Initiatives for Children and Families." In *New Approaches to Evaluating Community Initiatives: Concepts, Methods, and Contexts,* ed. James Connell et al. Washington, DC: Aspen Institute.

Challenges of Measurement in Community Change Initiatives

Michelle Alberti Gambone

Introduction

Community change initiatives (CCIs), as is clear to everyone associated with them, are very complex endeavors. Whatever the particular focus of individual initiatives, all CCIs have in common the ambitious goal of catalyzing and sustaining significant change in fundamental aspects of social, economic, and political structures and their functioning in communities. They all begin with the premise, in some form, that activities can be undertaken that will alter basic patterns of social interaction, values, customs, and institutions in ways that will significantly improve the quality of life of a community's residents.

This characteristic distinguishes CCIs from more traditional social or economic interventions, which typically attempt to meet social policy goals by using a relatively defined and discrete mechanism (such as a new service or program) to produce desired changes in the lives of targeted individuals. CCIs attempt to change the everyday environment in communities in ways that will result in better outcomes for everyone living within a designated geographic area. This crucial difference in strategy poses a new and complex set of challenges for those involved in implementing CCIs, and at the same time multiplies and complicates the issues that need to be addressed by those evaluating the initiatives.

This chapter builds on a meeting attended by evaluators and researchers convened by the Aspen Institute Roundtable on Comprehensive Community Initiatives for Children and Families focusing on the specific measurement-related challenges facing those who attempt to assess the progress and impact of these initiatives. Over the course of the meeting, the participants articulated the range of theoretical and methodological evaluation challenges that are surfaced by CCIs, raising questions that ran the gamut from the philosophical ("How do we attribute causality?") to the practical ("What instruments exist for the range of variables to be measured?"). At the same time, it was also apparent that the state of the field is such that evaluation strategies, generally, and measurement strategies, specifically, are unfolding as these community efforts proceed.

The purpose of this chapter is to identify and briefly discuss some of the most pressing issues that stem from the particular problem of measuring change in CCIs and, in so doing, to improve understanding of one of the key challenges in the overall process of researching community endeavors.

The Role of Theory
in Measurement

The most basic measurement-related questions facing evaluators of CCIs are the same as those facing any evaluator: What should be measured, how, and when? As other chapters in this volume make clear, such seemingly straightforward technical issues are complicated in CCIs both because of the comprehensive and evolving design of the interventions and because of the multiple purposes of evaluation, ranging from formative feedback to assessment of impact to social learning. Once again, theory helps orient the researcher, in this case on measurement issues.

First, no research design with finite time, money, and human resources can test all the possible relationships among activities, outcomes, and contexts in a community. As posited by Weiss (1995), a theory of change requires, first and foremost, that all stakeholders be clear about an initiative's intended goals, which in turn should provide general guidance about what to measure at baseline and over the long term. Also, a theory of change demands some level of clarity about the pathways intended for getting to the longer-term goals. Those pathways are generally made up of a series of activity-outcome sequences which are, in principle, measurable. Thus, a theory of change should help guide decisions about what aspects of an initiative should be measured and in what order the measurement should take place.

Second, given the experimental nature of CCIs, the "social learning" dimension of evaluation is critical and affects decisions about how to structure and carry out measurement. The progress of "normal science" is rooted in the principle that knowledge development occurs *only* when high-quality, reliable measurement strategies are combined with well-specified theories so that hypotheses can be tested. As the resulting information is used to confirm or discard hypotheses, new "knowledge" is gained, and disciplines make progress in their ability to explain and predict phenomena. Constructing research designs that yield valid and reliable information, therefore, is more than a matter of methodological mechanics. From this perspective, data collected without a theory has the status of "information" and is limited to describing phenomena, while data collection guided by theory produces what can be called "knowledge."

Thus, specifying the underlying theory of change of an initiative not only provides practical guidance about what to measure, how, and when, but is necessary if the field of community change is to progress. Having said this, it is also true that the field is, in many respects, so young that theory specification is as much an art as a science. This fact is at the center of the difficulty of designing the high-quality research that can best serve all CCI constituencies. The theories underlying these initiatives are often developed and elaborated while the initiatives are underway, and research teams are often integral participants, and sometimes even catalysts, in the process of specifying those theories.

Measuring Effects, Progress, and Context in CCIs

Evaluations of CCIs are intended to (1) assess the effectiveness of the initiatives in achieving the outcomes as specified; (2) provide information for monitoring and reporting on the progress made by initiatives in implementing the activities that are expected to catalyze and sustain change in a community; and (3) develop a knowledge base about the circumstances that facilitate or hamper positive or negative outcomes and the linkages specified in the initiative's theory of change.

In order to meet the first purpose, the research design needs to address the question of whether the CCI activities ultimately have the intended *effects* that are sought, over the long term as well as during interim periods. To meet the second purpose, a research design needs to address the question of whether *progress* is being made in catalyzing and sustaining change in a community, and if so, how. This entails designing a strategy for measuring what activities a CCI generates in a community, how it attempts to do so, and the outcomes of those activities. The knowledge development goal requires both of the above, as well as an examination of the *context* in

Figure. A Measurement Model for CCI Evaluations

Measuring Context	Measuring Progress	Measuring Effects
Historical conditions and ongoing dynamics	Activities and interim outcomes	Long-term outcomes
Question: Under what conditions is the initiative operating? (For example, history, geography, economics, politics, population, or relationships)	*Question: How are activities catalyzed and implemented?* (For example, involvement of individuals or groups, decision making, roles, facilitators, or obstacles)	*Question: What long-term outcomes result from CCI activities?* (For example, change at the level of individuals, family, organizations, institutions, or community)
	Question: What CCI activities are undertaken? (For example, mobilizing people or organizations, new or restructured activities, or new or restructured resources)	
	Question: What early and intermediate outcomes result? (For example, meeting predetermined thresholds for participation, civic activities, or events)	

which a CCI is undertaken. This requires that evaluators develop strategies for measuring the conditions under which change is attempted and the influence of those conditions on the implementation and effects of the CCI. The accompanying figure provides a graphic representation of a general measurement model that can serve these multiple purposes.

This section treats the three issues of measuring effects, progress, and context individually, describing the key dilemmas associated with each. The intention is not to resolve these dilemmas, since specific design decisions need to be made within the context of each initiative, but to elaborate on the issues that must be considered to produce a multi-purpose research design. The discussion notes how a theory of change can be one mechanism to guide evaluators through choices about the focus and timing of measurement.

Measuring the Long-Term Effects of CCIs

Specifying the expected long-term outcomes of a CCI effort in terms of measurable variables is in many ways the most traditional and straightforward aspect of developing a CCI evaluation plan. Whether the long-term goals are set by the designers of an initiative, local implementers, or community residents, they are usually specified earlier, with more clarity and consensus, and in more concrete terms than other elements of the theory. Nevertheless, the scope of a typical CCI—in both number and nature of effects sought—constitutes a major challenge for researchers. As with discrete social programs, the ultimate success or failure of these efforts will be judged on the basis of long-term, measurable outcomes. But developing a fair and interpretable strategy for assessing change in CCIs brings to the forefront several issues that differ from those of more traditional program evaluation.

WHAT AND WHEN TO MEASURE

A hallmark of CCIs is their intention to improve the overall quality of life in communities by effecting change across multiple "strands," such as housing quality and affordability, economic opportunities, civic pride and social cohesion, service quality, family health, and youth development. The first challenge for a CCI evaluation is simply to define and assemble a catalog of reliable measures for the long-term outcomes that stakeholders have defined as important.

A complicating issue in defining and measuring long-term outcomes is the expectation that CCIs will spark "synergy" across these multiple strands. Thus, change in one strand can have spillover effects or may even be a necessary condition for change in another. Therefore, relationships among long-term outcome areas need to be specified in advance as part of the theory of change in order to define precisely *what* should be measured, *when* it is most sensible to assess effects in a particular area, and a *framework* for interpreting findings. For example, an initiative may target housing quality and affordability, stability of neighborhood residence, and neighborhood cohesion as long-term outcomes for improvement. At the same time, the underlying theory of change may be that improved housing quality and affordability are expected to change migration rates and patterns within the target neighborhood, which in turn will increase the level of neighborhood cohesion. Therefore, under a highly specified and sequenced theory of change, the housing outcomes should be assessed first, with migration and cohesion outcomes evaluated only after the housing effects are evident.

A further issue in defining the measurement of long-term outcomes is the common CCI tactic of implementing activities in stages throughout a geographic area. An accurate assessment should recognize that some activities are focused initially on an area smaller than the "target community" as a whole. Continuing the previous example, a CCI might select a specific area of ten square blocks to redevelop first, and then move on to another area. This would have clear implications for how the numerator and denominator should be specified for assessing changes in housing stock, migration rates, and social cohesion at any particular point in time. The denominator for assessing changes in housing stock would be the number of dwellings in the smaller area, not the full target community. At baseline and at the earliest follow-up point, the numerator would consist of the number of substandard (or high priced) dwellings in the ten-block area. The need to calculate such effects at particular points in time has clear implications for how statistical, survey, and other types of data are collected from the start.

The complexity of CCIs also raises issues about what is considered significant change. Although the challenge of establishing causality is examined elsewhere in this volume, it bears noting here that assessing and interpreting the effectiveness of CCIs can be problematic because the thresholds that would define meaningful improvement are unknown or unspecified. There may be "tipping points" that must be reached before significant change can be expected in certain areas. Without a body of empirically based, practical knowledge about, for example, the degree of improvement in housing stock needed before change in migration rates becomes evident, it will be difficult to interpret the effectiveness of CCIs.

How to Measure

The sheer number and variety of long-term effects sought by CCIs present significant measurement challenges. Assembling the needed measurement "tools" and collecting the breadth of data can be an overwhelming task, especially in communities that have not been the subject of previous community-level research. The methodological issues surrounding the construction of small area data sets from administrative records, conducting neighborhood-level surveys, creating organizational capacity for record keeping, and other techniques for assessing neighborhood change are, fortunately, receiving increasing attention from researchers and evaluators (Sommer et al., 1996; Urban Institute, 1996). In addition, there is an effort underway to catalogue measures that are currently being applied to or developed and tested in CCIs and other community-based programs.[1] As progress is made in both these areas, the design and implementation of CCI evaluations will become increasingly efficient.

A significant challenge arises from the fact that most evaluations measure effects, even community effects, at the individual level. Aggregation of individual-level information to describe communities is more easily accomplished in some domains than in others. For example, Coulton, Korbin, and

Su (1996) found that aggregating perceptions of individual residents yielded promising levels of reliability in some key areas of interest to CCIs, such as facility availability, usage, and quality and block club activity. Other community-level outcomes, such as neighborhood social interactions, economic opportunity structures, and institutional coordination, require different measurement strategies that take significant time and resources to develop.

Finally, because most CCI neighborhoods have not been the subject of previous research, many measures that are used have been adapted from other research settings. One particular problem is that the populations of CCI neighborhoods are largely minority, and few existing measures have been developed with particular attention to their validity when applied to individuals of minority racial, ethnic, and cultural backgrounds. While there have been some efforts to test the reliability of common measures for minority groups (Jones, 1996), it is difficult to know in advance the validity of such measures in CCI settings.

Tracking Progress and Early Results

WHAT AND WHEN TO MEASURE

As with measuring the long-term effects of a CCI, measuring more immediate progress raises a set of issues and challenges that are somewhat more difficult than those encountered in traditional evaluation research. As long-term investments, CCIs are not expected to achieve their ultimate goals quickly, sometimes charting a course toward change over five, ten, or more years. Yet even early implementation steps have observable effects. The need for initiatives themselves to have access to information for formative feedback and the need for research in this field to contribute to knowledge development are both best served by specifying and measuring not only long-term outcomes, but also the early and interim effects that lead to them. This makes it critical that evaluation designs include mechanisms for assessing the progress these initiatives are making years before long-term effectiveness can be assessed.

On one hand, having a theory of change helps to move the initiative and its evaluators beyond what are traditionally called implementation data—that is, descriptive information about the intervention and how is it implemented—by tying such information directly to outcomes of interest. On the other hand, this careful specification and assessment of early, interim, and long-term outcomes, the linkages among them, and the strategies to be used closes off some traditional evaluation shortcuts to CCI evaluators. In more circumscribed program evaluations, aspects of the research design may be minimized or even excluded to conserve resources without causing significant loss to the utility of the study: this might be possible, for example, if the program model is predetermined and unchanging, if options for *how* it is to be implemented are relatively constrained, or if ultimate outcomes—the effects on individual participants—are available to be assessed in a relatively short time frame.

By contrast, measuring progress in CCIs requires that linkages be specified among the strategies and approaches a CCI undertakes, the activities it implements, and the early, interim, and longer-term outcomes it is expected to achieve, and that all these linkages be measured with equal intensity. No short-cuts are immediately apparent. For example, because CCIs are meant to be community-driven efforts to produce change, the questions surrounding *how* governing entities are formed and decisions are made need to be monitored throughout the life of the initiative. In turn, the degree and quality of implementation of activities should be specified and measured, and their early outcomes must be monitored. Thus, understanding and assessing progress toward ultimate effects require that three components—how a CCI is undertaken, what activities it implements, and what and when early and intermediate outcomes are achieved—be measured. A predictable feature of CCI evaluation is that this stage of the research design process is sure to be complex.

Perhaps the greatest obstacle to measuring activities and their intermediate outcomes is the dearth of well-developed theory or systematic data about the crucial elements for effective community mobilization, planning, and governance and how those aspects of a community initiative, in turn, lead to effective strategies for producing short-term and long-term outcomes. As a result, researchers must devote a great deal of effort to working with CCI operators to specify what activities will be undertaken in a community, why they have been chosen, and what indicators will mark interim progress or success. As with long-term outcomes, determining the threshold of activity required to meet goals is problematic, given the absence of existing systematic research to inform this process. Nevertheless, this time-consuming activity is a necessary step if benchmarks included in the research design are to carry weight with all the consumers of the evaluation, from program managers to funders to community residents. Progress is being made in the CCI context in conducting this type of research, and new knowledge will help the design and implementation of future evaluations to become more efficient.

Determining when progress should be measured can also be difficult. Depending on the outcome being studied, some data must be collected on a continuous basis, while others can be collected periodically. As new strategies are chosen and new activities planned over the life of the initiative, documenting baseline conditions in the target neighborhood can be an ongoing requirement of the research design.

How to Measure

To operationalize a plan for measuring progress in early and intermediate outcomes, CCI evaluators must first contend with the volume and variety of outcomes requiring documentation. Because there are so few existing, reliable measures of early and intermediate activities and outcomes, CCI researchers are usually left with the task of developing those measures as an initiative proceeds. Further, much of the data must be collected on a continuous basis, which means that CCI participants, on-site researchers, or both may be needed as partners in carrying out the research design.

For example, to collect information on meeting attendance, organizational participation rates, civic activities, and informal neighborhood events, evaluators might depend on strategies that can be incorporated into the CCI implementation or observations made as events occur. Working with community members to develop and incorporate data collection activities and recruiting and managing local data collectors are challenges that require ongoing attention and substantial resources.

Measuring Context

Measuring the context—social, economic, political, cultural, institutional, and so on—in which a CCI takes place raises issues that differ in degree but not kind from those previously discussed. Here again, theory and research to support the work are scarce, and therefore the researcher needs to apply the same degree of creativity in measurement design and breadth of measurement strategies that were required in measuring effects and progress. Once again, if the evaluation findings are to be interpreted and fully understood, linkages must be specified, in this case, among contextual factors, implementation strategies and activities, and their early, intermediate, and long-term outcomes.

WHAT AND WHEN TO MEASURE

Identifying what components of context are important to a CCI and deciding how and when to measure them is complicated, but necessary, because of the dynamic nature of communities and the interventions. Each community has a unique history, and ongoing dynamics are influenced by internal and external factors. These dynamics, in turn, affect the shape and progress of a CCI as it seeks to achieve its desired outcomes. Thus, even as a CCI is attempting to influence factors within its purview, the initiative is subject to the influence of factors over which it has little or no control. Understanding and comparing the circumstances under which CCIs can be effective requires that any theory of change take into account at least three types of contextual factors to be identified and measured as part of a research design: historical conditions, ongoing dynamics, and critical events.

In setting a CCI underway, a community starts from a particular point in its history, which forms the context into which change is introduced. The physical geography, local economy, political history, population, and other factors in both the target community and its broader surroundings (such as the city) need to be documented historically and at the time the initiative begins. It is also important to understand the community's trajectory: for example, although two communities may begin with similar poverty rates, one may be in the midst of a ten-year economic decline while the other has experienced economic growth over the last three years. Understanding how, when, and why a CCI works necessitates linking these conditions to the rate of progress seen in establishing activities and producing interim and long-term outcomes.

The ongoing dynamics of a CCI community are also important to measure and link with the other parts of the research model. These conditions include surrounding social, political, and economic factors—such as population dynamics, racial relations, or political activism—that are not directly targeted for change but can influence the extent to which the CCI activities are implemented and the strength of their results. For example, an initiative may not be targeting migration into and out of the community, but a growing foreign immigrant population or an out-migration of families with school-age children can have a significant impact on the CCI.

Clearly, these factors need to measured and linked with other research findings about progress and effectiveness. Even so, it is important to ensure that dynamics directly targeted by the CCI are treated as outcomes, and that only those not directly targeted are treated as contextual factors. These factors should be measured on a continuous basis over the course of a CCI.

A third group of contextual factors to be measured can be thought of as critical events; that is, discrete, powerful events that can directly or indirectly affect the progress of a CCI by changing the ongoing dynamics in a community. These factors include a broad range of possible events, such as the award of significant new grants (for example, through designation as an Empowerment Zone), natural disasters (such as floods or earthquakes), political change (such as an election, new legislation, or a school closing), or social relations (such as civil unrest or police conflict). It is important to document the occurrence of such events and trace those effects that can have an impact on CCI implementation and outcomes.

How to Measure

Measuring community context requires the full range of techniques at researchers' disposal. Social factors such as population, economic history, and political participation require the creative use of statistical data for the target area. Other contextual factors, such as outbreaks of civil unrest, shifts in political climate or racial relations, and existing attitudes toward key organizations or institutions, require careful qualitative data collection and analysis. These might be documented by site-based researchers or through key informants interviewed on a regular basis by a research team. In either case, it is important to ensure that sufficient financial and human resources are dedicated to this type of data collection or the understanding of a CCI's progress and effectiveness will be incomplete. Indeed, as noted by O'Connor (1995), understanding the contextual conditions under which CCIs are relatively more or less effective is one of the most important research and policy questions to answer.

Discussion and Recommendations

Conducting high-quality research on CCIs is critical if knowledge development is to occur, but doing it well is difficult and expensive. Whether one is inclined to devote resources to theory building and measurement development or to developing other techniques (such as random assignment within a community context or constructed comparison groups for attributing causality), intensive human and dollar investments are required. The complex nature of these initiatives demands that significant resources be devoted to the research design effort, both before and during implementation of the initiative. A few strategies and practices have the potential for moving the field forward and ultimately making evaluation research on CCIs more efficient.

Develop new measures. The demands of CCI evaluation research are extensive and diverse, largely by virtue of the sheer volume and newness of the needed measures. Although some measure development can and should be done within the context of specific initiatives, efforts specifically aimed at constructing and validating new tools or developing models of threshold points could yield significant benefits. Better tools and models could reduce CCIs' reliance on expensive community surveys, which to date have been used to collect much of the data during all phases of measurement.

Increase the availability of existing measures. CCI initiatives and evaluators should attempt to publish their evaluation designs and measures as early as possible. Although this is not standard practice in program evaluations (or is done only in conjunction with a final report), the CCI field needs to take a more active approach to sharing information if the field is to grow in the next five years, while initiatives are on their way toward measuring long-term outcomes and producing final reports.

Support the specification of underlying theories. Given that theory specification is a critical element in evaluation, funders could help by building in incentives for CCI stakeholders to specify their theories of change early and reassess those theories during the course of an initiative. Related incentives could encourage evaluators to incorporate a theory of change approach into their evaluation designs.

Undertake basic research on community change. One of the reasons that evaluators and others who are undertaking research on CCIs must spend so much time developing new methods and measures is because the "science" of community research is underdeveloped. The process of "natural" community change is poorly understood, and little investment has been made in the tools for undertaking such research. A longitudinal panel study of communities would provide a rich source of basic information about the processes and contextual factors associated with natural and planned change. It would also provide the context for development of new research methods.

Encourage the development of small area data in existing data collection efforts. Standard censuses and surveys still focus on individuals, giving little attention to the neighborhoods and community contexts in which they reside. The federal government is considering adding questions about small areas in the census to be conducted in the year 2000. Such information would greatly enhance both design and implementation of community-based initiatives.

Note

1 The Roundtable is developing an annotated catalogue of outcome measures, drawn from current and past evaluations of CCIs, other complex initiatives, and basic research on communities.

References

Coulton, Claudia, Jill Korbin, and Marilyn Su. 1996. "Measuring Neighborhood Context for Young Children in an Urban Area." *American Journal of Community Psychology* 24:5-32.

Jones, Reginald, ed. 1996. *Handbook of Tests and Measurements for Black Populations.* Hampton, VA: Cobb and Henry.

O'Connor, Alice. 1995. "Evaluating Comprehensive Community Initiatives: A View from History." In *New Approaches to Evaluating Community Initiatives Concepts, Methods, and Contexts,* ed. James Connell et al. Washington, DC: Aspen Institute.

Sommer, T. Erich, et al. 1996. *The Creation of a Community Information Infrastructure.* Chicago: Chapin Hall Center for Children.

Urban Institute. 1996. *Democratizing Information: The First Year Report of the National Neighborhood Indicators Project.* Washington, DC.

Weiss, Carol Hirschon. 1995. "Nothing as Practical as Good Theory: Exploring Theory-based Evaluation for Comprehensive Community Initiatives for Children and Families." In *New Approaches to Evaluating Community Initiatives: Concepts, Methods, and Contexts,* ed. James Connell et al. Washington, DC: Aspen Institute.

Measuring Comprehensive Community Initiative Outcomes Using Data Available for Small Areas

Claudia Coulton and Robinson Hollister

Introduction

Comprehensive community initiatives (CCIs), typically carried out within relatively small, geographically bounded communities, need information about those communities and their residents in order to plan and evaluate their work. Although extensive demographic, economic, and social indicators are available for the nation and other larger geographic units, neighborhood-level information is seldom produced routinely. Furthermore, because CCIs are comprehensive, they need information about a broad range of outcomes, tracked over multiple points in time. For all these reasons, it is desirable that CCIs draw upon existing data sources to derive information about small geographic areas.

Our purpose is to describe the many and varied kinds of data sources that have the potential to produce small area information for CCIs. The focus is on obtaining and using administrative, survey, and census data that are already being collected for other purposes and converting them into information for CCIs. We also address the important cautions and limitations of small area analysis and the application of data collected for other purposes to the measurement of community change. We attempt to cast a wide net by considering many domains that are important to CCIs, including housing, economic development, safety and security, education, service reform, and community building.

Advantages and Disadvantages of Available Data

The advantages of using available data to measure change are several. First, a retrospective baseline can be created because the measures use data that have already been collected. Second, communities can be compared with one another, since many data sources cover the entire city, district, or county within which the CCI target community is located. Third, geographic information system (GIS) technology makes it practical to manipulate data and build up to the desired units of geography through aggregation. Fourth, the data can be subjected not only to traditional time-trend and comparative analyses but also to spatial and ecological analyses.

There are, of course, disadvantages as well. Data collected for purposes other than the particular evaluation or planning needs of CCIs may only approximate the concepts of interest. Also, because the available data sources vary considerably in their accuracy, care must be taken to adjust for or avoid data elements that are vulnerable to well-known errors. Finally, most available data do not capture the important social processes that go on among community residents and within and between community organizations. These important outcomes of CCIs require special measures and original data collection activities.

Establishing Geographic Boundaries

Although "community," as used in the term "comprehensive community initiative," is a social unit, a CCI must establish clearly demarcated geographic boundaries to acquire and use available data. Geographically bounded communities are often thought of as neighborhoods (Chaskin, 1995). Neighborhood definition is not always an easy task, however, especially when CCI participants disagree about boundaries or when the target area encompasses several neighborhoods.

Researchers have traditionally used census geography for the purpose of data aggregation, with census tracts and block groups serving as proxies for neighborhoods. (A census tract is a geographic area containing between 2,500 and 8,000 residents. A block group is a number of contiguous blocks within a census tract designed to contain about 250-550 housing units. Both designations are established by the U.S. Bureau of the Census.) Research on resident perceptions has shown that residents seldom agree on neighborhood boundaries, but that the average size of their perceived neighborhood is somewhat larger than their block group but smaller than their census tract (Coulton, Korbin, Chan, Su, and Wang, 1997). For convenience and comparability, CCIs often link boundary definitions to census geography, although GIS technology can support resident-defined boundaries as well.

The use of available data sources may present some limitations on geographic definitions. For example, although it is always desirable to obtain data at the smallest geographic unit available, for confidentiality purposes some data sources contain only census codes or administrative districts rather than individual addresses. This can reduce the flexibility of the CCI to set and change boundaries and still make relevant calculations.

If measures built upon available data are to be sensitive indicators of change, it is also important that the geographic boundaries used for data aggregation are commensurate with the real targets of the CCI at a particular point in time. If, for example, the CCI is working on different outcomes or is at different stages in particular sections of the neighborhood, the data should be aggregated so as to capture those differences.

Administrative Data

There is a long tradition of using data collected for administrative purposes to produce social and economic indicators (Rossi, 1972; Annie E. Casey Foundation, 1997). The emphasis on outcomes and accountability in many social programs has raised additional interest in such information (Schorr, 1994). Most administrative agencies now have computerized record systems, and the advent of GIS technology makes it feasible to calculate indicators for smaller areas from those large data bases.

Numerous sources and types of data from administrative agencies can be used to produce measures useful for CCIs. Most data bases are maintained by local agencies, but a few state and federal data bases can be used for small area measures. Because of the local nature of much of the data, the descriptions in this chapter may not match exactly what is available in a particular locale. Although the list of data sources described here is long, it is not exhaustive. As shown in the table, the sources are grouped into six cate-

Table. Administrative Data Sources for Small Area Measures

HOUSING

Data Source	Indicator Examples	Availability
HMDA Information: Records of loan applications and approvals	• Conventional loans (%) • Loans denied (%) • Financial institutions making loans	Public records, available annually from the Federal Reserve Bank's Financial Institutions Council
Local Property Tax Data: Real property records	• Tax delinquent properties (%) • Median housing assessed values • Residential parcels (%)	Public records, maintained for taxing purposes, available from local tax assessor; format and ease of use vary by jurisdiction
Building and Demolition Permits: Records of permits issued	• Value of construction (%) • Buildings demolished	Public records, available from city building department; may not be computerized
Housing Code Enforcement Reports: Records of violations	• Properties with violations (%)	Public records, available from city building inspection department; may not be computerized
HUD Information: Records of public and subsidized housing units	• Total public housing units • Persons per unit in public housing	Available annually from federal Department of Housing and Urban Development in computerized format; geo-coding may be missing

ECONOMY

Data Source	Indicator Examples	Availability
ES202 Information: Employer industry classification, total employment, and payroll	• Change in total employment (%) • Employment in manufacturing (%)	Confidential employer reports filed with the state employment services agency; in many states, reports can be obtained for research purposes with proper safeguards
UI (Unemployment Insurance) Wage Record: Employee earnings and weeks worked	• Former welfare recipients in jobs (%) • Average earnings of training participants	Confidential individual records filed by employers with the state employment services agency; records do not include addresses, so must be merged with another data source for small area analysis; confidentiality protections as for ES202
UI Claimant File: Information on applicants for benefits	• Unemployment insurance claims filed • Average weeks of benefits paid	Confidential records of individual claims filed with the state employment services agency

Data Source	Indicator Examples	Availability
Business Directories: Selected listings of businesses, published by Cole's, Harris, Dun and Bradstreet, and others	• Total establishments, by industry • Change in establishments (%)	Commercially available from vendors
CDBG Information: Records of expenditures	• Dollars expended annually • Expenditures by category (%)	Available from local Community Development Block Grant administrator; difficult to allocate to small areas because many expenditures are not neighborhood specific
Municipal Income Tax Records: Employer tax withholding records	• Total dollars generated by employers • Increase in tax dollars	Highly confidential data; information aggregated to the neighborhood level may be available by request
Training Program Records: Records of trainees in public programs	• Persons in training • Trainees placed in employment (%)	Confidential records of trainees, maintained by state or local human service department (JOBS program) or state employment services agency (JTPA program)

SAFETY AND SECURITY

Data Source	Indicator Examples	Availability
Municipal Police Records: Records of crime reports, victims, suspects and arrests	• Crime rates • Crimes committed by residents (%)	Maintained by municipal police departments; availability varies by jurisdiction; most departments follow Uniform Crime Reporting procedures
911 System Data: Calls to local emergency dispatch system	• Calls reporting domestic violence • Change in calls (%)	Maintained by regional agency; availability varies by jurisdiction
Juvenile Court Filings: Records of charges filed	• Juvenile crime rate • Juvenile filings for violent offenses (%)	Confidential records, maintained by county court; availability and format vary by jurisdiction
Coroner's Reports: Records of deaths	• Homicides involving firearms (%) • Suicides involving drugs	Maintained by local coroner; availability varies by jurisdiction; may not be computerized
Child Maltreatment Reports: Records of reports to child protection authorities	• Children with maltreatment reports (%) • Reports that involve neglect (%)	Confidential records, maintained by local or state child protection agencies; availability limited and requires strict confidentiality protections
Liquor Licenses: Permits to sell alcoholic beverages	• Number and type of outlets	Public records, maintained by state bureau of liquor control

Table. Administrative Data Sources for Small Area Measures (continued)

EDUCATION

Data Source	Indicator Examples	Availability
Public school records: Records of students enrolled in public schools	• Children absent more than 20% of days (%) • Children passing proficiency exams (%) • Children with preschool experience (%)	Confidential records, maintained by local board of education; availability and format vary by jurisdiction; information reported to the state is usually aggregated to the building or district level and is therefore unsuited to small area analysis
Head Start Records: Individual records of students enrolled in Head Start	• Eligible children attending Head Start (%) • Average months enrolled	Confidential records, maintained by local Head Start agency or agencies; availability varies

HEALTH

Data Source	Indicator Examples	Availability
Vital Records: Birth, death, and fetal death certificates	• Pregnancies with adequate prenatal care (%) • Infant mortality rate • Teen birth rate • Births to unmarried mothers (%)	Available annually from state vital statistics office; may include census geographic codes; index portion of certificate with address available under confidentiality agreement for valid research purposes; matched birth-death file available but often delayed by several years
Communicable Diseases Information: Records of reportable disease incidence	• Cases of diseases, including STDs	Confidential records, maintained by state and local health officials; availability and format vary by jurisdiction
Immunization Records: Records of student immunization status	• Kindergartners fully immunized by age 2 (%)	Confidential records, maintained by local school districts; availability and format vary by jurisdiction
Medicaid Claims: Claims for medical services	• Annualized rates of ambulatory care utilization • Care obtained from emergency rooms (%)	Confidential records, maintained by state Medicaid agency; availability and format vary by state (as states move to managed care, use of claims and reporting requirements may change)
Hospital Discharge Files: Reports on hospital discharges	• Age-adjusted rates of hospitalization	Confidential information, published by zip code by some hospital associations; availability varies; low incidence may make rates

SOCIAL SERVICES

Data Source	Indicator Examples	Availability
Public Assistance Files: Monthly eligibility and payment files	• Recipients per 100 population • Total dollars paid per month • Long-term recipients (%)	Confidential records maintained by local or state human services agencies; format and availability vary; months must be linked to determine duration of recipiency
Subsidized Day Care Records: Records of children receiving day care subsidies	• Children in subsidized day care • Vouchers used in day care homes (%)	Confidential records, maintained by local or state human services agency; format and availability vary
Day Care Licenses: Records of licensed day care providers	• Day care slots by type • Increase in day care slots (%)	Confidential records, maintained by state licensing authority or local child care resource and referral agency; availability and format vary
Child Welfare Records: Records of children in custody or receiving protective services	• Children taken into care annually • Children under agency supervision • Children in foster placement	Confidential records, maintained by local and state child welfare agencies; availability and format vary
Mental Health, Alcohol, and Drug Services Records: Records of individuals receiving services through mental health and substance abuse treatment systems	• Persons in treatment • Clients keeping regular visits (%)	Confidential records, maintained by local boards; availability and formats vary

COMMUNITY RESOURCES AND PARTICIPATION

Data Source	Indicator Examples	Availability
Voter Records: Voter registration lists	• Eligible voters who are registered (%)	Public records, maintained by local board of elections; available for small areas
Membership Records: Local organizations' membership records	• Neighborhood residents who are members (%)	Organizations vary in recordkeeping methods and willingness to release information; if addresses are recorded, small area measures can be developed
Community Directories: Parks, playgrounds, churches, libraries, and other facilities	• Number and type of institutions	Directories vary in accuracy and specificity; computerized yellow pages have wide coverage but include only organizations that have chosen to be listed
Public Transit Information: Routes, schedules, and ridership	• Average travel time to key locations • Direct routes to neighborhood	Available from local transit authority; travel times and distances may be calculated using mapping software
Automobile Registrations and Licenses: Records of vehicles and drivers	• Automobiles per capita • Population with valid driver's licenses (%)	Public records; available for a fee from the state bureau of motor vehicles

gories: housing, economy, safety and security, education, health, social services, and community resources and involvement. These categories reflect
the primary uses to which the data have been put, although most sources are
applicable in several categories when combined with other information.

Housing-Related Data Sources

Many CCIs are interested in improving housing in their communities. Data
from a variety of sources can be used to develop indicators of housing
stock, conditions, and markets in small areas. Available information covers
housing characteristics, condition and quality, construction and demolition, and financing.

HOME MORTGAGE DISCLOSURE ACT (HMDA) INFORMATION

The Home Mortgage Disclosure Act (HMDA), enacted in 1975 and implemented by the Federal Reserve Board, requires covered institutions to compile
and disclose data about loan applications they receive and home purchase and
home improvement loans they originate or purchase during each calendar year.
Institutions required to file HMDA data include commercial banks, savings and
loans, credit unions, and mortgage companies that meet specific criteria.

The data are maintained in the institution's Loan Application
Register (LAR). Each LAR record contains loan/application information
such as type, purpose, amount, and action taken. Each record also contains
some applicant and co-applicant characteristics, such as race, gender, and
gross annual income. Information about the property location, such as the
census tract, county, metropolitan statistical area (MSA), and state is also
recorded. In addition, each record includes a few variables about the census
tract, such as population, number and percent of minority population,
median income, and number of owner-occupied units.

Another record, the Transmittal Sheet (TS), contains information
about each financial institution, including name, address, parent company
name and address, and tax identification number. The LAR and TS data can
be linked by using a respondent identification and agency code found on
both files.

These data, available on reel, cartridge, and CD-ROM from the Federal Reserve Bank's Federal Financial Institutions Examination Council (FFIEC), are issued annually, with each year's data released in the fall of the following year. An order form can be downloaded from http://www.ffiec.gov/hmda. Additional information about the data, such as reporting criteria and background information, can also be found on the web site.

Several small area indicators can be developed from the HMDA data. The total numbers of loans applied for, approved, denied, or withdrawn can be determined, along with reasons for denial. The purpose of the loan/application (to purchase, improve, or refinance a home) is available, as is the type (conventional, FHA, VA, or FmHA). Demographic characteristics of loan applicants and co-applicants are also available. From this information, evaluators can compute approval and denial rates for the small area based on race, gender, and income of applicants; approval and denial rates by financial institution; financial institutions' shares of lending in a particular area or to a particular group; and the lending patterns of specific financial institutions.

The data have been used by fair housing groups to examine lending patterns in communities and to test for evidence of discriminatory practices. Public officials have analyzed the performance of financial institutions in meeting the housing credit needs of their communities. The economic stability of a neighborhood can also be assessed by computing trends in commercial lending and conventional mortgage activity.

LOCAL PROPERTY TAX DATA

A wide variety of information about every parcel of property is collected and maintained by the local auditor or assessor office for the purpose of levying taxes. These records contain three types of information: tax billing records, characteristics data, and deed transfer data. The tax billing record includes parcel number, parcel size, owner name and address, land and building assessed values, property class, land use codes, gross taxes, special assessments, and delinquency status. The characteristics data include parcel number, number of rooms, year built, lot size, land use code, and roof type. The deed transfer data includes information about property sales and transfers, names of buyer and seller, address of property, sales amount, date of sale, and deed type. The tax billing and characteristics data are available annually, and the deed transfer data are available monthly. All three types can be linked by parcel number.

Although these are public records, obtaining them in useable formats for analysis can be difficult in some regions. Some local offices provide the data electronically, while others may not have the resources to do so.

Some of the same property information is contained in a commercial software product known as MetroScan, published for approximately 130 counties nationwide by Transamerica Information Management. Primarily intended for use by realtors, the MetroScan data base includes the census tract and block code for each parcel, as well as some school district information, and gives the user the ability to print county and street maps. The MetroScan data base can be searched by a number of variables, including tract, street, and property type. Although the data can be exported in several formats, the user can export only 5,000 records at a time. Although cumbersome for an area with a large number of properties, this process can be quite convenient for a more modest neighborhood. Information on MetroScan can be obtained at http://www.transamerica.com.

Small area indicators that can be developed from real property data include the market and assessed values of homes, median and average sales prices, volume of property sales and transfers, number of sales by deed type (such as sheriff, trustee, or warranty), and number of tax delinquent properties. All these indicators can be computed by property class (residential, commercial, or industrial), land use (single family, commercial warehouse, manufacturing plant, etc.), and geographic area.

The data have been used to study small area trends in housing values and the market for real estate. Other studies have examined the pattern of population movement by linking deed transfers for sale and purchase, thus tracking where individuals are buying and selling property. These and other indicators have been used together to assess neighborhood stability and condition.

BUILDING AND DEMOLITION PERMITS

Building and demolition permits—intended to ensure that zoning requirements, fire and structural standards, and other building standards are met—are collected and maintained within a municipality's building or housing department. Each permit includes the name of the owner, address of the property, parcel number, written description of work to be done, codes identifying work to be done, permit use class (such as commercial or residential), estimated cost of work to be done, and permit issue and expiration dates. In addition, the permit shows the name and registration number of the contractor performing the work, inspection date, building inspector, and permit fees. The permit information is public record and can be obtained in the appropriate city department, although its availability in electronic format varies by city.

Small area indicators that can be developed from this data include the number of permits by type (such as new construction or external rehabilitation) and by use class (such as commercial or residential). By calculating values associated with building permits by type and geographic area, it is possible to determine, for example, the level of investment being made in residential rehabilitation or new housing construction. Neighborhood groups have used the information to track housing demolition and, in conjunction with other housing indicators, to assess neighborhood stability and condition.

HOUSING CODE ENFORCEMENT REPORTS

Housing code enforcement information is available from a city's building inspection or housing division. The housing code attempts to ensure the health and safety of the occupants of a building by setting rules for basic maintenance and upkeep. Reports of housing code violations typically include the address and owner of the property with the violation, parcel number, code being violated, inspector name, date the violation was cited, time period to comply, compliance date, and whether or not legal action was taken. In addition to code violations, the records show complaints of nuisances or problems that make a neighborhood unattractive or unsafe. The information is available to the public from the appropriate city department, although not every city can supply it in electronic format. The data are frequently updated.

Indicators that can be developed from these data include number and rate of properties with violations, violations by type (for example, faulty wiring or paint needed) and severity, and number and rate of nuisances (abandoned buildings and cars, garbage improperly stored, etc.) by geographic area. Compliance rates and violations that result in legal action can also be calculated. The data have been used, in conjunction with other housing indicators, to assess the stability and condition of neighborhoods and to document success in enforcing compliance with code violations.

HUD INFORMATION ON PUBLIC AND SUBSIDIZED HOUSING

The U.S. Department of Housing and Urban Development (HUD) collects and maintains a variety of information about public and subsidized housing units, most of it gathered at the local level and reported to HUD. These data are available for census tracts and individual housing projects.

  . The HUD information includes the name and address of the housing project, total number of subsidized housing units by type (such as public housing or Section 8), percent of units occupied, average rent, percent of tenants who moved during the last year, average stay in unit, average number of months on waiting list, average number of persons per unit, average income, percent of persons in different income categories, where the majority of tenants' income comes from (such as welfare or wages), percent with assets over $5,000, average age of head of household, percent with disability, racial breakdown, average bedroom size, percent of residents by family type, percent overhoused (more bedrooms than people), and percent with utility allowance. Geographic information includes the zip code, latitude and longitude, census tract, and county. Additional tract-level information includes percent poor, percent minority, and percent households that are owner-occupied. This information is available through HUD's HUDUSER data base by project site or census tract. The data can be downloaded for inclusion in data bases, spreadsheets, and statistical packages. More information is available at http://www.huduser.org/data.html.

  Each local housing authority collects and maintain its own records regarding tenants and management of units. The locally maintained data bases may be more complete than information supplied to HUD and may provide more detail and flexibility than the national data set, which offers only aggregate information. The ease with which the information can be obtained may vary by housing authority.

Public housing data can be used to determine the economic status and mobility of public housing residents within the neighborhood. Combined with a total housing unit count from the census, it can be used to calculate the percentage of housing in the neighborhood that is publicly operated. The data have been used by a variety of researchers, evaluators, and housing administrators to profile the public and subsidized housing population and develop programs to assist tenants in moving from subsidized housing to home ownership.

Economic-Related Data Sources

Many administrative data sources contain information about the economic and job activity in an area, which can be useful in supporting CCI work toward economic development and related issues.

EMPLOYMENT DATA BASES

Although departments of employment services are the primary sources of employment information in states, these agencies do not usually publish information for small areas. Nevertheless, several of their data bases may be useful to CCIs in measuring aspects of employment within neighborhoods.

ES202 information. According to federal mandate, states must collect reports related to unemployment insurance from every establishment that employs more than one worker. The ES202 data base, generated from these reports, therefore covers nearly all paid employees, although self-employed individuals, such as doctors, and family businesses with no paid employees are largely unrepresented. This is the only government data base that provides company-level information along with geographic location.

The data contained in the ES202 file includes establishment name, legal name, address, city, zip code, state, county code, standard industrial classification (SIC) code, ownership code (indicating public or private ownership), number of employees, and total quarterly wages. Total monthly employment is provided for each establishment. Two variables, the unemployment insurance (UI) number and the reporting unit number (RUN), uniquely identify a company. A date indicates when the UI number was established, and successor and predecessor UI numbers may enable the user to link companies that have changed ownership over time. (These variables are not required and therefore may not be reported.) Another variable indicates whether the company is a multi-unit employer (such as a bank with multiple branches) or a single-unit employer.

The data are available quarterly from the state's bureau of employment services, with each quarter's data available in the same quarter of the following year. The information is available electronically, but the format may vary by state.

Although they provide unique establishment-level information, the ES202 data pose some well-known problems (White, Zipp, and McMahon, 1990; Leete and Bania, 1995; Waits, Rex, and Melnick, 1997). First, address information may not be accurate, since some firms mistakenly report all employment at the address of a headquarters or of an accountant who completes the report rather than the address of the actual employment location. There are additional problems if the user wants to look at establishments over time. Each establishment has unique UI and RUN numbers to link quarter by quarter, yet these numbers change if an establishment changes ownership. If the predecessor or successor UI number is not reported, there may be some difficulty linking establishments.

The advantage of the ES202 data is the accuracy of the total employment reported by each firm. The federal mandate carries with it a tax liability that encourages accurate reporting of employment. In addition, the ES202 employment numbers at the county level have been found to mirror other official government measures of employment closely.

Federal and state rules restrict who may obtain these data and how they may be used, and some confidentiality rules apply. For example, if there are only two employers in a geographic area with a particular SIC code, or if one establishment accounts for more than 80 percent of the employment in a particular SIC code, the data must be suppressed.

The ES202 data can be used to calculate several small area indicators on employment. Employment, wages, and number of establishments can be calculated by SIC code and geographic area. Average payroll per employee by industry and geographic area can also be calculated. If data are analyzed over time, the number of business openings, closings, and relocations and associated employment and wages can be determined. Employment gains and losses by geographic area and SIC code can also be computed. The ES202 employment data have been used to measure employment change by SIC in small areas, develop estimates of employment in various geographic areas, determine location of specific types of employment, and estimate locations of expected job openings.

UI wage record. The unemployment insurance (UI) wage record is also available from each state's bureau of employment services and collected under the same federal mandate as ES202. In addition to information about the employer, the wage record file contains specific information about the employee, including name, social security number, quarterly wages paid, and weeks worked. Employer information includes name, address, city, zip code, state, SIC code, and UI number. Like the ES202 data, UI wage records are available quarterly and are subject to some restrictions on obtaining and using the files.

The UI wage records cannot be used alone to develop small area indicators because they do not contain individual wage earners' home addresses. Even so, some researchers have linked address-coded public assistance records to UI records to determine the employment experiences of welfare recipients within a geographic area. Links could be made to other agency records as well.

UI claimant file. The UI claimant file, collected under the same federal mandate as ES202 data and the UI wage record, contains specific information about individuals who have filed for unemployment compensation. The data include the claimant's social security number, address, birth date, sex, and race. Additional information includes weekly benefit amount, average weekly wage, number of qualifying weeks, date of claim, date of separation from job, pay rate, and employer UI account number. These data are confidential, and state and federal regulations restrict who may obtain them and how they may be used. The file is available quarterly from the state's bureau of employment services.

Small area indicators that can be developed from these data include percent of persons receiving benefits, average length of time on unemployment, and percent who have exhausted benefits. Demographic characteristics of unemployment compensation recipients can be also computed. The data have been used, in conjunction with other data sources, to target recipients who have exhausted benefits and provide access to job training programs.

BUSINESS DIRECTORIES

Business directories can be helpful sources of employment information. Only a few directories are listed here, but most libraries maintain a catalogue of the directories available and the types of information provided by each. On their own, the directories may not be a complete source of employment information, but they can enhance the accuracy of addresses and establishments in a geographic area when used in conjunction with ES202 data (Carlson, 1995).

Cole's Business Directories. A directory is published for each state by American Directory Publishing Company in Omaha, Nebraska, and distributed by Cole Publications. Directories are available in print and electronic (CD-ROM) formats. The data base has several drawbacks. Unlike ES202 files, it contains employment ranges only, not actual employment levels, and firms are under no legal requirement to be listed. In addition, the directory is updated continuously, making it difficult to establish a list of firms for a single point in time. The listing is based on telephone directories, and so firms not listed in the telephone book are unlikely to be included.

Various versions are sold as electronic "national yellow page" listings for businesses, primarily intended for other businesses marketing products to firms in particular industrial classes. Other electronic business directories include ProPhone Business Listing, PhoneDisc PowerFinder, and Select Phone Business Listings, each with similar shortcomings.

Dun and Bradstreet Indicators. Based on Dun and Bradstreet credit rating data, the Dun Market Indicators (DMI) file is limited to firms that actively seek out a credit rating record with Dun and Bradstreet. Smaller firms and those without a credit history are unlikely to be included. DMI is also likely to contain outdated data, since firms that close or move have no incentive to update their records. Additionally, firms may understate or overstate employment levels in an effort to improve credit ratings. DMI does not attempt to track employment for every establishment location, therefore employment counts may represent county or area totals for a given firm.

Harris Directory. The Harris Directory is published annually by Harris Publishing Company of Twinsburg, Ohio, and is available for selected Midwestern and Southern states. Most of the firms listed are manufacturing companies. Like DMI, the Harris Directory does not necessarily report employment by establishment location, therefore the employment count may represent a firm total. It may also contain some of the same problems as the other business directories listed.

COMMUNITY DEVELOPMENT BLOCK GRANT INFORMATION

The Community Development Block Grant (CDBG) program is funded by the Department of Housing and Urban Development and administered by communities that are receiving funding. This entitlement program provides annual grants to central cities of metropolitan statistical areas, other cities with populations of at least 50,000, and qualified urban counties with populations of at least 200,000. The purpose of the grants is to assist communities in carrying out a wide range of community development activities directed toward neighborhood revitalization, economic development, and the provision of improved community facilities and services. Specifically targeted are areas with high concentrations of low- and moderate-income residents. Each city allocates funding to projects it deems appropriate and consistent with HUD regulations and submits to HUD an annual report of funded activities. Activities include housing rehabilitation and new construction and improvements to or construction of public facilities, such as neighborhood centers, parks, streets, and health facilities.

The data are prepared and maintained by each community receiving the funding, usually by a local department of community development or planning. The data available from CDBG include name and address of the funding recipient, census tract and political boundary, description of the activity funded, activity codes, amount of funding, month and year of the activity, amount expended in a given period, geographic area served by the activity (census tract, political boundary, or city as a whole), and number of residents or households served. The racial and income characteristics of residents or households served by particular activities are also available. National objective codes indicate whether the area being served is considered low/moderate income, slum/blighted, or in urgent need of assistance.

Although the information is public record, the ease of obtaining and using it varies by community, as does its availability in electronic format. The data contain some ambiguities, particularly when the user is focusing on neighborhood analysis. For example, it is difficult to assign the financial benefit of some projects to a particular neighborhood, since activities may target multiple neighborhoods or a project based in one neighborhood may operate citywide. Such expenditures must either be apportioned across many neighborhoods or left out of neighborhood-level analyses.

Small area indicators that can be developed from these data include estimated CDBG funding by geographic area, estimated per capita funding by geographic area, types of activities being funded, and racial and income profiles of populations being assisted. The data have been used to study the impact of CDBG funding on residential rehabilitation and other community development activities in specific communities and to determine the investment being made in various CDBG activities.

MUNICIPAL INCOME TAX RECORDS

Many states allow municipalities or counties to collect taxes on income earned by their residents and by nonresidents who work within their boundaries. These taxes are withheld by the employer and collected by the jurisdiction imposing the tax or by a central collection agency on its behalf. The information collected by the jurisdiction or collection agency includes the employer name and address, total amount of local taxes withheld from employees, taxes paid based on net profit of business, and federal identification number. Generally, the taxes are paid on a monthly or quarterly basis, although this varies by state. Confidentiality rules may make this information difficult to obtain in some localities. Typically, the tax collection agency produces aggregate data for selected neighborhoods in response to a special request.

Small area indicators that can be developed from these data include income tax generated by businesses in a geographic area. If appropriate confidentiality agreements can be crafted, it might be possible to link these data with other data sources, such as ES202 files, using federal identification numbers. This would allow additional indicators to be developed, such as income tax generated by particular industries (using SIC codes) and total wages and number of employees by geographic area and industry.

TRAINING PROGRAM RECORDS

Federally funded training programs generate data that can be used to determine levels of participation in these activities in local communities. Although the programs may undergo significant changes in the next few years as a result of block grants and welfare reform, their data bases are likely to continue to record the same basic information.

Job Opportunities and Basic Skills program information. From 1988 to 1997, Job Opportunities and Basic Skills (JOBS) was the federally mandated program aimed at helping families make the transition from welfare to self-support through job search, work experience, education, training, and other services. (It has since been superseded by the Temporary Assistance to Needy Families program.) JOBS was governed by federal and state regulations, and its data systems were operated primarily by state departments responsible for public assistance administration. Under welfare reform, states and local welfare-to-work initiatives are likely to maintain similar, perhaps improved, data bases.

The JOBS information is located in two files, one containing demographic information about public assistance recipients obtaining JOBS services and the other containing information about recipients' activity histories in the JOBS program. The demographic information includes social security number, address (street, city, zip code, and county), race, sex, date of birth, educational level or school enrollment status, marital status, cash benefit from Aid to Families with Dependent Children, and length of time on assistance. Program information, updated monthly, includes a chronological history of an individual's participation status, including eligibility, job assessment, job assignment, attendance record, exemptions (for long-term illness, very young children, etc.), failure to participate, sanctions, and employment history. The two files can be linked by social security number. Obtaining data may depend on the purpose for which it is sought, since the files contain confidential information about each JOBS participant.

Small area indicators that can be developed from the JOBS data include the average time between a job assessment and assignment to an activity, the participation rate among recipients, participation rates by JOBS activity, sanction rates, and employment rates of participants. Data from the JOBS program have been used to determine participation rates in welfare-to-work programs and, in conjunction with public assistance records, participation by long-term recipients in JOBS activities (Coulton, Verma, and Guo, 1996).

Job Training Partnership Act records. The Job Training Partnership Act of 1982 (JTPA) established the nation's largest employment and training program for disadvantaged adults and youths facing serious barriers to employment. The goals of the program are to increase employment and earnings and reduce welfare dependence. Program participation is voluntary, but candidates must meet certain criteria to receive JTPA services. The program provides classroom vocational training, on-the-job training, job search assistance, and other related training services. It is administered by the states, with service delivery provided locally.

JTPA program data include participant information, such as social security number, birth date, sex, race, address, eligibility status, employment history and status, educational status, and participation in public assistance programs. Application date, termination date, and services provided are also recorded, as is information regarding the aptitude, ability, and skill level of each participant. Employment and public assistance status are recorded approximately three months after termination from the program. The data are collected and maintained by the state's bureau of employment services and are available quarterly. Like the other employment related data files, restrictions apply regarding who may obtain these data and how they may be used.

Several small area indicators can be developed from JTPA data, including participation rates overall and by race and sex, percent of participants on welfare, and education and skills levels of participants. The data have been used to document participant demographics and outcomes, such as drop-out rates, employment rates, average wage when employed, and decreased reliance on welfare.

Data Sources Related to Community Safety and Security

Neighborhood safety and security is a major concern of almost all CCIs. Information regarding these issues can be found in several sources.

MUNICIPAL POLICE RECORDS

Each police department maintains a record of each incident of crime reported in its jurisdiction. These records contain a significant amount of information about the crime, the victim, and, when available, the suspect or arrestee. The crime reports contain specific information, such as crime location, type of crime, time, date, weather conditions, and information about the arresting officer, including name and badge number. Types of crime include homicide, rape, aggravated assault, robbery, burglary, arson, auto theft, domestic violence, simple assault, menacing, and drug-related violations such as trafficking or possession. Some crime reports also contain a file of information about the victim, including race, sex, address, age, and date of birth.

Police departments also maintain an arrest data base. Included in each arrest report are address, race, sex, age, and date of birth of the arrestee. Information is also available about suspects, including geographic and demographic information and physical characteristics according to witness or victim descriptions. Information is also available regarding weapons used during incidents of crime. Crime reports can be linked to victim, arrest, and suspect reports using a report number.

Most police department data are available electronically and are released annually. Since this information is confidential and sensitive, the willingness of police departments to release these data may vary by jurisdiction.

Among the small area indicators that can be developed with these data are numbers and rates of crime by geographic area. Many researchers consider only serious crimes, called Part I crimes under the terminology of the Uniform Crime Report (UCR). Crimes can also be disaggregated by the race, sex, and gender of victims and assailants or by the victim-assailant relationship. For example, the reports can be used to identify crimes in which the victim and offender live in the same area or are of the same race. Weapon use by crime type can also be calculated. Crime data have been used to document crime levels in communities, to determine the need for violence prevention or community policing programs, and to understand possible causes and effects of crime.

Most police departments have adopted the UCR codes for crime reporting and standardization of offense definitions, which allow crime statistics to be compared across police jurisdictions. The UCR program compiles and maintains nationwide crime statistics, using data provided through the voluntary participation of local and state law enforcement agencies. The Federal Bureau of Investigation administers the program. Each year, the FBI releases a report entitled *Crime in the United States,* which contains data collected through the UCR program. The report provides data by state, county, and municipality (for cities and towns with 10,000 or more in population), including crime rates, number of crimes by type, and number of arrests by sex, race, and age. *Crime in the United States* can be found in libraries or purchased from the U.S. Government Printing Office. More information is available at http://www.fbi.gov.

911 SYSTEM DATA

Most 911 emergency systems are operated by county agencies, with 911 calls for emergency service processed by the appropriate police, fire, or emergency medical service department. Data available from 911 calls include the name, address, and phone number of the caller, although this information is not always complete because some callers are reluctant to identify themselves. Information about the emergency includes the exact location, date, and time of call, description of the emergency, whether an ambulance is required, and a priority and alarm level based on type of emergency. The time a call is received by the police, time of arrival at the scene, whether a contact is made, and a description of the result of the call are also available.

The data are organized by priority level, with 1 being the most serious and 4 being the least. The calls are also categorized according to whether the call indicates a crime against a person, an accident (involving, for example, hazardous waste), a danger to public safety (such as a bomb threat), a property crime, or general assistance (such as transporting a prisoner or assisting with a traffic stop). The data are available annually and may vary in format by jurisdiction.

Small area indicators that can be developed from these data include police response times and number of 911 calls by priority level. In addition, the calls can be categorized according to the description of the emergency. For example, the number of 911 calls indicating violent crime (such as homicide, robbery, or domestic violence), property crimes, or public safety issues can be calculated. Data about 911 calls can supplement other crime-related information. For example, some 911 calls are precipitated by incidents—such as altercations within households or minor disturbances—that do not result in crime reports. Data regarding response times can be useful to police departments and communities as a whole, since slow response times may indicate a need for more staffing during particular periods or in certain geographic areas.

JUVENILE COURT RECORDS

The juvenile court handles cases of delinquency, unruliness, and dependency for all individuals under the age of eighteen. A record is maintained for each juvenile who enters the court system, including age, sex, race, date of birth, and census tract.

Offenses that come before the juvenile court include violent crimes, such as homicide and robbery; property crimes; drug violations; and less serious offenses, such as disorderly conduct, curfew violations, and truancy. Information collected by the court includes the location, date, and type of each offense, case number and type, source of the complaint (parent, school, etc.), judge, and disposition and disposition date. In addition, the records contain information regarding probation, such as probation officer, days on probation, and, where applicable, detention home location and release date.

The court maintains records of the addresses of offenders, victims, and offense locations, but researchers' ability to obtain those data varies by court system. Access to demographic characteristics of victims also varies. Detailed information about individual victims and offenders, such as address, race, sex, and age, is confidential. The court may release an annual report aggregating data to the municipality or county level, but neighborhood indicators are seldom published.

Small area indicators that can be developed include delinquency rates, number and type of crimes committed by juveniles, and race, sex, and age of offenders. If victim information is obtained, the victim-offender relationship by sex, race, age, and geography can also be determined at an aggregate level. The data have been used to determine the level of juvenile crime and develop strategies and programs to reduce it. The federal Office of Juvenile Justice Prevention provides information at http://www.ncjrs.org/ojjdp/html/pubs.html.

CORONER'S REPORTS

The coroner determines the circumstances, manner, and cause of each violent, sudden, unusual, or unattended death and prepares a detailed report outlining the findings. Coroner's reports contain confidential information about the victim and, when applicable, the assailant. Information about the victim includes age, sex, race, and address, along with any findings regarding drugs or alcohol in the victim's system at the time of death. Information about the death includes place, date, time, day of the week, type of death (homicide, suicide, etc.), and mode of death (firearm, stabbing, etc.), and, where applicable, caliber of weapon. Information about the assailant includes sex, race, age, address, and previous offenses. The data are available from the local coroner's office annually, but the format and rules for access may vary by jurisdiction. In some localities, for example, much of the report is not computerized.

Small area indicators that can be developed from these data include suicide and homicide rates, places of death, times and days when deaths occur, and how deaths occur. Information about victims and assailants, such as race and sex, and about victim-assailant relationships by age, race, sex, and geography can also be determined. Coroner's reports are more detailed than police department crime reports and can be used in conjunction with those reports to enhance information regarding homicides and suicides.

CHILD MALTREATMENT REPORTS

Incidents of child abuse and/or neglect are reported to local child protection agencies, which investigate claims and determine whether abuse or neglect has occurred or is occurring. A record is maintained for each reported incident of abuse and/or neglect. The data available from reported cases of child abuse include location of alleged abuse and/or neglect, person making the report (teacher, doctor, victim, etc.), type of alleged abuse and/or neglect (sexual, physical, or emotional), and whether the allegation was substantiated, indicated, or unsubstantiated. Information about the victim is also available, including address, age, gender, and victim's relationship to the perpetrator. Perpetrator information includes age and gender. The confidentiality and sensitivity of this information is an important issue, particularly at the address level. Obtaining these data depends on the purpose for which they are sought. Generally, the data are available annually and electronically.

Indicators that can be developed from these data include child abuse rates, types of abuse and/or neglect being reported, and numbers of substantiated and unsubstantiated incidents. The age and gender of victims can be determined, as can victims' relationships with perpetrators of abuse and those reporting abuse. The data have been used to document child maltreatment and determine factors that may contribute to it.

The National Center on Child Abuse and Neglect, part of the U.S. Department of Health and Human Services, collects and maintains national and state-level information on abused and neglected children through its National Child Abuse and Neglect Data System (NCANDS), available at http://www.caliber3.calib.com/nccanch. The system does not release information regarding small areas. Participation by states is voluntary, but most states provide data to the system. The NCANDS annual report includes information regarding reporters of maltreatment; number of reports substantiated, indicated, and unsubstantiated; types of maltreatment; and perpetrator and victim characteristics, such as age, race, and gender.

LIQUOR LICENSE RECORDS

In each state, the Department of Liquor Control is responsible for issuing permits to manufacture, sell, and distribute alcoholic beverages. Records of those permits are public information and include the name of the permit holder, address of permit location (street, city, zip code, county, and taxing district), and permit class (carryout beer only, wine only, etc.). The address of the outlet as listed on the permit is inaccurate in some cases, but the name of the permit holder may provide some clue to its true location.

A few small area indicators can be developed from these data, including the number of alcohol outlets in a geographic area, the number per capita, and the types of outlets, such as carryout stores or bars. Investigators can also determine the type of alcohol sold (beer, wine, hard liquor, or all three) and how late alcohol can be sold. Researchers have used these data to examine and document the relationship between the density of alcohol outlets and the level of violent crime in an area.

Education-Related Data Sources

Educational outcomes are important indicators of the well-being of a community and the functioning of its systems. CCIs often focus on children and young people since education is a fundamental component of development (Thorton, Love, and Meckstroth, 1994). Public school systems typically generate reports for the state or the community as a whole, but seldom produce data for small areas. Only limited data are available for private and parochial schools, which maintain separate and unique record systems.

PUBLIC SCHOOL RECORDS

Most public school districts maintain computerized files of individual student records. These records are confidential but, with proper protection agreements, can be used to develop measures for small areas. The files include each student's address, school attended, school transfers or leavings, scores on standardized achievement and proficiency tests, attendance and disciplinary records, free lunch eligibility, and family status.

The data can be used to calculate attendance rates and average achievement for students by school or by neighborhood. School and residential mobility can be calculated by matching students' records across years to determine movement. By matching records for a cohort of students—usually from the 8th grade onward—to determine those who graduate, school completion can be calculated. School entry records have also been used to document immunization status and school readiness. The nature of these records varies considerably across districts.

HEAD START RECORDS

Area Head Start agencies maintain records on children enrolled in Head Start and on individual Head Start programs. The files contain each child's address, Head Start center location, enrollment date, and other selected family and child information. These records are confidential and their format and availability differ across local agencies.

Head Start records can be geo-coded and aggregated to calculate rates of Head Start enrollment in small areas and distances between children's homes and the centers they attend. Matched with school enrollment files, Head Start records can be used to calculate preschool participation rates.

Health-Related Data Sources

Health is defined not merely as the absence of disease but as overall physical, mental, and social well-being. Although vast improvements have been made in the area of preventive health in the last 50 years, health indicators in many low income communities in the United States compare unfavorably with the overall high national standard of health (Geronimus, Bound, Waidmann, Hillemeier, and Burns, 1996). Well-established methods allow researchers to track many of those indicators using small area data (Gould, Mahajan, and Lucero, 1989).

VITAL RECORDS

The registration of births, deaths, fetal deaths, and other vital events is a state and local function. The civil laws of every state provide for a continuous, permanent, and compulsory vital registration system. The state vital statistics office issues certificates of live birth, fetal death, or death, either directly or through a local registrar, and typically compiles records of these events.

Birth information is available in two sections. The first section, known as the index portion, contains a unique birth certificate number, mother's name, address, and other demographic and identifying information. Some localities include a census tract designation. The index portion is confidential and is released only upon approval of a special request justifying the need for such information. The other portion, called the statistical file, contains the birth certificate number along with such additional information as prenatal care, congenital anomalies, and birth weight. Some jurisdictions also include the census tract. The statistical portion is widely available for public health research. The death file consists of a unique death certificate number, name, social security number, and other indicators such as cause of death. The fetal death file has almost the same information as the birth file but also includes the cause of death.

Many small area indicators can be calculated from birth certificate data. Recorded birth weights can be analyzed to arrive at the number of low birth weight infants. Information about mothers' prenatal care can be used to calculate the adequacy of prenatal care according to Kessner's index, which considers number of gestation weeks, timing of entry into care, and total number of prenatal care visits (Kessner, Singer, Kalk, and Schlesinger, 1973). Death files can be analyzed to derive such information as leading causes of death and infant death rates, which can then be compared with local, state, and national standards. Excess mortality can be calculated by comparing age-specific deaths in the neighborhood with expected deaths based on a standard population (McCord and Freeman, 1990). Prenatal information can be analyzed from the fetal death file to identify small geographic areas of risk for such outcomes.

Most state and local governments publish vital statistics reports, some containing small area data. The state and local departments of vital statistics can be contacted for these reports. The National Center for Health Statistics (NCHS) publishes monthly and annual reports for the nation, states, counties, cities, and regions. Selected NCHS publications can be viewed at http://www.cdc.gov/nchswww/nchshome.htm.

COMMUNICABLE DISEASES INFORMATION

Physicians are required by law to report certain diseases, such as tuberculosis, syphilis, and AIDS, to local and state health officials. Records of these reports are maintained by departments of health, and in some cases are computerized. Health department data usually contain addresses, although for reasons of confidentiality these data can be released only if special justifications are made. Furthermore, small geographic areas may have incidences so small that no meaningful analysis can be carried out. Indicators that can be developed include incidence of disease in a particular area or within a specific population group.

Data about some communicable diseases are available from the World Health Organization   at http://www.who.ch/programmes/ emc/emc_home.htm. The Centers for Disease Control publishes information on communicable diseases in selected metropolitan areas at http://www.cdc.gov/publications.htm.

EMERGENCY MEDICAL SERVICE RECORDS

Emergency medical services are delivered with a sense of urgency to patients, such as accident or heart attack victims, in need of immediate attention. Information about patients transported via the public emergency medical service (EMS) system is recorded in 911 data. For an example of how these data are used in Durham County, North Carolina, see http://www.durhamems.com/Research.htm.

Many medical emergencies are treated in emergency rooms but do not appear as 911 calls. A more complete measure of these emergencies could come from emergency room records. In cities where local emergency rooms collaborate on an injury registry system, it is possible to calculate injury rates for small areas. Among the important indicators are rates of intentional and accidental injury by age group (Rivara, Calonge, and Thompson, 1989). Among young people in particular, injuries are a good indicator of health risk as well as social control in a community (Prothrow-Stith, 1991). Although hospitals in most cities do not maintain a common data base for emergency room visits, there is a considerable interest in injury surveillance (Centers for Disease Control, 1988). The availability of emergency service codes in the International Classification of Disease System makes it possible to establish data systems, and a growing number of communities are exploring such systems.

IMMUNIZATION RECORDS

The immunization status of a population is considered an important measure of the adequacy of preventive health care, indicating not only the protection afforded by the vaccine itself but regular contact with a medical professional. Although states are not required to collect data on immunization, some states conduct surveys to estimate the number of children immunized, while some communities are experimenting with computerized immunization tracking systems. Local area school registration gives some indication of immunization status, since schools and day care centers are mandated to ask for proof of immunization before they admit students.

Some small area indicators can be developed from available data, such as the percentage of children without health insurance at the point of entry into school or who did not receive vaccinations at the appropriate age. The incidence of communicable diseases for which vaccines are available is another indicator of lack of immunization. More information is available from the Centers for Disease Control and Prevention at http://www.cdc.gov/nip/home.htm.

MEDICAID CLAIMS

Claims filed by medical providers for services delivered under Medicaid—which provides health insurance coverage to low income individuals and families—may be a valuable source of data on health and medical services for populations in small geographic areas. Administration of the Medicaid program varies from state to state, and most states enter only a limited number of variables into the computerized system. Even so, available data usually includes provider description, classification of illness, procedure codes, service dates, and service charges. The recipient's address, necessary for small area analysis, may need to be merged into the claim from an eligibility file. Researchers may need to file a special request justifying the need for the data, owing to confidentiality issues.

Several small area indicators can be developed using these data, such as annualized rates of medical care utilization by type (emergency, inpatient, ambulatory, etc.), patient health status and age, and diagnosis or procedure. National statistical information, compiled by the Health Care Financing Administration, can be viewed at http://www.hcfa.gov/medicaid/mcaidpti.htm. For additional national information, see http://www.census.gov/ftp/pub/prod/1/gen/95statab/health.pdf.

Claims data have been used extensively in health services research, but the formats in which they have been provided are likely to change under managed care. Managed care providers may be required to submit encounter forms to states for their Medicaid enrollees, but some states may accept aggregate reports of services provided for population groupings. This would preclude address-based small area analysis.

HOSPITAL DISCHARGE FILES

Hospital discharge files are maintained by some state hospital associations and government agencies. Many state hospital associations maintain and publish data on patient age, payer, clinical service, sex, length of stay, diagnostic related group (DRG), hospitals, beds, and admissions, aggregated at the zip code level. Patient-level data exist, but confidentiality rules govern their release. "Hospital Statistics," published by the

American Hospital Association, provides some hospital information with address data.

Small area indicators can be developed from these data, including average cost by severity of diagnosis, number of inpatients and outpatients, incidence of the most prevalent preventable conditions per 1,000 population, average length of stay, and number of beds and hospitals. Utilization rates have also been compiled across geographic areas using discharge data (Wennberg, Freeman, and Culp, 1987). The National Association of Health Data Organizations (NAHDA) addresses some data-related issues at http://www.nahdo.org/index.html.

Social Services Data Sources

Social services are public and private programs rendered to individuals and families to improve their economic, social, physical, and mental well-being. They are relevant to CCI evaluation, both because service reform is an important objective of many initiatives and because service provision and utilization are useful indicators of the status of the population in a small geographic area.

PUBLIC ASSISTANCE FILES

Public assistance programs, most of which operate under state and federal law but are delivered locally, supply various forms of cash and in-kind assistance to eligible persons who qualify under means testing criteria. These programs include Temporary Assistance for Needy Families (which replaces the federal Aid to Families with Dependent Children program), food stamps, Medicaid, emergency assistance, and local general assistance.

Data on public assistance benefits are available through state or local departments of human services. Computerized individual records, including name and address, case and recipient numbers, program participation, eligibility status, and benefit amount, are contained in monthly files. Records can be extracted for assistance units or for individual recipients. A few states maintain longitudinal records, but in most places these need to be created by merging monthly records to create individual histories.

Public assistance files are confidential and can be released only for valid purposes, with proper protection agreements in place. Some departments can supply monthly files geo-coded by census tract, rather than name and address, reducing confidentiality problems. However, without recipient identifiers, longitudinal or matched files cannot be created.

Monthly files can be used to calculate participation in various public assistance programs by neighborhood residents. Longitudinal files can be used to calculate rates of long-term and short-term welfare participation. When public assistance records are merged with UI wage records, rates of moving from welfare to work in small geographic areas can be calculated.

SUBSIDIZED DAY CARE RECORDS

Child care programs operating under the Personal Responsibility and Work Opportunity Act maintain records on children receiving day care subsidies, their families, and day care providers. These data are confidential but may be available through state or local departments of human services for valid research purposes with proper protections. Records include name of parent and child, address, eligibility status, service hours per week, estimated cost per week, at-risk indicator, family size, income, education, and caretaker. The records are organized by month and include children whose families qualify for day care subsidies under public assistance or low income working status.

Subsidized day care participation of families in small geographic areas can be calculated, along with the amount of the subsidies and the types of providers chosen. The research and publications department of the U.S. Department of Health and Human Services offers statistics on day care indicators at http://aspe.os.dhhs.gov/GB/sec12.txt.

DAY CARE LICENSES

Every state requires child care providers to meet certain training and staffing criteria in order to obtain a license. Data on day care providers may be obtained through the state or local licensing agency or from local child care resource and referral agencies. Confidentiality guidelines limit the release of these data, but information without addresses or other identifiers can ordinarily be released to users who justify the need and guarantee protection.

Records contain the name and address of the licensee, numbers of slots for infants, toddlers, preschoolers, and school age children, and some additional information. Indicators that can be developed include numbers, types, and locations of slots relative to employment locations and homes of welfare recipients and working poor residents. Some information about day care can be found at http://www.careguide.net/.

CHILD WELFARE RECORDS

Child welfare services include preventive services such as social support, investigation of reported child abuse or neglect, services for abused and neglected children, crisis intervention, and other related services. Child welfare records are maintained by county and state departments of child welfare or child protection. These records are confidential.

Although federal requirements stipulate that child welfare information be computerized, the data vary in their completeness and accuracy. Records may include name, address, income, school, education, religion, ethnicity, marital status, and other demographic information. Dates and status of child abuse and neglect reports, entry into and exit from custody, foster care, residential treatment, protective services, and special programs are also important pieces of information for analysis.

Small geographic area indicators can be developed using geo-coded records. The number of children in custody or in foster care can be calculated, along with rates of reported child maltreatment. Child welfare records can be merged with other agency records to examine relationships among services provided by various child-serving agencies and to track outcomes (Goerge, Van Voorhis, and Lee, 1994). Although such matching and merging is a challenging task, it has the potential to produce information useful to CCIs in targeting local service reform. More information on child welfare data bases can be found at http://aspe.os.dhhs.gov/hsp/cyp/chapin1.pdf.

Mental Health, Alcohol, and Drug Services Information

Mental health, alcohol, and other drug abuse services are delivered by a wide range of public, nonprofit, and for-profit organizations. Although no single agency maintains data on all programs, those operated under public authority may generate data useful for developing small area measures. Local service providers often maintain confidential, computerized records that contain the client's name, address, and dates and types of service, including admissions to inpatient facilities or treatment centers. The availability and format of these records vary considerably from one agency to another.

Small area indicators that can be developed from the geo-coded records include numbers and rates of residents under treatment, demographic characteristics of patients, prior treatment histories, criminal justice histories, social services, addiction severity, duration of treatment episodes, key services received, program staffing, ownership, resource base, and costs. National information is available through the Substance Abuse and Mental Health Services Administration (SAMHSA) at http://www.samhsa.gov/.

Data Sources on Community Resources and Participation

Building or rebuilding community infrastructure, capacity, and participation are among the goals of many CCIs. These phenomena are difficult to capture using administrative data, but a few possible sources are listed here.

Voter Records

Voter registration and participation records, maintained by local boards of elections, are open to the public but vary in their format and accessibility. The number of registered voters may be reported by ward or other political jurisdiction, but addresses can be used to calculate the rates of participation and registration within the boundaries of a CCI. Voter records have been used to measure participation by neighborhood and ethnicity; for an example of research tracking voter participation by Latinos, see http://naid.sppsr.ucla.edu/southwest/test1.html.

MEMBERSHIP RECORDS

Membership in neighborhood organizations is another indicator that may be useful to CCIs, since membership growth may be an indicator of rising social participation. Although organizational membership records vary in quality and format, those organizations that actively recruit, collect dues, or provide services to members are most likely to have up-to-date, computerized records. If individual addresses are available, these records can be geocoded to obtain counts of members for small geographic areas.

COMMUNITY DIRECTORIES

As community assets, community organizations are of considerable interest to CCIs. Unfortunately, no single data base provides information on organizations operating within a small area, yet some partial listings may be useful. For example, addresses in computerized yellow pages can be geo-coded and mapped by neighborhood. Other possible sources include lists of libraries, available from the American Library Association; churches, available from a local inter-church council; neighborhood development corporations and neighborhood centers, available from a local economic development agency; and parks and playgrounds, available from the local parks department. Although these lists can provide geographic locations of community assets, information about the magnitude of their operations or contributions may need to be obtained directly from the organizations. Information about computerized yellow pages is available at http://www.nctweb.com/cds/selphone.html.

PUBLIC TRANSIT INFORMATION

Public transportation may offer some important indicators for CCIs, since civic participation depends on access to key locations outside the neighborhood and convenient transit stops within the neighborhood, particularly for non-drivers such as elderly, impoverished, and disabled residents. To measure access, evaluators can use bus and train schedules to calculate travel times to key destinations from the CCI neighborhood if computerized information is not available from local transit authorities. Transit stops can be geo-coded, mapped, and used in calculating distances from residents' homes to stations. These data can also aid in calculating average commuting time to areas of employment growth, a crucial factor in economic development (Coulton, Verma, and Guo, 1996). In addition, average commutes to service providers might be a useful indicator for service improvement. Some national information is available from the American Public Transit Association at http://www.apta.com/.

Automobile Registrations and Licenses

Other indicators of a neighborhood's access to regional services and its general level of resources are auto registrations and licensed drivers. Records of auto registration and licenses are open to the public and can be obtained for a fee from the state's bureau of motor vehicles. Some states use dynamic data bases, updated as changes are made, thus allowing researchers to obtain a "snapshot" of all available data at a given point in time. Data are available with addresses and zip codes by type and classification (commercial, passenger, etc.) of vehicle registered, which can be used to assign census tracts using existing geo-coding software. Indicators that can be developed include number of annual registrations, per capita automobiles owned, and average vehicles owned by a family.

Issues and Challenges in Using Administrative Data

Using administrative data to construct small area measures presents a series of challenges. How successfully these problems can be overcome depends upon the type and source of the data and specific local circumstances. Some general issues may or may not become barriers in particular locales or situations.

Confidentiality

Many administrative data sources contain individual information that is protected either by law or custom. Unless the data base already contains census block or tract codes, the CCI evaluator must request the release of confidential information about individuals' street addresses to conduct small area analysis. Even information aggregated to the level of the census tract may breech confidentiality if only a handful of cases fall into a particular category and could thus be identified.

Administrative agencies can enter into confidentiality protection agreements with researchers who have a valid purpose for using the data to develop community measures. The researchers must follow standard methods for guarding data with identifiers, assuring that only necessary and secure personnel have access to the data and guaranteeing that confidential data will not be released. Researchers affiliated with institutions with federally approved institutional review boards should have their confidentiality protection methods reviewed by those bodies. Some agencies have well-established guidelines for releasing confidential data, while others have little experience in this area. However, with the exception of a few agencies that are strictly prohibited by law from releasing confidential data, most agencies can release data if the researchers are made agents of the agency and agree to abide by agency rules.

Community measures based on confidential data must be calculated for areas large enough to avoid revealing individual identities. This issue arises for categories based on rare events or small groups. For example, employment in a particular industry in a small area could be concentrated in one or two identifiable firms. If so, such figures could not be released.

The decision to release confidential information requires consideration of the risk-benefit ratio. The agency must judge the reputation of the research institution and its expertise in protecting human subjects to determine the risk that an inadvertent breech of confidentiality will occur. It should also weigh the benefit to itself and the community of making small area data available. Many agencies do not have the internal resources to look carefully at their data by small area. Thus, the benefits of releasing the data (under strong and binding confidentiality protections) for geographically based analysis is often significant if the agency is assured that information will be provided to them in return.

DATA ACCURACY

Small area information produced from administrative records suffers from four types of accuracy problems: inaccuracies in the records themselves, bias in reporting, small numbers in particular categories, and distortions related to averaging.

Inaccuracies can be a problem in any data base. Users of administrative data should check with the supplying agency about each data element and make a judgment about its accuracy and possible sources of inaccuracy. Many researchers have found that the most accurate data elements tend to be those that are essential to the agency's work or subject to quality control. Thus, for example, public assistance payroll records stemming from the issuance of checks are more likely to be accurate than intake information that has no bearing on eligibility, such as educational attainment. Especially important to small area analysis is the accuracy of addresses for particular events that are being analyzed. Unfortunately, agency data bases often overwrite original addresses with address changes, thus eliminating the location current at the time of the event.

A second problem is reporting bias, which can influence the accuracy of records that are generated only when particular events are reported. For example, crimes are known to be underreported to the police (O'Brien, 1985), and law enforcement jurisdictions differ in their response to crime reports (Sherman, 1989). These two factors can affect whether a crime record is generated and how the crime is classified. Child abuse and neglect reports are vulnerable to similar problems (O'Toole, Turbett, and Nalpeka, 1983).

Third, accuracy can be affected when the number of particular events in an area is small. Infant deaths, for example, occur in very small numbers in a CCI during a given year. A change in even one death can raise the infant death rate markedly without reflecting a true change in health status of the population or quality of health services. The literature on sample size and accuracy suggests that, for rare events, evaluators can use multi-year averages or group neighborhoods together to achieve numbers from which estimates can be generated with confidence (Lemeshow, Hosmer, Klar, and Lwanga, 1990).

Population estimates for small areas are a final source of inaccuracy in developing measures from administrative data. Many indicators—such as crime incidence—are calculated as rates in order to make them comparable across small areas that differ in size. Also, although the decennial census is considered the best count of the population, its numbers are quickly outdated. Population estimates can be used for the years between censuses, but there are well-known problems with accurately estimating the population in small areas (Smith and Cody, 1994). Thus, many measures are made even more inaccurate by errors in both the numerator and denominator.

DATA EXTRACTION AND MANAGEMENT

Administrative records come in many different formats. Most easily useable by CCIs are those that have already been aggregated to the relevant units of geography. For example, many local health departments routinely produce counts of births, deaths, infant deaths, and other useful statistics by census tract. Most data, however, have not been converted to this format. Typically, administrative data files contain individual-level records, with information on a single individual appearing in multiple records across multiple files. Some files are extremely large and contain cases and records irrelevant to small area analysis. Considerable work often goes into understanding the file formats, extracting the relevant records, geo-coding the addresses, and aggregating the data to the required units of geography.

A complicating factor in using administrative data is assuring that the correct records have been extracted for the desired measure. Decisions must be made about the "window" of time to be considered, whether the unit is persons or events, whether to count all cases or new cases only, and how to handle duplicates. For example, a child maltreatment report is an event that involves one or more children. In a given year, the same child may be reported multiple times, or a single event may yield several reports. Child maltreatment cases may be carried as open records in the agency data base over several months or years. Such data make possible several different measures for a small geographic area, including the total number of maltreatment reports in a year, individual children reported as maltreated at least once in a year, maltreatment cases served by the agency at a point in time during the year, and maltreated children ever served during the year by the agency. Researchers need to be clear about exactly how their calculations are made and what the resulting measures mean.

MATCHED AND LONGITUDINAL FILES

Administrative data are often organized by month, quarter, or year. Most data bases are event driven, generating a record, for example, when a person is eligible for a program, a payment is made, a deed transfers, or a child is born. However, CCIs may require some measures that reflect that these events happen over time to an individual, building, firm, or some other entity. To develop this type of measure, longitudinal records must be created by matching events across separate records using a constant identifier such as a parcel number or a case number.

Although longitudinal measures require considerably more effort to process than individual records, they are frequently more reflective of important outcomes. For example, a CCI that was less interested in reducing public assistance use than in eliminating long-term dependency might want to calculate the number of long-term welfare recipients in a small area by matching monthly eligibility files for each individual over a number of years.

A similar challenge occurs when measures require that data be matched across multiple agencies or multiple data sets from a single agency. For example, a CCI may be interested in assuring that preschool children of mothers moving from welfare to work are still able to take advantage of Head Start programs in the neighborhood. A match would need to be made between public assistance, employment, and Head Start records to monitor progress on this outcome.

Matching across multiple agencies may require the use of probabilistic matching procedures when there is no universal or reliable individual identifier (Jaro, 1995; Newcombe, 1988). For example, social security numbers are erroneous or not available in many data files, but names, birth dates, addresses, and other identifiers can be used to improve the accuracy of matching. Matching across data bases has the potential to create sensitive and refined measures, which could be useful in capturing the synergistic effects of CCIs (Goerge, Van Voorhis, and Lee, 1994).

Census Products, Surveys and Related Sources

CCI evaluators can also find useful information in data generated by the U.S. Bureau of the Census and by special surveys and censuses on economic, housing, and other issues relevant to community regeneration.

U.S. Census of Housing and Population Data

In its decennial census, the U.S. Bureau of the Census strives for complete coverage of housing stock and population and provides data down to the level of census tracts for almost all characteristics measured and to the level of block groups for many characteristics. The major drawback of census data is that they are gathered only once every ten years.

The census asks two levels of questions: the short form (sometimes referred to as the "100 percent"), which contains 7 basic population and 7 housing questions pertaining to each person and housing unit; and the long form (sometimes referred to as the "sample"), which covers 26 population and 19 housing items, answered by approximately one in six households (17 percent) nationally. Census population data are available in two major forms: summary tape files and public use microdata samples. Information on the data files can be found at http://www.census.gov.

SUMMARY TAPE FILES (STFs)

Summary tape files provide cross-tabulations of characteristics identified for specified geographic areas, usually in finer detail than printed census reports. These machine readable collections of summary statistics are available on computer tape; certain STFs are also available on microfiche or CD-ROM.

The STF3A is probably the most widely used file in this group because it contains long form responses regarding employment, income, trip to work, duration of residence, and housing characteristics, tabulated to the census tract level and sometimes to the block group level. It should be remembered, however, that the sample of approximately 17 percent of households is subject to some level of sampling error.

STF1 files. This collection of 100 percent, or short form, summary statistics covers congressional districts (101st Congress), counties, county subdivisions and places, census tracts and block numbering areas (BNAs, roughly equivalent to census tracts in areas where no tracts have been designated), and block groups and is available on microfiche and CD-ROM. STF1B, which covers counties, county subdivisions and places, census tracts and BNAs, block groups, and blocks, also covers metropolitan areas and urbanized areas. It is available on microfiche and CD-ROM, with only partial data for blocks. STF1C covers counties, places, and (in selected states) county subdivisions of population greater than 10,000 and metropolitan areas and urbanized areas. It is available on CD-ROM. STF1D covers congressional districts, counties, and places and (in selected sates) county subdivisions of population greater than 10,000.

STF2 files. These contain a more detailed collection of 100 percent summary statistics. STF2A covers counties, places of population greater than 10,000, and census tracts and BNAs. STF2B covers counties, places of population greater than 1,000, and county subdivisions. STF2C covers counties, places, and (in selected states) county subdivisions of population of greater than 10,000, along with metropolitan areas and urbanized areas and all county subdivisions of New England metropolitan areas.

STF3 files. These files contain a less detailed collection of sample, or long form, summary statistics. STF3A covers counties, county subdivisions and places, census tracts and BNAs, and block groups and is available on microfiche and CD-ROM. STF3B, covering five-digit zip codes, is available on CD-ROM. STF3C covers counties, places, and (in selected states) county subdivisions of population greater than 10,000, and metropolitan areas and urbanized areas. It is available on CD-ROM. STF 3D covers congressional districts, counties, and places and (in selected states) county subdivisions of population greater than 10,000.

STF4 files. This collection includes a more detailed set of sample summary statistics. STF4A covers counties, places with population greater than 10,000, and census tracts and BNAs. STF4B covers counties, places, and (in selected states) county subdivisions of population greater than 2,500; it also covers all county subdivisions in New England metropolitan areas. STF4C covers counties, places, and (in selected states) county subdivisions of population greater than 10,000, and metropolitan areas and urbanized areas.

PUBLIC USE MICRODATA SAMPLE (PUMS)

These files contain individual microdata taken from the 1990 census long form samples. Each record includes essentially all the 1990 census data collected about each person in a sample household and the characteristics of the housing unit. Unlike the STF files, which include fixed cross-tabulations for a given geographic area, these files enable users to prepare their own cross-tabulations or conduct multivariate analysis. In order to preserve confidentiality, locations are indicated in PUMS designated areas, identified as areas containing at least 100,000 population and not crossing state lines. The data are available in two files, one containing a 5 percent sample of housing units where location can be groups of counties, a single county, a place, or a grouping of census tracts, and the other containing a 1 percent sample of housing units with location indicated by metropolitan area or other large area, the boundaries of which may cross state lines.

ADDITIONAL DATA SETS BASED ON THE DECENNIAL CENSUS

Some specialized data sets developed from 1990 census data are also available.

   County-to-County Migration File. Based on the 1990 census, this file gives summary descriptions of intrastate and significant interstate county-to-county migration streams, including counties of origin and destination and characteristics of members of the migration stream. It is available on CD-ROM.

   Commuting Zones and Labor Market Areas. Developed from 1990 journey-to-work data, these units include 741 commuting zones (CZs), delineated for all U.S. counties and county equivalents, and 394 labor market areas (LMAs), aggregated from the commuting zones to meet the Bureau of Census criterion of 100,000 population minimum. CZs and LMAs can be used as geographic boundaries and combined with other data sources to track changes over time in economic activity. A CD-ROM and information about the methodology are available at http://www.lapop.lse.edu.

1990 Census Transportation Planning Package. This set of special tabulations of 1990 census data is tailored to meet the needs of transportation planners. It has two elements (statewide and urban) and three parts (residence, workplace, and journey-to-work). An urban element data set was created for each metropolitan planning organization across the country according to formats specified locally (for example, a customized geographic area or standard census tracts and block groups). It includes tabulations by area of work and area of residence, mode of travel to work, type of work, and time to get to work. It is available on CD-ROM through the U.S Department of Transportation at http://www.bts.gov.

American Housing Survey Information

The American Housing Survey (AHS) collects data on housing, including apartments, single-family homes, mobile homes, vacant housing units, household characteristics, income, housing and neighborhood quality, housing costs, equipment and fuels, size of housing unit, and recent movers. National data are collected every other year, with a sample on average of 55,000 homes. Data from each of 47 selected metropolitan areas are collected about every four years, with an average of 12 metropolitan areas included each year. The sample in each metropolitan area is 2,500 or more homes.

The AHS returns to the same housing units year after year to gather data, adding new units identified from permit listings. The data therefore provides a picture of household flows through a constant representative set of housing units. Because of sample size limits, however, valid estimates are possible only down to geographic units of 100,000 or more (like the PUMS data), even in metropolitan areas covered by the area surveys. Even so, by providing an indication of how housing stock and residents are changing in the broader context, the survey can be valuable to evaluators interested in smaller areas within the 47 designated metropolitan areas. When using these data to examine income or poverty of residents, evaluators should note that the AHS has historically under-reported income and over-reported poverty compared with the Current Population Survey, and that both surveys tend to under-report income and over-report poverty compared with tax returns and national income accounts. Information on the survey can be found at http://www.census.gov/hhes/housing.

1992 U.S. Economic Census Data

Gathered every five years since 1967, the U.S. Economic Census covers specific industry types: retail trade; wholesale trade; service industries; construction industries; manufacturers; mineral industries; financial, insurance, and real estate industries; transportation; communication; and utilities. Reports on the various industries give number of establishments, number of employees, revenue, and payroll, as well as some industry-specific information. Most are available on CD-ROM and can be converted into data files. However, confidentiality concerns dictate a fairly high level of geographic aggregation, usually by metropolitan area or metropolitan area and county and occasionally by zip code.

County Business Patterns Series

This annual series reports the number of establishments by employment size, industry group (agriculture, forestry, and fishing; mining; construction; manufacturing; transportation and utilities; wholesale trade; and retail; finance, insurance, and real estate), and payroll. The geographic unit is counties, but zip code data are also available. County Business Patterns are based primarily on administrative records and reports from current surveys, unlike the 1992 Economic Census, which is based on responses from individual establishments. These data are available on CD-ROM. Information is available at http:/www.census.gov/epcd/cbp.

Consolidated Federal Funds Report, Volume 1, County Areas

Consolidated Federal Funds Report (CFFR) data are obtained from federal government agencies and published in an annual series covering federal expenditures or obligations in the following categories: grants, salaries and wages, procurement contracts, direct payments to individuals, other direct payments, direct loans, guaranteed or insured loans, and insurance. Dollar amounts represent either actual expenditures or obligations. For more information on CFFR data, see http//www.census.gov/govs/www/cffr.html.

County and City Data Book

This source contains data from 1987 through 1992, including more than 220 data items for states and counties, almost 200 data items for cities, and 33 items for places of 2,500 population or more. Items include age, money and personal income, population, education, health care and human services, housing ownership and value, births, deaths, poverty, local government finance, employment, business, banking, climate, elections, and social programs. It is available on CD-ROM. Information on the data is available at http://www.census.gov/stat_abstract/ccdb.html.

Regional Economic Information System

This series, updated periodically, presents annual estimates of local area economic data for states, counties, and metropolitan areas for the years 1969-94. Statistics in the data base include personal income and earning variables, full and part employment variables, transfer payment variables, and farm income and expenses variables. Some breakdowns are given by industry, or SIC code. The data estimates are derived from a number of sources, many of which are used for the National Income and Product Accounts estimates. For example, earnings and employment estimates are derived mostly from the Bureau of Labor Statistics ES-202 series. Earnings are estimated by both place of work and place of residence. The data are available on CD-ROM. For further information, see http://www.bea.doc.gov or http://www.lib.virginia.edu/soscsci/reis/reis1.html.

Federal-State Cooperative Program for Population Estimates

This program generates several series of population estimates, including annual estimates of county populations and biannual estimates of city or place populations. Each set starts from 1990 census figures, then estimates components of change in population from birth and death records, domestic migration (based on federal income tax returns), international migration (based on statements to the Immigration and Naturalization Service by legal immigrants and refugees), and undocumented immigrants (based on 1990 census figures on recent foreign born immigrants to specified places). Because federal program allocations are based on these estimates, cities and places often challenge the estimates, and periodic updates reflect those challenges and the reconciliation process specified by law. Although the estimates are carefully made, caution should be used in applying them to small areas and especially to subgroups by age, race, and sex. For example, one study using these estimates as the numerator in a calculation of nonwhite teen birthrates at the county level found a rate in excess of 100 percent in 7 percent of the county-years in the sample (Kane and Staiger, 1996). The estimates can be downloaded from http://www.census.gov/population/www/estimates/popest.html.

Small Area Income and Poverty Estimates

The Bureau of the Census recently initiated a program to update selected income and poverty estimates at the state and country levels. Estimates are made of median household income, per capita income, number of persons below the poverty level, number of children under age 5 below the poverty level, number of children 5 to 17 years old below the poverty level, and number of persons age 65 and over below the poverty level. At a later stage, the project may attempt estimates of children in poverty at the school district level. A committee of the National Academy of Sciences is monitoring this project and advising on methodology. State and county estimates for 1993 are available at http://www.census.gov/hhes/www/saipe/saipe93/ftp93.html.

U.S. Department of Education Data

Some information about local school districts and schoolchildren is compiled by the federal Department of Education and made available to the public.

THE SCHOOL DISTRICT DATA BOOK

The School District Data Book (SDDB) is an education database and information system that contains the most extensive available set of data on children, their households, and the nation's school systems. The SDDB includes demographic and cartographic CD-ROMs and provides up to 200,000 data items for school districts, including detailed information from the 1990 census school district special tabulation for states, counties, and districts. Its mapping features enable users to view maps of all individual school districts in the nation. Information is available at http://www.ed.gov/NCES/surveys/SDDB/introd.htm.

THE COMMON CORE DATA

The Common Core Data (CCD) is a comprehensive, annual, national statistical database of all public elementary and secondary schools and school districts, which contains data that are comparable across all states. CCD presents three categories of information: general descriptive information on schools and school districts; data on students and staff; and fiscal data. The general descriptive information includes name, address, phone number, and type of locale; information on students and staff includes demographic characteristics; and fiscal information covers revenues and current expenditures.

The CCD is made up of a set of five surveys sent to state education departments. Most data are obtained from administrative records maintained by the state education agencies. Statistical information is collected annually from public elementary and secondary schools (approximately 87,000), public school districts (approximately 16,000), and the 50 states, the District of Columbia, and outlying areas. For further information see http://www.ed.gov/NCES/ccd/index.html.

Geographical Information Systems

A geographical information system (GIS) is a computer program that allows the user to organize and analyze information geographically. Nearly all the information discussed in this paper is about specific places and can be tracked to specific addresses, census tracts, wards, or neighborhoods. The major use of GIS programs is to take these kinds of data and create visually striking and informative thematic maps, some of which brand or shade areas of a territory along a single variable (such as percent of the population over age 65), while others highlight specific addresses or events (such as crime incidents).

GIS programs are also useful in analyzing data. Mapping programs allow the user to overlay one thematic map on top of another, showing, for instance, the relationship between concentration of minority population and delivery of public services. GIS programs can also provide descriptive statistics about geographical areas.

All GIS programs plot geographical data. To do so, however, GIS programs require electronic base maps, including street and address ranges, census tracts, blocks and block groups, and other common geographic areas such as wards or zip codes. There are a number of ways to get these base maps, either by purchasing the maps from a private vendor (which can be expensive) or converting the U.S. Census Bureau TIGER files into maps that can be used by a specific GIS program. The TIGER files are available at many libraries and universities, but converting them to a format that can be read by a GIS program requires additional software.

There are several GIS software programs available for the microcomputer. These include ArcInfo, ArcView, Mapinfo, and MapQuest. The two most accessible to new users are Mapinfo (available at 1-800-FASTMAP, or www.mapinfo.com) and ArcView. Both allow researchers to use geographic information, geo-code and manipulate data, and create thematic maps for presentation.

Once a user becomes familiar with these programs, they are very easy to work with, although it is important to add that ease of use neither assures accuracy nor prevents the creation of distorted maps. The accuracy of geo-coding, for instance, is dependent upon the quality of the street and address ranges of the base maps being used. It is worth noting that the TIGER files have significant gaps, particularly in quickly developing areas. Geo-coding based on TIGER files will likely produce a high number of addresses that cannot be accurately assigned X and Y coordinates. Also, many GIS programs have programmed a number of defaults in the creation of thematic maps, which can easily lead to the creation of maps that provide a distorted picture of the data.

Despite the ease of use features of all available GIS programs, new users will frequently find that they have questions or unique problems. Fortunately, many colleges and universities teach courses on GIS mapping, and many have GIS labs. The staff of a geography department or GIS lab at a local university is a good place to ask for assistance and training. Indeed, it might be advisable to find out what GIS software is being used by local educational institutions before making a purchase.

Building Local Capacity
for Small Area Information

CCIs are not the only members of their communities that can benefit from ready access to information about neighborhoods or other sub-city geographic units. Indeed, there is growing recognition of the need for this information, and growing capacity to use it, among government agencies, advocacy groups, planning councils, and neighborhood residents (Urban Institute, 1996; Sawicki and Craig, 1996).

Neighborhood information systems now exist in Cleveland, Providence, Denver, Oakland, Boston, Atlanta, and a few other cities. In each place, one or more local organizations has undertaken the development of neighborhood measures across a comprehensive range of topics and has agreed to assist local organizations in using that information to guide action. A common theme among these efforts is that neighborhood information is an essential element of community building. A community cannot truly create a responsible and responsive agenda for change without knowing a lot about itself.

Existing neighborhood information programs are run by local organizations that are either independent or part of universities or foundations. Each has built strong relationships with the agencies that provide the data, obtaining and processing information continuously, turning it into neighborhood measures or indicators, and returning geographic analyses to the agencies that supplied the data. The programs vary in how they disseminate the neighborhood information. Cleveland, for example, makes it available on line for census tracts, neighborhoods, and municipalities (Chow and Coulton, 1996). Other programs make the information available as part of a community planning or action agenda and to individual groups or organizations upon request.

Neighborhood information capacity is vital to CCIs because they can seldom afford to obtain and process large amounts of available data just for the few neighborhoods they target. There is an economy of scale when measures are created for all neighborhoods in a county or region. For example, finding birth certificates from a single neighborhood in the vital records file and calculating a low birthweight rate for that neighborhood would cost almost as much as conducting the same activity for all of the neighborhoods in a city.

The experience gained in setting up these neighborhood information capacities is now becoming available to other cities. The Urban Institute's National Neighborhood Indicators Project is coordinating such an effort; for information, see http://www.urban.org. Examples of comprehensive neighborhood indicator programs are also available for Cleveland from Case Western Reserve's Center on Urban Poverty and Social Change, at http://www.cwru.edu/CWRU/Dept/MSASS/poverty/cupsc.htm, or for Providence at http://www.providenceplan.org.

Using Small Area Information in CCIs

CCIs have unique needs for information for several reasons. First, they evolve over extended periods of time, so their information needs are ongoing and dynamic. Second, they are comprehensive, so their information needs range across sectors. Third, they attempt to change entire communities, so they need information pertaining to the communities' residents, organizations, systems, physical conditions, social structures, and economies. Finally, they are action oriented, so that they need information that is timely but consumes only modest resources for data gathering and analysis.

Using available data is consistent with these unique information needs. Collected regularly and periodically and stored so that retrospective baseline information can be created, these data allow evaluators to examine trends and dynamics of change and support the creation and analysis of community change. Because the data are gathered for other purposes, they do not require the effort and expense of original data collection.

However, there is a danger that CCIs can drown in available data if the measures sought are not part of a carefully constructed theory of change. Available data have the potential to measure early, interim, and ultimate outcomes along a well-considered pathway. In this respect, it is essential that the time frame during which the available data are collected be carefully linked to the timing of change anticipated by the theory. Further, the measures will be much more meaningful if the theory specifies thresholds for the amount of change anticipated by the theory.

The ready availability of some but not other types of data can also lead to the light post fallacy—that is, looking for change where it is easiest to observe. CCIs generally anticipate many outcomes that cannot be measured with available data, especially those that relate to community perceptions or processes. Nevertheless, the available data sources reviewed in this chapter are key resources for the totality of information CCIs need for planning, action, and evaluation. Today's information technology makes these data an important and practical tool, deserving serious methodological attention and further development.

Note

This paper was prepared for the Aspen Institute's Roundtable on Comprehensive Initiatives. The assistance of Lisa Nelson and Venky Chakravarthy is gratefully acknowledged.

References

Annie E. Casey Foundation. 1997. *City Kids Count*. Baltimore: Annie E. Casey Foundation.

Carlson, Virginia L. 1995. "Identifying Neighborhood Businesses: A Comparison of Business Listings." *Economic Development Quarterly* 9: 50-59.

Centers for Disease Control. 1988. "Public Health Surveillance of 1990 Injury Control Objectives for the Nation." *Morbidity and Mortality Weekly Report* 37: 27-68.

Chapin Hall Center for Children. 1996. *Creation of a Community Information Infrastructure.* Chicago.

Chaskin, Robert. 1995. *Defining Neighborhoods: History, Theory and Practice.* Chicago: Chapin Hall Center for Children.

Chow, J., and Claudia Coulton. 1996. "Strategic Use of a Community Data Base for Planning and Practice." *Computers in Human Services* 13: 57-72.

Coulton, Claudia, Nandita Verma, and Shenyang Guo. 1996. *Time-Limited Welfare and the Employment Prospects of AFDC Recipients in Cuyahoga County.* Cleveland: Case Western Reserve University.

Coulton, Claudia, Jill Korbin, Tsui Chan, Marilyn Su, and Edward Wang. 1997. *Mapping Resident Perceptions of Neighborhood Boundaries.* Cleveland: Case Western Reserve University.

Geronimus, Arline T., John Bound, Timothy A. Waidmann, Marianne M. Hillemeier, and P. Burns. 1996. "Excess Mortality among Blacks and Whites in the United States." *New England Journal of Medicine* 14: 491-98.

Goerge, Robert, John Van Voorhis, and B. J. Lee. 1994. "Illinois Longitudinal and Relational Child and Family Research Database." *Social Science Computer Review* 12: 351-65.

Gould, J. B., N. Mahajan, and M. Lucero. 1989. "Improving Perinatal Outcome through Data Management: The Design of Small Area Analysis Systems." *Journal of Perinatal Medicine* 16: 305-14.

Jaro, M. A. 1995. "Probabilistic Linkage of Large Public Health Data Files." *Statistics in Medicine* 14: 491-98.

Kane, Thomas, and Douglas Staiger. 1996. "Teen Motherhood and Abortion Access." *Quarterly Journal of Economics:* 478.

Kessner, D. M., J. Singer, C. E. Kalk, and S. Schlesinger. 1973. *Infant Death: An Analysis by Maternal Risk and Health Care.* Washington, DC: National Academy of Sciences.

Leete, Laura, and Neil Bania. 1995. *Assessment of the Geographic Distribution and Skill Requirements of Jobs in the Cleveland-Akron Metropolitan Area.* Cleveland: Case Western Reserve University.

Lemeshow, S., D. W. Hosmer, J. Klar, and S. K. Lwanga. 1990. *Adequacy of Sample Size in Health Studies.* New York: John Wiley and Sons.

McCord, C., and H. P. Freeman. 1990. "Excess Mortality in Harlem." *New England Journal of Medicine* 322: 173-77.

Newcombe, Howard B. 1988. *Handbook of Record Linkage: Methods for Health and Statistical Studies, Administration, and Business.* Oxford: Oxford University Press.

O'Brien, R. M. 1985. *Crime and Victimization Data.* Beverly Hills, CA: Sage Publications.

O'Toole, R., P. Turbett, and C. Nalpeka. 1983. "Theories, Professional Knowledge, and Diagnosis of Child Abuse, in *The Dark Side of Families: Current Family Violence Research,* eds. D. Finkelhor, R. Gelles, G. Hotaling, and M. Strauss. Newbury Park, CA: Sage Publications.

Prothrow-Stith, Deborah. 1991. *Deadly Consequences.* New York: Harper-Collins.

Rossi, P. H. 1972. "Community Social Indicators," in *The Human Meaning of Social Change,* eds. A. Campbell and P. E. Converse. New York: Russell Sage.

Rivara, F. P., N. Calonge, and R. S. Thompson. 1989. "Population-Based Study of Unintentional Injury Incidence and Impact during Childhood." *American Journal of Public Health* 79: 990-94.

Sawicki, David S., and W. J. Craig. 1996. "Neighborhood Indicators: A Review of the Literature and an Assessment of Conceptual and Methodological Issues." *Journal of the American Planning Association* 62: 240-53.

Schorr, Lisbeth. 1994. "The Case for Shifting to Results-Based Accountability with a Start-up List of Outcome Measures with Annotations." Cambridge, MA: Harvard Project on Effective Services.

Sherman, L. 1989. "Hot Spots of Predatory Crime: Routing Activities and the Criminology of Place." *Criminology* 27: 27-56.

Smith, S. K., and S. Cody. 1994. "Evaluating the Housing Unit Method." *American Planning Association* 60: 209-21.

Thornton, C., J. Love, A. Meckstroth. 1994. "Community-Level Measures for Assessing the Status of Children and Families." Paper presented at the annual research conference of the Association for Public Policy and Management, Chicago.

Waits, M. J., T. Rex, and R. Melnick. 1997. "Cluster Analysis: A New Tool for Understanding the Role of the Inner City in a Regional Economy." Paper presented at the Community Outreach Partnership Conference, U.S. Department of Housing and Urban Development, Phoenix.

Wennberg, John E., Jean L. Freeman, and William J. Culp. 1987. "Are Hospital Services Rationed in New Haven or Over-Utilized in Boston?" *Lancet:* 1185-88.

White, Sammis B., John F. Zipp, and William F. McMahon. 1990. "ES202: The Data Base for Local Employment Analysis." *Economic Development Quarterly.*

Urban Institute. 1996. *Democratizing Information.* Washington, DC: Urban Institute.

Establishing Causality in Evaluations of Comprehensive Community Initiatives

Robert C. Granger

Introduction

Causal attribution is difficult in all sciences, and by its nature the comprehensive community initiative (CCI) is an especially complex case. Like
many domestic social programs, CCIs are meant to create positive changes
in the well-being of low income children and families. They try to do this
by combining some or all of the following elements in a manner that
encourages synergy across the strategies: expansion and improvement of
social services, such as child care and family support; health care; economic development; housing rehabilitation; community planning and organizing; adult education; job training; and school reform. Moreover, most of
today's CCIs operate on the premise that power must devolve to the community as part of the effective change process (Connell, Kubisch, Schorr,
and Weiss, 1995).

CCIs work across sectors while trying to change individuals, families,
institutions, and communities. They are situated in particular places and
historical moments; as interventions they tend to evolve slowly and flexibly
with attention to a large number of interacting processes; and they try to
affect a broad range of outcomes (Connell, Aber, and Walker, 1995; Rossi,
1996). They also tend to involve a large number of individuals and
groups—funders, community leaders, community residents, the "down-
town" political structure. All these factors make it extremely challenging to
determine whether or not CCIs make a difference and, if so, how.

Given the obvious evaluation challenges presented by CCIs, it takes
courage, and perhaps some folly, to address the issue of causality in CCI
evaluations. Yet that is the focus of this paper, necessitated by the fact that
the interventions themselves seem too promising to be ignored or given

short shrift by the evaluation community. The paper especially tries to assess the promise of theory-based evaluations in advancing the assignment of causality to changes within CCI communities.

The paper begins with a brief discussion of the theory of change approach being articulated by James Connell, Anne Kubisch, and other colleagues from the Aspen Institute Roundtable on Comprehensive Community Initiatives for Children and Families. The theory of change approach is then submitted to a "test" for evaluations developed by Chen (1990): that is, any evaluation, regardless of its specific purpose, should be responsive to the needs of stakeholders and produce credible and generalizable results. The paper concludes that theory-based approaches can help on these counts if evaluators attend to the need for sufficiently credible counterfactuals at all stages of their work. Doing so will require that they develop strong theories, use multiple methods of inquiry to search for and confirm patterns in data, creatively blend research designs, and refrain from rushing to judgment based on findings from individual studies. The paper places this discussion in context by considering what is meant by "cause," the role of counterfactuals in estimating effects and their causes, and the consequences of mistakes in causal inference.

Causality and the Theory of Change Approach

A theory of change approach to evaluation assumes that underlying any social intervention is an explicit or latent "theory" about how the intervention is meant to change outcomes (Weiss, 1995; Schorr, 1995). This notion has been around for some time (Weiss, 1972; Cronbach et al., 1980). In the earlier literature not directed toward CCIs, theory is most typically suggested as a guide for getting within the "black box" of social programs, in order to understand the relative contribution of specific programmatic mechanisms or components to any estimated effects. Further, having an explicit theory about how various processes and outcomes might be linked can direct data collection and analysis. With this map in hand (so the argument goes), evaluators and their clients can measure near-term outcomes with some confidence that observable change in those outcomes will be followed by changes in longer-term outcomes (Chen, 1990). They can also measure the processes that link (and perhaps cause change in) those outcomes. In short, theory can help evaluators pull apart and understand social interventions.

While the general notion of a theory of change approach is not new, the literature does not contain many examples that describe in detail how to develop such a theory for an intervention. There appears to be a consensus that theories about CCIs will come from a combination of existing "social science knowledge" and "practitioner wisdom," with local practitioners in a CCI playing an important role (Weiss, 1995). There are good reasons why local wisdom is required. First, current social science and practitioner knowledge alone are in no way up to the task. As yet, there is neither a scientific literature nor a consensus among practitioners about how to put CCIs in place or how to assure that certain activities will lead to desired results.[1] Second, getting local stakeholders involved is consistent with the "community empowerment" ethos of CCIs. Third, knowledge of how an initiative should (or could) be implemented demands local knowledge about such things as community capacity and culture. Thus, a potential role of the evaluator is to "surface" the latent theory. This process tends to take the form of a dialogue that either begins with a description of the first steps of the intervention and moves across outcomes or starts with long-term outcomes and creates a "map" back to the intervention (Brown, 1995). The intent of this guided process is to create a written, explicit description of how stakeholders expect to move from activities to their goals.

Developing a theory of change requires both art and science. In CCIs, stakeholders and groups commonly hold different (and not necessarily compatible) theories. Regardless of its theory, each group seems to feel more sure about its ultimate goals and the near-term strategies, activities, and benchmarks than about activities and outcomes that will presumably occur between current events and long-term results. In addition, stakeholders tend to view their theories as dynamic. They want to revisit their hypotheses about how events will unfold as time passes and experience suggests that revisions are necessary. This means that our current theories of change are not fixed guides that evaluators and others can use in a rigid way. Rather, as with most things in the natural sciences, they are at best well-informed propositions about how highly complex events are related at a particular time and place.

What Does "Cause" Mean?

The state of social science knowledge allows us to adopt only a rather modest standard about causal inferences. As Holland (1988) notes, since Aristotle, philosophers of science have been trying to define what it means for A to cause B. In the social sciences, the statement "A causes B" is often misleading. At best, even in situations where we can use true experimentation, we are able to make quite general, undifferentiated statements about the discrete causes of any effects. In part, this is because most social interventions are multifaceted, and their elements interact in ways we cannot predict. Holland extends this idea, referring to what he calls "encouragement" studies (where individuals are encouraged to participate in an intervention). His point is that humans exhibit varied behavior in response to such things as the "opportunity" to enter a program. Some attend and some do not, and the extent and pattern of attendance for those who come vary in unpredictable ways. Thus, it may be credible to say that X, Y, and Z are the effects of a particular CCI, but it will be virtually impossible to know with any precision what aspects of the CCI caused those effects.

Accepting that it will not be possible (or desirable) to try to pull a CCI apart for causal attribution, we are still left with questions like, "If we do all of X, will we get Y?" Think of this as seeking 100 percent predictability. While complete predictability may be a goal, as Cook and Campbell (1986) note, it will not come soon. Cook and Campbell eloquently write that "this is partly because of the quality of current social science theories and methods, partly because of the belief that society and people are ordered more like multiple pretzels of great complexity than like any structure implied by parsimonious mathematical formulas . . . [and] scientists assume that the world of complex, multivariate, particularistic, causal dependencies . . . is ordered in probabilistic rather than deterministic fashion."

Thus, evaluations of CCIs and most other social interventions, even those aided by well-articulated theories of change, will at best help us make some fairly imprecise inferences about the causal ingredients within the intervention.

How Important Is a Counterfactual to Understanding Cause?

Causal inference requires estimating effects, and one cannot estimate effects without a counterfactual. Even in disciplines where experimentation is unavailable, such as astrophysics, history, political science, and geology, causal attribution requires counterfactual inference (Tetlock and Belkin, 1996). While this is widely understood in the scientific community, it is surprising how quickly discussions about evaluating social programs lose the distinction between outcomes (a measure of the variables that follow all or some of an intervention) and effects (the outcome minus an estimate of what would have occurred without the intervention). To make this point clear, consider the following summaries of two social projects:

Summary 1

A number of children participate for up to two years in a high-quality early childhood intervention. Long-term follow-up shows that 33 percent do not finish high school or earn a general educational development (GED) certificate, 31 percent are detained or arrested, 16 percent of their school years are spent in special education, and the teen pregnancy rate for females in the program is 64 per 100.

Summary 2

A number of teen mothers and their children participate for up to 18 months in a high-quality comprehensive program meant to improve their educational achievement and credentials, increase their employment and earnings, and decrease their reliance on public assistance. After long-term follow-up, the proportion hold-

ing a high school diploma or a GED certificate has increased from
6 percent to 52 percent, the employment rate during the year pre-
ceding measurement has grown from 37 percent at baseline to 53
percent at follow-up, just 20 percent earned more than $500 dur-
ing the year before baseline but at follow-up 48 percent have done
so, and Aid to Families with Dependent Children (AFDC) receipt
has fallen from 95 percent to 75 percent.

Query

Which intervention made a difference?

Answer

The early childhood intervention described in Summary 1.

Readers may realize that summary 1 describes the program group
outcomes for participants in the Perry Preschool Project at age 19
(Berrueta-Clement et al., 1984). This small social experiment involving
123 families is arguably one of the most influential demonstration studies in history. The intervention made a positive difference across a range
of important outcomes. Summary 2 represents the 42-month outcomes
from the New Chance Demonstration, a program for high school
dropouts who had their first children as teenagers and were on AFDC.[2]
The evaluation shows that many of the young women moved forward in
many ways, yet, consistent with findings from other interventions for this
subset of teenage parents, the program group did not advance farther
than their control group counterparts in most respects. The accompanying table contains selected measures from these two studies and makes
the point that a strong counterfactual is fundamental to having a good
estimate of effects.[3]

Before moving on, it may be useful to explore a limit of the previous
example. The table may suggest that a counterfactual is important only
when we are interested in judging an intervention's effects on long-term
outcomes. This is not so. Rather, a counterfactual is needed for other evaluation purposes, such as refining a program. For example, suppose the
developers of the Perry model wanted to know if certain staff development

Table. Selected Findings from the Perry Preschool Study and the New Chance Demonstration

Outcome	Program Group	Control Group	Difference
Perry Preschool (at age 19)[a]			
High school graduation or equivalent (%) (N = 121)	67	49	18**
Ever detained or arrested (%) (N = 121)	31	51	-20**
Percent of years in special education (N = 112)	16	28	-12**
Teen pregnancies (females only, per 100) (N = 49)	49	64	-15*
Sample size	58	65	
New Chance Demonstration[b]			
Percent with GED or diploma			
at baseline	6.4	5.3	1.1
at 42-month follow-up	51.9	43.8	8.1***
Prior year employment (%)			
at baseline	36.6	37.1	-0.5
at 42-month follow-up	53.3	50.5	2.8
Prior year earnings (%)			
at baseline			
$0-$500	79.9	80.8	-0.9
$501 or more	20.1	19.2	0.9
at 42-month follow-up			
$0-$500	51.7	53.2	-1.6
$501 or more	48.3	46.8	1.5
On AFDC (%)			
at baseline	95.0	94.7	0.3
at 42-month follow-up	75.4	73.5	2.0
Sample size	**1,401**	**678**	

Sources: Data on the Perry Preschool Study are from John Berrueta-Clement et al., *Changed Lives: The Effects of the Perry Preschool Program on Youths through Age 19* (Ypsilanti, MI: High/Scope Educational Research Foundation, 1984), Table 1. Manpower Demonstration Research Corporation.

Data on the New Chance Demonstration are from Manpower Demonstration Research Corporation research, including the project's final report; see Janet Quint, Hans Bos, and Denise Polit, *New Chance: Final Report on a Comprehensive Program for Disadvantaged Young Mothers and Their Children* (New York: MDRC, forthcoming).

Notes: Statistical significance levels are indicated as ***= 1 percent; **= 5 percent; *=10 percent.

[a] N=number responding to survey.

[b] Calculations include data for sample members who had values of zero for outcomes and for program group members who did not participate in New Chance. Rounding may cause slight discrepancies in sums and differences.

activities were "paying off" in changes in teacher behavior, which in turn were creating differences in student performance. To complete this analysis, they would need to assess the effects on each of these variables in the presumed causal chain. To do so, they would have to address questions such as the following: How much staff development are teachers getting? Are they getting more of it than they would have without us? Do doses of staff development predate change in teacher behavior? Do teachers who are not getting staff development also change their behavior? Does performance by students differ between those whose teachers are and those whose teachers are not receiving staff development? At each stage of the analysis, the strength of any causal attribution would rest on the strength of the counterfactual and the validity of the theory undergirding the analysis. Without the counterfactual, it would not be possible to estimate the effects on the outcomes of interest. And without the theory, it would not be possible to link those effects in a causal chain.

Of course, for practical reasons, evaluations have to pay more attention to certain effects and causes than to others. For instance, in the above example it probably makes sense to worry more about the link between teacher behavior and student effects than between effects on staff development and the link to teacher behavior. This raises the question, "When are a counterfactual and a causal inference good enough?"

What Is the Appropriate Standard for Credibility?

Establishing a simple, uniform threshold for credibility may not be possible. Instead, since evaluations are done to help people make decisions, the credibility of any causal inference should be commensurate with the importance of the judgment it will influence. A causal judgment is really a probabilistic statement about the likelihood that one thing leads to another. As with all probabilities, there is always the chance that a particular attribution is wrong. Sometimes we will assert that a CCI caused some effect and we will be mistaken; that is, the *appearance* of cause might exist simply due to chance or some unobserved (or uncontrolled for) phenomenon. Similarly, we may say that a CCI is not getting us what we hoped, when in fact it is making a positive difference. Accepting that mistakes are always possible, the question becomes something like, "In the scheme of things, what sorts of mistakes are more tolerable than others?"

It seems that the decisions with the greatest consequence have to do with whether or not the CCI is causing effects on the longer-term outcomes of interest. If we make a mistake on that question, two scenarios are possible, depending on the nature of the error. If we mistakenly attribute positive effects to a CCI, some people will erroneously assume that the CCI should be continued and (perhaps) replicated elsewhere. On the other hand, if we mistakenly say that the CCI is not making a difference (or is making a negative difference), then the effort may be inappropriately stopped. Are these mistakes serious? Quite possibly. Their seriousness depends on such considerations as the importance of the CCI's effects (if any) on the participants and society at large, the cost of the CCI, and the need elsewhere for the resources consumed by the CCI (in economic terms, the "opportunity costs" of the CCI). In contrast to this example, causal misattribution regarding the exact nature and effect of some program implementation strategy, such as staff development, is of less concern. At worst, staff members might participate in some activities that are not crucial to the program's success, or some worthwhile program development activities might be inappropriately stopped.[4]

The lesson here is that the credibility of inferences becomes more important as the consequences of making a mistake become graver. Furthermore, the ramifications of making a mistake must be considered from the multiple vantage points of the different stakeholders. Important consequences demand lots of credibility, and minor consequences demand some.

Testing the Value of the Theory of Change Approach

As Chen noted in *Theory-Driven Evaluations* (1990), debates regarding evaluation tend to be method oriented. That is, most discussions involve the relative merits of various experimental and quasi-experimental designs and their interaction with various data collection methods (nomothetic/quantitative versus idiographic/qualitative)[5] and purposes (problem documentation, program refinement, and summative program assessment). Chen provides a framework for these discussions that is useful in considering the theory of change approach. He observes that evaluation results should provide evidence of four characteristics:

- **responsiveness,** by being relevant and useful to the needs and concerns of decision makers, program managers, program staff, clients, and funders

- **objectivity,** by being reliable, valid, comfirmable, factual, and free from bias

- **trustworthiness,** by being both convincing and free from confounding factors ("internally valid" in common evaluation terms)

- **generalizability,** by being pertinent to circumstances, populations, and problems beyond the immediate evaluation ("externally valid" in common evaluation terminology)

How does the theory of change approach measure up against each of these dimensions when the task is to make causal inferences?

Responsiveness

Given the current state of practitioner and social science knowledge about how CCIs work, stakeholders are going to be closely involved in the development of any theory of change. As Stake has pointed out, evaluations are more responsive to various stakeholders if those stakeholders are involved in selecting the evaluation's questions, measures, and methods (1975). This is an important consideration given the political nature of most evaluation work. Common agreements, in advance, about such things as early benchmarks can help stakeholders avoid controversy and contention.

The theory of change approach goes beyond simple involvement to using credibility among stakeholders as the touchstone for assessing a theory. Even if an evaluator suggests that a CCI should import ideas documented elsewhere, the ground rule that seems to be emerging is that these ideas need to be "owned" by the local groups. Local stakeholders must believe that the theory of change makes sense. Therefore, a theory of change approach, and the causal links it depicts, ought to be highly responsive, as long as all views are considered and thoughtfully weighed.[6]

Objectivity

Laying out a theory *a priori* makes potential causal relationships explicit. Thus, it seems that a theory of change approach should increase the objectivity of causal judgments. Yet achieving such a benefit may take some work. Experience shows that different stakeholder perspectives lead to different theories, while several sources in the literature suggest that cognitive and emotional biases may systematically influence the way individuals attribute cause in indeterminate situations (Tetlock and Belkin, 1996; Granger and Armento, 1980).

One factor that appears to influence our judgments of causality is the degree to which we see outcomes as normative (Kelley, 1973). If an outcome is seen as typical, we are likely to decide that it was caused by "environmental" factors outside a program. However, if an outcome is seen as atypical, we are more likely to believe that the outcome was shaped by the program under review. Cognitive psychologists have shown that a number of factors, such as prior expectations of the attributer, perspective (having a role either inside or outside an intervention), and the "vividness" of the results all shape the judgment of normalcy (Tversky and Kahneman, 1971, 1973, 1974; Borgida and Nisbett, 1977). For example, one very vivid and recent episode in an event-outcome sequence (such as "my Toyota just broke down") tends to crowd out "pallid" baseline data (the maintenance record in *Consumer Reports*, for instance). Similarly, being an actor in a situation (as opposed to being an observer) seems to influence judgments about cause. Although the empirical literature on this topic contains some nuances, participants tend to assign the cause of events to forces outside themselves, while observers tend to emphasize the causal role of participants. Not surprisingly, however, some researchers have observed an emotional side to these biases. We tend to attribute perceived success to our own actions and failure to external factors, unless it is likely that we will be proven wrong (Bradley, 1978).

Given these well-documented biases in the psychological literature, it is likely that theories of change will vary by stakeholder in rather predictable ways. The solution probably lies in doing just what evaluators and CCI stakeholders are doing: laying out the various theories, critiquing each others' conceptions, developing a consensus (or consciously leaving competing theories "on the table" for consideration), and revising theories prospectively to avoid *ex post* justifications.

Trustworthiness

Armed with a consensually developed theory of change that arguably makes causal inferences more responsive and credible, the evaluation inevitably has to confront the test of trustworthiness. Are the results convincing and free from confounding factors? Determining how to answer that question often engenders a fairly acrimonious debate about the fallibility of various evaluation designs. Some line up for social experimentation with random assignment and decide that other approaches are a distant second best (Hollister and Hill, 1995). Another camp asserts that random assignment is not practically possible with CCIs and that it leads to misleading and rigid analyses (Schorr, 1995). Both positions have some merit, but the debates do not move us very far forward.

The call for random assignment is driven by a desire to estimate a counterfactual in a way that controls for selection bias, along with other confounding factors that might compete as causal explanations for any estimated effects.[7] Selection issues have been a major problem in the evaluation of social programs (Lalonde, 1986; Fraker and Maynard, 1987; Friedlander and Robins, 1995), and in most interventions targeted on individuals, they must be seriously addressed through randomization or very strong quasi-experimental methods. At this moment, however, the questions dominating CCIs do not demand counterfactuals that are free from selection bias in order to produce credible results. Furthermore, if CCIs reach a point where such counterfactuals are needed, randomization alone may not be the best solution.

Although CCIs have existed in various forms at other times in our domestic policy history (O'Connor, 1995; Halpern, 1994), the current resurgence is quite recent. As most stakeholders tell us, CCIs are now facing contexts that may well be more depleted than before. This means that the threshold questions facing CCIs have to do with program implementation and refinement. At this time, we do not have agreed-upon methods for creating CCIs that are sufficiently durable and strong to drive even mid-term benchmarks. In spite of pressure from funders, summative assessment of CCIs seems premature.

The process of program refinement demands causal inferences in order to allocate scarce resources. Questions include "Are the planned activities happening?" and "Do they seem to be leading to (or causing) short-term benchmarks in ways that are responsive and credible to those who need to make decisions (about staying the course, revising the approach, or revising the theory)?" Answering such questions demands a counterfactual. At issue is how strong that counterfactual must be. It appears excessive to seek counterfactuals for such estimates beyond a clear theory, careful documentation of the activities and outcomes (including intended and unintended outcomes), lots of transactions between evaluators and stakeholders about the emerging picture, and some clear-headed "counterfactual reasoning." Measuring counterfactuals is not cost-free; most near-term events are within the control of an intervention (for example, it is hard to imagine "village councils" spontaneously springing up in four neighborhoods in Cleveland without CCI activity); and mistakes about causal inference at this stage are not likely to carry high stakes.

That said, there will soon come a time when stakeholders reasonably ask about the mid-term accomplishments of CCIs. Are we on the right track? Answering such a question demands a stronger counterfactual than we are likely to get solely from a theory of change and the good work of evaluators. When this time comes, some will suggest a design that randomly assigns communities as the way to proceed. Their intent will be to create a counterfactual where there is no selection bias. (The communities in the two groups will be equivalent if a sufficient number of communities are included in the lottery.) But such a design alone will not be sufficient because it will not fully answer the first-order questions regarding what it takes to get a CCI implemented, and the relationship between implementation and subsequent effects.

Because random assignment has been characterized as "the gold standard" (Hollister and Hill, 1995), it may be useful to step back and assess what random assignment might mean at the community level. First, we would be faced with a decision about the composition of our research sample. A concern for generalizability would suggest that we should recruit a broad sweep of communities. On the other hand, a broad sweep would undoubtedly take in many communities without the will or resources to implement a CCI. Failures of implementation would be costly to the evaluation; specifically, resources would be spent on studying communities that never get a CCI going. Therefore, we would probably proceed fairly far along, using prescreening criteria, before we chose the final sample for the research. For example, we might screen out communities that did not express a strong willingness to start a CCI. Then, assuming that there were not enough CCI start-up resources to go around, we would use the lottery-like process of random assignment to allocate the finite resources, creating a "program" group of communities and a "control" group of communities.

Given the nature of CCIs, even with our prescreening, some experimental communities would only partially implement the initiative. Conversely, some communities in the control condition would begin their own CCIs. The only unbiased estimates would compare all the communities in the program group with all those in the control group—an unsatisfactory comparison, given the mixed levels of implementation in each group. When policymakers, practitioners, and funders ask about the intermediate effects of CCIs, they do not want answers that include lots of sites where implementation has failed. Nor do they want to muddy the estimation of CCI effects by comparing CCIs in some communities with different CCIs in others. Rather, the two likeliest questions are, "When a CCI is in place, does it make a difference?" and "What does it take to put a successful CCI in place?"

Assuming those two questions, three strategies can help generate trustworthy causal inferences, especially if they are used in tandem: creatively blend designs to create reasonably strong counterfactuals; explicate and test for patterns within and across sites and time; and investigate possible causes and effects using mixed data collection methods and modes of analysis. All are assisted by a clear theory of change. An overarching recommendation about causal inference in CCIs is to come to such inferences slowly, especially if the stakes regarding a misattribution are large.

Blend designs. Quasi-experimental methods were born of the inability to use experimental methods sensibly in all situations (Campbell and Stanley, 1963; Cook and Campbell, 1986; Cook, 1991). Since Campbell's and Stanley's seminal *Experimental and Quasi-Experimental Designs for Research*, the language of "internal" and "external" validity has dominated most discussions about causality and design. Hollister and Hill (1995), drawing in particular on a study that compared experimental and quasi-experimental estimates from the same data sets (Friedlander and Robins, 1995), raised important questions about relying on any one quasi-experimental approach. That is not what I have in mind.

The recommendation instead is for the sort of planned and creative blending of designs that has long been advocated by researchers including Cook, Campbell, and Stanley. For example, as noted above, assume that a first-order "effects" question for CCIs is, "When a CCI is in place, does it make a difference?" One quasi-experimental design that could help us answer that question is an interrupted time series (Campbell and Stanley, 1963; Cook and Campbell, 1979). The design estimates effects by longitudinally taking a number of pre-intervention observations to establish a pre-intervention trend. Then the series is "interrupted" by an intervention (that is, the implementation of the CCI), followed by the collection of further longitudinal data. If the trend in the data changes with the advent of the intervention, the change (or effect) is attributable to the intervention.

In an interrupted time series, selection bias is controlled for by using each site as its own control in the time series analysis. This feature of the design helps with the problem of sites achieving different levels of implementation by allowing the evaluator to compare the deviations from the trend for different levels of implementation, with each deviation being free from selection effects.

The main threat to the validity of this causal inference is that some other event outside the intervention might cause us to miss—or mistakenly find—some effects. For example, a sudden general economic downturn that coincided with the beginning of a CCI might mask its effects on a variety of economic outcomes. Conversely, a general improvement in the economy that was unrelated to a CCI but coincided with its implementation might create some positive effects that the evaluation would mistakenly attribute to the CCI.

Some recent studies are trying to guard against such misattribution by adding data from nonintervention sites to the design. Here, some form of matching of communities, or matching coupled with randomization (referred to as "stratified" random assignment), can be helpful. For example, as reported in Rossi (1996), the evaluation of the Rapid Early Action for Coronary Treatment (REACT) public health intervention involves the random assignment of ten communities, five to a program group that receives the REACT intervention and five to a control condition.[8] Similarly, in the Jobs-Plus demonstration, the Manpower Demonstration Research Corporation (MDRC) has created program and comparison sites by having six communities each nominate two or three public housing developments for the intervention.[9] MDRC then randomly assigned one development in each city to the program group and the remainder to the comparison group. The REACT and Jobs-Plus evaluation teams do not believe that their randomization of a few communities has created a fully unbiased counterfactual in either evaluation. But it has addressed the potential concern that the interventions somehow "stacked the deck" in their favor.

Furthermore, the Jobs-Plus team is gathering time series data on both intervention and comparison sites. This strengthens the overall design in two important ways. First, it helps minimize the threat of history. If the time series data show an improvement (measured as the deviation from the historical trend) in the treatment communities that exceeds the deviation in the comparison communities, it is more likely that the estimated effects are the result of the intervention. Conversely, if a deviation in the treatment communities is matched by an equivalent deviation in the comparison communities, the results imply that some other co-occurring event is driving the change.

The time series data especially helps with the potential problem that some communities chosen for the "noninterruption" time series cohort will implement CCIs on their own. (The closer the equivalence of the two groups, the more this scenario is likely.) Because each community serves as its own control, we can include such communities in the time series analysis as "interrupted" cases. Second, we can examine these cases to understand how they managed to create a CCI without the (presumably necessary) help available to those communities in the program group. This will get us closer to understanding what it takes to create community change.

The use of an interrupted time series with an attendant, uninterrupted comparison series is not a panacea. The design demands the ability to gather longitudinal data, and few current administrative record systems are up to the task. Second, such designs tend to work best when the intervention "interrupts" the time trend abruptly and the effects are large. Neither may be the case with a particular CCI. However, the time series approach seems more appropriate in this situation than randomization alone.

Explicate and test for patterns. While a blend of time series data appears promising for evaluations of CCIs, we have to go farther to get trustworthy causal inferences. In simple terms, one person's cause is another's effect. That is, we look for causality by understanding how patterns of effects (estimated by comparing the intervention cases with their counterfactuals) are linked together in the data. For example, CCIs tend to assume that participation in various cross-sector planning bodies will lead to more resources coming to the community. It is tempting to estimate only the effect on resources, because that is a long-term outcome of inter-est. But to link any estimated effect back to the presumed cause of increased participation, one needs first to estimate the effect on that out-come. That is, has participation changed significantly (using some reliable counterfactual like the historical trend)? Then, does that change seem to be related in a predictable way to any changes in resources? Several authors have suggested that a finely drawn theory of change can guide the testing for such patterns in results (Weiss, 1972; Chen, 1990; Trochim and Cook, 1992; and Rossi, 1996). The suggestion, following Cook and Campbell (1979), Freedman (1991), and others, is to rely on design (as opposed to statistical modeling) as the primary vehicle for estimating effects. Then, these design-driven estimates of effects can be included in more sophisti-cated models.

Integrate methods. A third recommendation is to enhance causal analysis in CCIs by integrating methods in a predetermined way. Most eval-uators recognize that the integration of methods makes good sense. Different methods are better suited to learning about different phenomena. For example, quantitative techniques are typically better for such tasks as assessing the prevalence of discrete phenomena in a community (such as the rate of housing starts), while qualitative techniques more usefully expose context, certain processes, and the meanings people attach to events.[10]

At first blush, the *a priori* statement of a theory of change may seem antithetical to the qualitative paradigm. After all, some people would argue that the "theory" should emerge developmentally over time, influenced by the unfolding events. That sounds right, and fortunately it is consistent with the behavior of evaluators pursuing a theory of change approach to CCI evaluation. As described earlier, current theories of change are incom-plete, particularly in the space between close-in (short-term) program activities and long-term outcomes of interest. This implies that field researchers should be close to stakeholders over time, presenting the stake-holders with information (from both quantitative and qualitative methods) and extracting their revised theories about the future. Without these refinements, it is going to be impossible to make intelligent guesses about effects or their potential causes.

A second reason to mix methods involves the need to measure things well. Measurement error can obscure potential effects, while measurement bias (systematic measurement error) can distort results and lead to mistaken notions about cause. As described in the literature, theories of change are arrayed as sets of outcomes that are connected by processes or mechanisms. Many current "theories" present significant measurement challenges: just what does it mean for the community to "feel empowered" or for residents to "participate in decision making," and how can these be measured? This situation demands a mix of qualitative and quantitative work to generate a consensus (via convergence of results from different methods) that events, processes, and outcomes have occurred and are in fact linked. Thus, we need to take some qualitative and some quantitative measures of the same phenomena.

Methods may be mixed iteratively (for example, field work leads to a survey, which leads to more field work), or in a more integrated fashion (Greene, 1995; Ragin, 1989). While a discussion of the relative merits of these approaches is beyond the scope of this paper, a concern for causality probably steers one toward integration.

Generalizability

Chen (1990) discusses the idea that the results of an evaluation should be pertinent to other people, places, times, and related problems. This concept of generalizability has been in common conversation among applied social scientists since Campbell and Stanley (1963), and it has been refined in subsequent publications (Bracht and Glass, 1968; Campbell, 1986).

Multi-site demonstrations are common in applied social science research, as is the finding that an intervention can seem to "work" in some sites but not in others (Riccio and Orenstein, 1996). This is the sort of variation that ought to make anyone nervous about firmly latching onto a causal attribution based on results from one CCI evaluation. When interventions occur in multiple contexts, many things vary. Chief among these are the people involved (participants, staff, and others), the community context, the "quality" of the intervention, the moment in time, and any interaction involving some subset of these factors. As developed by Campbell (1957), Cook (1990), and others, the key to generalizability is replication across people, places, and time. The goal here is not that effects always be the same but that they occur in some predictable fashion.

Armed with a strong theory, evaluators are better prepared to antici-pate and then examine how between-site variation may shape effects. For example, a theory may suggest that a CCI emphasizing employment will make more of a difference for poorly skilled unemployed persons in a weak labor market (where they must compete with others in a pool of unem-ployed persons who are relatively skilled) than in a strong one (where most can get jobs without much special assistance). Such hypotheses can be explored if we pay attention to developing some common baseline and out-come measures for cross-site work.

It is going to take time and considerable coordination of evaluation activities before we can use variation across different studies as a way to pursue theory-driven hypotheses about how results should differ. But until we have done so, decision makers should be cautious.

In Closing

This paper has echoed much of what others have said about program eval-uation research in the past thirty years. The advice, that is, is to use theory as a guide, mix methods, seek patterns that corroborate each other (both within and across studies), and creatively combine various designs. None of this will surprise applied social scientists, nor will it be particularly reas-suring to those who call for redefining the standards of proof or discarding questions about effects. In short, the recommendation is to do the conven-tional work better, recognizing that CCI evaluation is helped in many ways by a theory-based approach.

This analysis suggests that a theory of change approach can assist in making causal inferences, regardless of an evaluation's immediate purpose. It is easier to document problems when a clear theory is available that will direct the baseline analysis and help a community design a CCI that can cause change. Program refinement demands causal analyses that can help decision makers allocate start-up resources, and these decision makers will be assisted by thinking through the links between strategies and early outcomes. Summative program assessment demands strong counterfactuals (the stakes regarding misjudgments are high at this stage), multiple measures of effects, and strong theory to lead the search for confirming patterns in those effects. Finally, generalizability to other persons, places, and times requires a theory to help us make and investigate such generalizations. All this seems especially true with CCIs, given their extreme complexity.

The main caution for the CCI community (including funders) is that a premature push for "effects" studies is likely to be very unsatisfying. Too much time will be spent gathering too much data that will not get synthesized across efforts. In contrast, funding of CCIs should rest on the *prima facie* merit of their activities at the present time. Funders should encourage mixed-inquiry techniques, theory building, and cross-site communication so the field can aggregate useful information over time.

Notes

1 This does not mean that we know nothing or that all theories have equal merit. For example, Connell, Aber, and Walker (1995) have described elements of what we know with some surety about the design of programs for children, youth, and families.

2 The author directs this study under the auspices of the Manpower Demonstration Research Corporation.

3 In the Perry Preschool Study and the New Chance Demonstration, the counterfactual is represented by the experiences and outcomes of members of the research sample who were assigned, in these studies at random, to the "control" group. At the point of random assignment, this group is equivalent to their counterparts randomly assigned to the "program" group. Thus, any subsequent differences between the groups that are large enough not to be due to chance are reasonably described as effects of the intervention.

4 Weighing the consequences of mistaken judgments about short-, mid-, and long-term effects is not straightforward. In asserting the importance of long-term outcomes, I recognize that CCIs must show "effects" all along the way, in

order to steer their implementation efforts and justify their resources. But given how little we know about the causal pathways from activities to effects, I am assuming that funders will not "pull the plug" prematurely, unless there is a pervasive failure to meet early benchmarks.

5 Nomothetic research attempts to establish general, universal, abstract principles or laws, while idiographic research deals with individual, singular, unique, or concrete cases.

6 It also may be the case that the very act of having local stakeholders participate in the "surfacing" process will improve the intervention. This follows from Schöen (1983) and others who have argued that "reflective" practitioners who have consciously considered their own assumptions and strategies will do a better job.

7 To understand selection bias, imagine we are estimating the effects of a CCI by comparing the results from one set of communities with those from a set of matched pairs. Extraneous influences on our outcomes might be controlled for by this design, but they also might exist due to factors related to how we selected communities into our CCI and comparison samples. Therefore, the argument goes, counterfactuals should be created through a lottery process so that the procedures for creating the counterfactual do not unwittingly bias the findings.

8 The REACT intervention seeks to improve the survival rate of heart attack victims by shortening the time between a heart attack and administering appropriate medication. The intervention consists of an educational campaign aimed at persons at risk, emergency personnel, and primary care physicians.

9 The Jobs-Plus demonstration seeks to increase employment and earnings in public housing through a combination of employment and training, financial incentives, and community organizing. See Bloom (1996) for a discussion of the demonstration and the research design.

10 This recommendation takes a pragmatic position regarding the "paradigm debates" involved in the mixing of various methods (Greene and Caracelli, 1997; Rossman and Wilson, 1985). The position here is that it is possible to integrate methods in a manner that preserves the integrity of their root assumptions.

References

Berrueta-Clement, John, Lawrence J. Schweinhart, W. Steven Barnett, Ann S. Epstein, and David P. Weikart. 1984. *Changed Lives: The Effects of the Perry Preschool Program on Youths through Age 19.* Ypsilanti, MI: High School Educational Research Foundation.

Bloom, Howard S. 1996. "Building a Convincing Test of a Public Housing Employment Program Using Non-Experimental Methods Planning for the Jobs-Plus Demonstration." Paper commissioned by the Manpower Demonstration Research Corporation, in partnership with the U.S. Department of Housing and Urban Development and the Rockefeller Foundation. Excerpted from "Research Design Issues and Options for Jobs-Plus," Howard S. Bloom and Susan Bloom, March 1996.

Borgida, E., and R. E. Nisbett. 1977. "The Differential Impact of Abstract vs. Concrete Information on Decisions." *Journal of Applied Social Psychology* 7: 258-71.

Bracht, Glenn H., and Gene V. Glass. 1968. "The External Validity of Experiments." *American Educational Research Journal* 5 (4):437-38.

Bradley, G. W. 1978. "Self-Serving Biases in the Attribution Process: A Reexamination of the Fact or Fiction Question." *Journal of Personality and Social Psychology* 36:56-71.

Brown, Prudence. 1995. "The Role of the Evaluator in Comprehensive Community Initiatives." In *New Approaches to Evaluating Community Initiatives: Concepts, Methods, and Contexts,* ed. James P. Connell et al. Washington, DC: The Aspen Institute.

Campbell, D. T. 1986. "Relabeling Internal and External Validity for Applied Social Scientists." In *Advances in Quasi-Experimental Design and Analysis,* ed. W. M. K. Trochim. San Francisco: Jossey-Bass.

Campbell, D. T. 1957. "Factors Relevant to the Validity of Experiments in Social Settings." *Psychological Bulletin* 54:297-312.

Campbell, D. T., and J. C. Stanley. 1963. *Experimental and Quasi-Experimental Designs for Research.* Chicago: Rand-McNally.

Chen, Huey-tsyh. 1990. *Theory-Driven Evaluations.* Newbury Park, CA: Sage Publications.

Chen, Huey-tsyh, and Peter H. Rossi, eds. 1992. *Using Theory to Improve Program and Policy Evaluations.* New York: Greenwood Press.

Connell, James P., J. Lawrence Aber, and Gary Walker. 1995. "How Do Urban Communities Affect Youth? Using Social Science Research to Inform the Design and Evaluation of Comprehensive Community Initiatives." In *New Approaches to Evaluating Community Initiatives: Concepts, Methods, and Contexts,* ed. James P. Connell et al. Washington, DC: Aspen Institute.

Connell, James P., Anne C. Kubisch, Lisbeth B. Schorr, and Carol H. Weiss, eds. 1995. *New Approaches to Evaluating Community Initiatives: Concepts, Methods, and Contexts.* Washington, DC: Aspen Institute.

Cook, Thomas D. 1991. "Clarifying the Warrant for Generalized Causal Inferences in Quasi-Experimentation." In *Evaluation and Education at Quarter Century,* ed. M. W. McLaughlin and D. Phillips. Chicago: National Society for Studies in Education.

Cook, Thomas D. 1990. "The Generalization of Causal Connections: Multiple Theories in Search of Clear Practice." In *Research Methodology: Strengthening Causal Interpretations of Nonexperimental Data,* ed. Lee Sechrest, Edward Perrin, and John Bunker. Washington, DC: US Department of Health and Human Services, Public Health Service Agency for Health Care Policy and Research.

Cook, T. D., and D. T. Campbell. 1986. "The Causal Assumptions of Quasi-Experimental Practice." *Synthesis* 68:141-80.

Cook, T. D., and D. T. Campbell. 1979. *Quasi-Experimentation: Design and Analysis Issues for Field Settings.* Chicago: Rand-McNally.

Cronbach, Lee J., S. R. Ambron, S. M. Dornbusch, R. D. Hess, R. C. Hornik, D. C. Phillips, D. F. Walker, and S. S. Weiner. 1980. *Toward Reform of Program Evaluation.* San Francisco: Jossey-Bass.

Fraker, T., and R. Maynard. 1987. "The Adequacy of Comparison Group Designs for Evaluations of Employment-Related Programs." *Journal of Human Resources* 22:194-227.

Freedman, D. A. 1991. "Statistical Models and Shoe Leather." In *Sociological Methodology* 21:291-358.

Friedlander, Daniel, and Philip K. Robins. 1995. "Evaluating Program Evaluations: New Evidence on Commonly Used Nonexperimental Methods." *American Economic Review* 85(4):923-37.

Granger, R. C., and B. Armento. 1980. "Debate Concerning Program Evaluation Results: A Natural Event." Paper presented at the Annual Meeting of the American Educational Research Association, Boston.

Greene, Jennifer C. 1995. "The Paradigm Issue in Mixed-Method Evaluation: Towards an Inquiry Framework of Bounded Pluralism." Draft. Cornell University.

Greene, Jennifer C., and Valerie J. Caracelli. 1997. "Defining and Describing the Paradigm Issue in Mixed-Method Evaluation." In *Advances in Mixed-Method Evaluation: The Challenges and Benefits of Integrating Diverse Paradigms,* ed. Jennifer C. Greene and Valerie J. Caracelli. San Francisco: Jossey-Bass.

Halpern, Robert. 1994. *Rebuilding the Inner City: A History of Neighborhood Initiatives to Address Poverty in the United States.* New York: Columbia University Press.

Holland, Paul W. 1988. "Causal Inference, Path Analysis, and Recursive Structural Equations Models." *American Sociological Association* 13:449-50.

Hollister, Robinson G., and Jennifer Hill. 1995. "Problems in the Evaluation of Community-Wide Initiatives." In *New Approaches to Evaluating Community Initiatives: Concepts, Methods, and Contexts,* ed. James P. Connell et al. Washington, DC: Aspen Institute.

Kelley, H. 1973. "The Process of Causal Attribution." *American Psychologist* 28:107-28.

Lalonde, R. J. 1986. "Evaluating the Econometric Evaluations of Training Programs with Experimental Data." *American Economic Review* 76:604-20.

O'Connor, Alice. 1995. "Evaluating Comprehensive Community Initiatives: A View from History." In *New Approaches to Evaluating Community Initiatives: Concepts, Methods, and Contexts,* ed. James P. Connell et al. Washington, DC: Aspen Institute.

Ragin, C. C. 1989. *The Comparative Method: Moving Beyond Qualitative and Quantitative Strategies.* Berkeley: University of California Press.

Riccio, James A., and Alan Orenstein. 1996. "Understanding Best Practices for Operating Welfare-to-Work Programs." *Evaluation Review* 20(1):3-28.

Rossi, Peter H. 1996. "Evaluating Community Development Programs: Problems and Prospects." Discussion draft. Amherst, MA: Social and Demographic Research Institute, University of Massachusetts.

Rossman, G. B., and B. L. Wilson. 1985. "Numbers and Words: Combining Quantitative and Qualitative Methods in a Single Large Scale Evaluation Study." *Evaluation Review* 9:627-43.

Schoën, Donald A. 1983. *The Reflective Practitioner.* New York: Basic Books.

Schorr, Lisbeth B. 1995. "New Approaches to Evaluation: Helping Sister Mary Paul, Geoff Canada and Otis Johnson while Convincing Pat Moynihan, Newt Gingrich and the American Public." In *Getting Smart, Getting Real: Using Research and Evaluation Information to Improve Programs and Policies.* Baltimore: Annie E. Casey Foundation.

Stake, R. E., ed. 1975. *Evaluating the Arts in Education: A Responsible Approach.* Columbus, OH: Merrill.

Tetlock, Philip E., and Aaron Belkin. 1996. "Counterfactual Thought Experiments in World Politics." *Social Science Research Council* 50(4):77-85.

Trochim, William M. K., and Judith A. Cook. 1992. "Pattern Matching in Theory-Driven Evaluation: A Field Example from Psychiatric Rehabilitation." In *Using Theory to Improve Program and Policy Evaluations,* ed. Huey-tsyh Chen and Peter H. Rossi. New York: Greenwood Press.

Tversky, A., and D. Kahneman. 1974. "Judgment under Uncertainty: Heuristics and Biases." *Science* 185:1124-31.

Tversky, A., and D. Kahneman. 1973. "Availability: A Heuristic for Judging Frequency and Probability." *Cognitive Psychology* 5:207-32.

Tversky, A., and D. Kahneman. 1971. "Belief in Small Numbers." *Psychological Bulletin* 76:105-10.

Weiss, Carol Hirschon 1995. "Nothing as Practical as Good Theory: Exploring Theory-Based Evaluation for Comprehensive Community Initiatives for Children and Families." In *New Approaches to Evaluating Community Initiatives: Concepts, Methods, and Contexts,* ed. James P. Connell et al. Washington, DC: Aspen Institute.

Weiss, Carol Hirschon 1972. *Evaluation Research: Methods for Assessing Program Effectiveness.* Englewood Cliffs: Prentice Hall.

Acknowledgements

The author would like to thank the following people for their helpful comments: Howard Bloom, James Connell, Thomas Cook, Janet Quint, James Riccio, and Peter Rossi.

Acknowledgements

The activities of the Roundtable on Comprehensive Community Initiatives for Children and Families have been funded by eleven foundations: the Annie E. Casey Foundation, the Ford Foundation, the Robert Wood Johnson Foundation, the Pew Charitable Trusts, the Foundation for Child Development, the Rockefeller Foundation, the John D. and Catherine T. MacArthur Foundation, the Charles Stewart Mott Foundation, the W. K. Kellogg Foundation, the Edna McConnell Clark Foundation, and the Spencer Foundation. The work of the Steering Committee on Evaluation is part of the ongoing efforts of the Roundtable and is therefore funded, in part, through the sources listed above. It has also received specific grant funds from the following sources: the U.S. Department of Health and Human Services, the U.S. Department of Housing and Urban Development, the Pew Charitable Trusts, the Ford Foundation, and the Annie E. Casey Foundation. The members of the Roundtable and the Steering Committee on Evaluation thank these funders for their support of this work.

The editors thank, first and foremost, the authors who contributed their work to this volume. We are grateful as well to Huey-Tsyh Chen, John Gaventa, Lynn Kagan, Michael Patton, Dennis Rose, Peter Rossi, Gertrude Spilka, Charles L. Usher, Mary Wagner, and Robert Yin, who participated in the telephone interviews that helped shape this volume. We also benefited from the thoughts and insights of Brett Brown, Robert Chaskin, Hector Cordero-Guzman, Claudia Coulton, Michelle Gambone, Bennett Harrison, Reginald Jones, Jack Kraskopf, Margaret Spencer, Abraham Wandersman, and Carol Weiss, who attended the meeting in late 1996 at which many of the issues covered here were discussed.

In addition, several people made production of this book possible, and we are grateful to them all: Rick Landesberg, Caroline Mengon, Sylvia Pear, and Rebecca Weaver. Anne Mackinnon, as always, did much more than editing to keep this publication on track. The Roundtable staff who were critical to this process all along are Crystal Hayes, Andrea Anderson, Debra Chinnery Smith, and Michelle Roberts. And, finally, none of this would have been possible without the wisdom and guidance of the members of the Steering Committee on Evaluation and the leadership of the co-chairs of the Roundtable, Harold Richman and Lisbeth Schorr.

The authors and editors are solely responsible for the accuracy of the statements and interpretations contained in this publication. Such interpretations do not necessarily reflect the views of the contributing foundations or of the federal government.

Contributors and Participants

About the Authors

Andrea Anderson is a research associate with the Roundtable on Comprehensive Community Initiatives for Children and Families at the Aspen Institute, where she is editing a forthcoming compilation of community-level outcome measures. Before joining the Roundtable, she was a senior analyst in the Housing, Income Security and Employment area of Abt Associates Inc.

Prudence Brown is a research fellow at the Chapin Hall Center for Children at the University of Chicago, where she is involved in the design, documentation, and evaluation of comprehensive community initiatives. She was formerly deputy director of the Urban Poverty Program at the Ford Foundation

James Connell is co-founder and president of the Institute for Research and Reform in Education, based in Philadelphia. He was previously an associate professor of education and psychology at the University of Rochester and director of research at Public/Private Ventures and has published numerous articles on youth development and community and school influences on urban youth.

Claudia Coulton is Lillian F. Harris Professor and co-director of the Center for Urban Poverty and Social Change at Case Western Reserve University. Through the Center she works with community-based organizations and initiatives to reduce poverty and related conditions in urban neighborhoods.

Karen Fulbright-Anderson is a research fellow with the Roundtable on Comprehensive Community Initiatives for Children and Families of the Aspen Institute. Prior to joining the Roundtable, she served as director of research at the Vera Institute of Justice and worked in the area of youth development at the Ford Foundation and the Commonwealth Fund. She has also held faculty appointments at the New School for Social Research and the Massachusetts Institute of Technology.

Michelle Alberti Gambone is currently a consultant to the Academy for Educational Development's Center for Youth Development, the Aspen Institute Roundtable on Comprehensive Community Initiatives, the Corporation for National and Community Service, and the Institute for Research and Reform in Education, among others. She was previously deputy director of research at Public/Private Ventures, where she served as principal investigator on several major studies.

Robert Granger, senior vice president at the Manpower Demonstration Research Corporation (MDRC), divides his time between leading research on MDRC projects on young parents and children and serving as the organization's chief financial officer. He is co-author of *Alternative Approaches to Educating Young Children* and co-editor of *Demythologizing the Inner City Child;* he is also the author of numerous professional articles.

Scott Hebert is a senior associate at Abt Associates, Inc., and currently serves as Abt's project director for the national evaluations of the Annie E. Casey Foundation's Jobs Initiative and the Empowerment Zones and Enterprise Communities Program of the U.S. Department of Housing and Urban Development. Prior to joining Abt, he was involved in designing and administering community revitalization, housing, and antipoverty programs at the local and state levels.

Robinson G. Hollister, Jr., is Joseph Wharton Professor of Economics at Swarthmore College. His previous positions include chief of research and plans for the Office of Economic Opportunity, co-principal investigator for the evaluation of the National Supported Work Demonstration, and chair of the Committee on Youth Employment Programs, National Academy of Science.

Sharon Lynn Kagan, senior associate at Yale University's Bush Center in Child Development and Social Policy, is a frequent consultant to the White House, Congress, the National Governors' Association, the U.S. Departments of Education and Health and Human Services, and numerous states, foundations, corporations, and professional associations. Presently, she is president-elect of the National Association for the Education of Young Children and co-chair of the National Education Goals Panel on Goal One. She is the author of the recently published *Not By Chance,* the report of the Quality 2000 Initiative and co-editor of *Reinventing Early Care and Education* and *Children, Families and Government.*

Anne C. Kubisch is director of the Roundtable on Comprehensive Community Initiatives for Children and Families at the Aspen Institute. Previously, she was deputy director of the Ford Foundation's Urban Poverty Program, where she was responsible for grants supporting comprehensive community initiatives and reforms in human service delivery systems.

Sharon E. Milligan is associate professor at the Mandel School of Applied Social Sciences and co-director of the Center on Urban Poverty and Social Change, Case Western Reserve University. In addition to her teaching responsibilities, she directs several research projects focusing on health, minorities, and technology for evaluating neighborhood-based initiatives in poor communities.

Susan Philliber is founder and senior partner of Philliber Research Associates, which specializes in the evaluation of human service programs. She has held faculty positions at the University of Utah, the University of Cincinnati, Columbia University, and the State University of New York, College at New Paltz, and has published extensively.

Ronald Register is executive director of the Cleveland Community-Building Initiative and chairman of the executive committee of the National Community Building Network, a national membership organization of practitioners, funders, policymakers, and evaluators.

Peter J. York, a research officer at the Center for Assessment and Policy Development in Philadelphia, is currently a doctoral candidate at Case Western Reserve University's Mandel School of Applied Social Sciences.

The Aspen Institute Roundtable on Comprehensive Community Initiatives

Harold Richman (Co-Chair)
Director
Chapin Hall Center for Children
University of Chicago

Lisbeth B. Schorr (Co-Chair)
Lecturer in Social Medicine
Director, Project on Effective
   Interventions
Harvard University

Michael Bailin
President
Edna McConnell Clark Foundation

Douglas Besharov
Resident Scholar
American Enterprise Institute
   for Public Policy Research

Angela Blackwell
Senior Vice President
Rockefeller Foundation

Barbara B. Blum
Senior Fellow in Child
   and Family Policy
National Center for Children
   in Poverty

Geraldine Brookins
Vice President — Programs
W. K. Kellogg Foundation

Geoffrey Canada
Executive Director
Rheedlen Centers for Families
   and Children

Peter Edelman
Professor of Law
Georgetown University Law
   Center

John W. Gardner
Haas Professor of Public Service
Stanford University

Sid Gardner
Director
Center for Collaboration
   for Children
California State University,
   Fullerton

Stephen Goldsmith
Mayor
City of Indianapolis

Patricia Graham
President
Spencer Foundation

Ralph Hamilton
Director of Florida Philanthropy
John D. and Catherine T.
   MacArthur Foundation

Ruby Hearn
Senior Vice President
Robert Wood Johnson Foundation

David Hornbeck
Superintendent
School District of Philadelphia

Craig Howard
Program Officer
James Irvine Foundation

Otis Johnson
Executive Director
Chatham-Savannah Youth Future
　Authority

Anne C. Kubisch
Director
Roundtable on Comprehensive
　Community Initiatives
Aspen Institute

Jack Litzenberg
Program Officer
Charles Stewart Mott Foundation

Susan Lloyd
Director
Building Community Capacity
John D. and Catherine T.
　MacArthur Foundation

Anita Miller
Program Director
Comprehensive Community
　Revitalization Program
Surdna Foundation

William A. Morrill
President
Mathtech, Inc.

Ralph Smith
Vice President
Annie E. Casey Foundation

Terry Peterson
Counselor to the Secretary
U.S. Department of Education

Ronald Register
Executive Director
Cleveland Community-Building
　Initiative

Julius B. Richmond
Department of Social Medicine
Harvard University

Michael Stegman
Macrae Professor of Public Policy
University of North Carolina

Gary Walker
President
Public/Private Ventures

Roundtable Steering Committee on Evaluation

J. Lawrence Aber
Director
National Center for Children in
  Poverty
Columbia University

Prudence Brown
Research Fellow
Chapin Hall Center for Children
University of Chicago

Philip L. Clay
Associate Provost
Professor of City Planning
Massachusetts Institute of
  Technology

James P. Connell
President
Institute for Research and Reform
  in Education

Claudia Coulton
Co-Director
Center for Urban Poverty and
  Social Change
Case Western Reserve University

Karen Fulbright-Anderson
Research Fellow
Roundtable on Comprehensive
  Community Initiatives
Aspen Institute

Robert Granger
Senior Vice President
Manpower Demonstration
  Research Corporation

Robinson G. Hollister, Jr.
Joseph Wharton Professor of
  Economics
Swarthmore College

Langley Keyes
Department of Urban Studies and
  Planning
Massachusetts Institute of
  Technology

Anne C. Kubisch
Director
Roundtable on Comprehensive
  Community Initiatives
Aspen Institute

Joyce Lashof
Dean Emerita
School of Public Health
University of California, Berkeley

Ronald Register
Executive Director
Cleveland Community-Building
  Initiative

Harold Richman
Director
Chapin Hall Center for Children
University of Chicago

Lisbeth B. Schorr
Lecturer in Social Medicine
Director, Project on Effective
    Interventions
Harvard University

Mercer Sullivan
Senior Research Fellow
Vera Institute of Justice

Gary Walker
President
Public/Private Ventures

Carol Weiss
Professor
Graduate School of Education
Harvard University

Heather Weiss
Director, Harvard Family
    Research Project
Graduate School of Education
Harvard University